JESUS the MESSIAH

A SURVEY OF THE LIFE OF CHRIST

Robert H. Stein

InterVarsity Press
Downers Grove, Illinois
Leicester, England

To my grandchildren—
Timothy, Benjamin, Elianna, Taylor, Christopher, Lydia—
with the prayer that they will come
to love and serve the Jesus of this book

InterVarsity Press
P.O. Box 1400, Downers Grove, Illinois 60515, U.S.A.
38 De Montfort Street, Leicester LE1 7GP, England

InterVarsity Press®, U.S.A., is the book-publishing division of InterVarsity Christian Fellowship®, a student movement active on campus at hundreds of universities, colleges and schools of nursing in the United States of America, and a member movement of the International Fellowship of Evangelical Students. For information about local and regional activities, write Public Relations Dept., InterVarsity Christian Fellowship, 6400 Schroeder Rd., P.O. Box 7895, Madison, WI 53707-7895.

Inter-Varsity Press, England, is the publishing division of the Universities and Colleges Christian Fellowship (formerly the Inter-Varsity Fellowship), a student movement linking Christian Unions in universities and colleges throughout the United Kingdom and the Republic of Ireland, and a member movement of the International Fellowship of Evangelical Students. For information about local and national activities in Great Britain write to UCCF, 38 De Montfort Street, Leicester LE1 7GP.

Scripture quotations, unless otherwise noted, are from the New Revised Standard Version of the Bible, copyright 1989 by the Division of Christian Education of the National Council of the Churches of Christ in the USA. Used by permission. All rights reserved.

Cover illustration: Scala/Art Resource, NY. Masaccio. Tribute Money. Brancacci Chapel, S. Maria del Carmine, Florence, Italy.

UK ISBN 0-85111-750-3
USA ISBN 0-8308-1884-7

Printed in the United States of America ∞

Library of Congress Cataloging-in-Publication Data

Stein, Robert H., 1935-
    Jesus the Messiah: a survey of the life of Christ/Robert H.
Stein.
      p.   cm.
    Includes bibliographical references and indexes.
    ISBN 0-8308-1884-7 (alk. paper)
    1. Jesus Christ—Biography. I. Title.
BT301.2.S687   1996
232.9'01—dc20
  [B]   96-32172
                        CIP

British Library Cataloguing in Publication Data

A catalogue record for this book is available from the British Library.

18	17	16	15	14	13	12	11	10	9	8	7	6	5	4	3	2	1
11	10	09	08	07	06	05	04	03	02	01	00	99	98	97	96		

Abbreviations

Adv. Marc.	Tertullian, *Against Marcion*
Ant.	Josephus, *The Antiquities of the Jews*
ANT	*The Apocryphal New Testament*, edited by J. K. Elliott
b.	indicates tractates from the Babylonian Talmud
BT	Babylonian Talmud
CD	*Damascus Document*
CIL	*Corpus inscriptionum latinarum*
Eccl. Hist.	Eusebius, *The Ecclesiastical History*
GT	*Gospel of Thomas*
IDB	*Interpreter's Dictionary of the Bible*
j.	indicates tractates from the Jerusalem Talmud
L	material unique to the Gospel of Luke
Loeb	Loeb Classical Library
M	material unique to the Gospel of Matthew
m.	indicates tractates from the Mishna
PT	Palestinian Talmud
Q	material found in Matthew and Luke but not in Mark
1QH	Thanksgiving Hymns of the Dead Sea Scrolls found in Cave 1
1QM	War Scroll of the Dead Sea Scrolls found in Cave 1
1QS	Manual of Discipline (or Rule of the Community) of the Dead Sea Scrolls found in Cave 1
4Q372	Fragment 372 of Cave 4 of the Dead Sea Scrolls
War	Josephus, *The History of the Jewish War*
Wisdom	Wisdom of Solomon (in the Apocrypha)

Preface

The present work seeks to introduce readers to the life of Christ. After each chapter is a list of references that can be investigated as desired. Due to the particular audience targeted by the present book, only works in English have been included.

The present work has been written without footnotes, for the problem of adequately footnoting a life of Christ and doing extensive work in the secondary literature is so great that one wonders if such a work could ever be written. The two large volumes *The Death of the Messiah* by Raymond E. Brown illustrate how an entire life of Jesus written in such a manner would be an impossible task in any one lifetime.

Translations of primary material, unless specifically stated, are from the following works: biblical quotations (New Revised Standard Version), rabbinic quotations (Babylonian Talmud [Soncino] and Mishna [Herbert Danby]), Josephus (Loeb Classical Library), second-century pagan writers and the early church fathers (Loeb Classical Library), the Tosefta (Joseph Neusner), *Gospel of Thomas (Synopsis Quattuor Evangeliorum)*, the *Infancy Gospel of Thomas* and the *Gospel of the Nazareans* (*The Apocryphal New Testament*, edited by J. K. Elliott [1993]).

I would like to express my appreciation to the people who were instrumental in my writing: my teaching assistants, Scott W. Johnson and Timothy J. Johnson, for their extensive checking of all the references and bibliographic data, as well as their stylistic suggestions; my colleague Dr. Thomas Schreiner, who was kind enough to read an early edition of the manuscript and make valuable suggestions; Gloria Metz, the faculty secretary, who once again provided her expertise to one of my writing projects; and my wife, Joan, who likewise read the manuscript, made many helpful suggestions and encouraged me throughout the project.

Introduction

The writing of books such as this has had a curious history. In the nineteenth century the writing of a life of Christ was almost a required exercise for New Testament scholars. Unfortunately the product was all too frequently autobiographical in nature, for the resultant Jesus of the researcher looked like, acted like and cherished the same values as the author. By the second decade of the twentieth century, however, the quest to produce a life of Christ had ebbed. Several factors led to the demise of this undertaking.

On the one hand, grave doubt arose as to whether historical research could arrive at the Jesus of history. People such as William Wrede, the historian Wilhelm Dilthey and the form critics raised serious questions as to the feasibility of writing such a life. They demonstrated that, far from being objective and dispassionate works, our Gospels were written from the perspective of the believing community. That was always recognized, but now there arose doubt as to whether the historian could ever penetrate behind the faith of the believing community and arrive at the "real" Jesus of history. In addition, the question arose whether historical research could ever be objective and neutral.

On the other hand, along with doubt in the ability to arrive at the historical Jesus, there also arose doubt as to the value of such an undertaking. Martin Kähler, Albert Schweitzer and Rudolf Bultmann questioned whether the result of such a "historical" investigation could ever prove an asset for faith. It was evident that the liberal, nonsupernatural Jesus of the historian could provide little assistance to the Christian believer. What faith sought and needed was not a Jesus who was similar to us. Yet the Jesus of historical research by definition could only be like us. He had to be by definition a Jesus stripped of the supernatural and miraculous. At best, such a Jesus could serve only as an example.

It is true that the humanity of Jesus (his being like us) is important and is emphasized in Scripture (see, for example, Heb 2:14-18; 4:14-16). Yet whenever Jesus' humanity is emphasized in Scripture it is never without stressing at the same time that he is even more significantly unlike us. He is without sin, he came from the Father, and he is the "only Son" (Jn 3:16). That is why he can bring to the believer victory over sin, death and the devil.

The quest that dominated New Testament studies in the nineteenth century ebbed and remained dormant for the most part until 1953. In October of that year Ernst Käsemann read a paper in which he pointed out that making an absolute distinction between the "historical" Jesus and the Christ of faith was ultimately a form of doceticism (an early Christian heresy that denied the true humanity of Jesus Christ). Furthermore, from a purely historical perspective one could not deny that information about Jesus of Nazareth was available to the historian. Thus a "new quest" for the historical Jesus began. The original quest emphasized a discontinuity between the Jesus of "history" and the Christ of the Gospels and sought to free the "real Jesus" from the Christ of the church and the creeds. The new quest, on the other hand, sought to find continuity between them.

Unfortunately, this new quest continued to work under the same historical-critical method, thus excluding the possibility of the supernatural (see chapter one). As a result, it was doomed from the start. The continuity that the new quest sought lay not in the essence and being of Jesus (that the historical Jesus and the Christ of faith are one and the same). Rather, the continuity was sought in the similarity of the message of the Jesus of history and the Christ of faith. A continuity was seen in that both the historical Jesus and the Christ of faith proclaimed and brought about the same existential encounter with God.

The popularity of the new quest waned quickly, for it could not bridge the gap between the purely human Jesus and the preexistent and supernatural Son of God of Christian faith. Furthermore, there did not appear to be any real difference between the existential encounter proclaimed by the Jesus of history and the Christ of faith and that proclaimed by the early church and the Old Testament prophets. Thus the continuity between the Jesus of history and the Christ of faith was no greater than that between the Old Testament prophets and the Christ of faith.

Today we are experiencing a renewed interest in the Jesus of history. This has been called by some the "third quest." In this third quest the Jewishness of Jesus is being emphasized and new sociological models are being used to assist in understanding the social and political situation of the first century. However, the results so far are disappointing. The same historical-critical method remains foundational for many of the researchers. Any research on the life of Christ that eliminates at the beginning the possibility of the supernatural will always produce a "historical Jesus" who is by definition radically different from the Christ of the Gospels. Without an openness to the supernatural, the result of any investigation of the life of Christ has predetermined that the resulting Jesus will be radically different from the Jesus who was born of a virgin, was anointed by the Spirit, healed the sick, raised the dead, died for the sins of the world, rose from the dead and ascended into heaven. Yet it is this supernatural Jesus that humanity desperately needs, for only this supernatural Jesus can bridge the gap between human sin and God's holiness. What the world so critically needs is a Savior, but only a supernatural Jesus can be a Savior.

In writing this work I have assumed the presence of the supernatural in the life of Jesus. In other words, this life of Christ has been written from a believer's viewpoint. It assumes that the Gospel accounts are reliable and that the burden of proof for the investigator lies not with those who affirm the historicity of the events and sayings found in the Gospels. It is rather the denial of their historicity that must be demonstrated. The Gospel stories are presumed truthful unless proven otherwise.

Jesus the Messiah consists of two parts. The first, "Key Issues in Studying the Life of Christ," contains three chapters and deals with introductory questions. The initial chapter discusses the presuppositions involved in such a study. Here I discuss my approach to the supernatural and the miraculous in the life of Jesus. One cannot investigate the life of Jesus of Nazareth without bringing to that study certain presuppositions. All too often discussion and debate about the historicity of a reported miracle in the life of Jesus involves not a discussion of the accounts or the event but the presuppositions concerning the supernatural. In the past much "life of Christ" research has assumed at the start that no miracle could have occurred. Such a presupposition should be stated openly and forth-rightly to the reader.

After discussing the presuppositions or ground rules for investigating the life of Jesus, I examine the sources available for such an investigation. Chapter two analyzes the Jewish, Greek and Christian (both biblical and nonbiblical) sources that are available for studying the life of Jesus and evaluates which ones will be most useful. Chapter three discusses what we can know concerning the chronological boundaries of the life of Jesus. Here I investigate the evidence available for dating various events in Jesus' life.

The second part of *Jesus the Messiah* consists of "The Life of Christ": the virginal conception (chapter four), the boyhood of Jesus (chapter five), the baptism (chapter six), the temptation (chapter seven), the call of the disciples (chapter eight), the message of Jesus (chapter nine), Christology (chapter ten), the confession of Peter (chapter eleven), the transfigura-tion (chapter twelve), the events of Palm Sunday (chapter thirteen), the cleansing of the temple (chapter fourteen), the Last Supper (chapter fif-teen), Gethsemane, the betrayal and arrest (chapter sixteen), the trial (chapter seventeen), the crucifixion (chapter eighteen), and the resurrec-tion and ascension of Jesus (chapter nineteen).

For some readers the first part of this work may prove to be more technical than they care for. If so, they may want to skip part one (chap-ters one to three) and begin immediately their reading in part two (chap-ters four to nineteen).

Part One
KEY ISSUES IN STUDYING THE LIFE OF CHRIST

1

WHERE YOU START DETERMINES WHERE YOU FINISH

The Role of Presuppositions in Studying the Life of Jesus

D URING MY FIRST YEAR AT SEMINARY I REMEMBER HEARING ONE OF the leading scholars of the day say the following in an address: "We would all like to believe that regardless of where one starts or how one approaches the evidence, as long as we are honest and objective we will all arrive at the same results when investigating a historical text." As a recent graduate in biology with a minor in chemistry, I readily nodded my head. After all, that was the essence of good science. No matter how one approached the evidence, if one were objective and honest the results would be identical with those of anyone else who approached the evidence honestly and objectively. I was shocked, therefore, when he went on to say, "We would all like to believe this, but it is simply not true. Where one starts one's investigation determines the results one will obtain." I will never forget my disappointment. At first I simply refused to believe my professor, but over the years the truth of what he said has been confirmed in my experience time and time again. Where a person starts powerfully shapes where he or she finishes.

Coming to Grips with the Miraculous

A basic issue involved in the study of the life of Jesus is the problem of miracles. No one can investigate his life without first coming to grips with the issue of the miraculous. The Gospels contain more than thirty miracles associated with the life and ministry of Jesus. In Mark alone 209 of the 661 verses deal with the miraculous. We read about various healings involving fever (Mk 1:29-31), leprosy (Mk 1:40-45), paralysis (Mk 2:1-12), a withered hand (Mk 3:1-6), hemorrhage (Mk 5:25-34), muteness (Mt 9:32-34), blindness (Mk 8:22-26), epilepsy (Mk 9:14-29), deformed limbs (Lk 13:10-17), dropsy (Lk 14:1-6), demon possession (Mk 1:21-28) and even a sword wound (Lk 22:49-51). There are raisings from the dead (Mk 5:35-43; Lk 7:11-15; Jn 11:1-44) and various nature miracles, such as the feeding of the five thousand (Mk 6:30-44) and the four thousand (Mk 8:1-10), the stilling of a storm (Mk 4:35-41), the cursing of a fig tree (Mk 11:12-14, 20-25), walking on water (Mk 6:45-52), the catching of a fish with a coin (Mt 17:24-27), a miraculous catch of fish (Lk 5:1-11; Jn 21:1-14), the turning of water into wine (Jn 2:1-11), a virginal conception (Mt 1:18-25; Lk 1:26-38) and an ascension into heaven (Lk 24:50-53; Acts 1:9). It is evident that a person cannot come to terms with the life of Jesus without coming to terms with the issue of miracles.

Furthermore, at the very heart of the Christian faith and message lies a miracle—the resurrection of Jesus. Paul states in this regard, "If Christ has not been raised, your faith is futile and you are still in your sins" (1 Cor 15:17; compare also v. 14). To deny the miraculous is to deny historic Christianity.

It would be nice to say that no matter how we approach the life of Jesus and the many miracles associated with that life, we will all come to the same conclusions as long as we deal with the evidence honestly. It would be nice, but it would be wrong. The fact is that before anyone ever investigates the miraculous accounts associated with Jesus' life, he or she has predetermined certain outcomes. Does one approach the Gospel accounts with an openness to the supernatural and thus the possibility of miracles? Or does one approach the accounts with the view that we live in a closed continuum of time and space in which there is no possibility of miracles occurring? Needless to say, the latter position has predetermined the possible results of any investigation into the life of Jesus. Each view is based on a faith commitment made prior to investigating the evidence. Openness to the supernatural allows certain conclusions that are impossible if one is closed to the possibility of the supernatural.

The Nonsupernatural Approach

In the study of the life of Jesus, many scholars have taken the nonsupernatural approach. The most famous liberal New Testament scholar, Adolf von Harnack, wrote at the beginning of the twentieth century, "We are firmly convinced that what happens in space and time is subject to the general laws of motion, and that in this sense, as an interruption of the order of Nature, there can be no such things as 'miracles' " (*What Is Christianity?* [New York: Putnam, 1901], pp. 28-29). We can also compare the view of Rudolf Bultmann, the leading German New Testament scholar of the twentieth century:

> The historical method includes the presupposition that history is a unity in the sense of a closed continuum of effects in which individual events are connected by the succession of cause and effect. . . . This closedness means that the continuum of historical happenings cannot be rent by the interference of supernatural, transcendent powers and that therefore there is no "miracle" in this sense of the word. Such a miracle would be an event whose cause did not lie within history. . . . It is in accordance with such a method as this that the science of history goes to work on all historical documents. And there cannot be any exceptions in the case of biblical texts if the latter are at all to be understood historically. (*Existence and Faith* [London: Hodder & Stoughton, 1961], pp. 291-92)

Earlier the English philosopher David Hume had eliminated miracles by the following philosophical argument: "[1] A miracle is a violation of the laws of nature; [2] and as a firm and unalterable experience has established these laws, [3] the proof against a miracle, from the very nature of the fact, is as entire as any argument from experience can possibly be imaged" (*An Enquiry Concerning Human Understanding: Of Miracles* 10.1). In other words, according to Hume we have the following syllogism:

A miracle is a violation of the "laws of nature."

The "laws of nature" are inviolable.

Therefore, a rational person is never justified in believing that a miracle actually happened.

Perhaps no one has better presented this approach to the study of history than the German theologian Ernst Troeltsch. According to Troeltsch, three principles should typify all historical investigation. The first is the *principle of criticism:* all historical judgments are and will always remain provisional. They are at best approximate and can deal only with probabilities. Thus any historical conclusion concerning Jesus can only be more or less probable and is always open to revision. If that is true, then it is impossible, or risky to say the least, to base one's eternal hope on any event of the past. The second is the *principle of analogy,* which assumes the uniformity of nature (that past experiences are similar to our present experience). Since our present experience is nonmiraculous, our interpretation of the past must be nonmiraculous. With respect to the life of Jesus, this means that his life must be interpreted as having been nonmiraculous. This principle is an extremely important one. Those who accept it without qualification must conclude that miracles cannot happen and that all biblical miracles are either mythical or misrepresentations of what actually happened. The third principle is the *principle of correlation,* which argues that historical explanation must always take into consideration the preceding and subsequent events and be interpreted in light of them.

An example of how this historical-critical method works may be helpful. A person investigating the account of the resurrection of Jesus found in Matthew 28:1-10 would proceed as follows.

He or she would investigate the account to find out such things as the Matthean editorial and theological contribution to the account, how this fits in with Matthew's emphases found elsewhere in the Gospel and so on. Frequently the term *redaction criticism* is used to describe such investigation. A historian would then seek to proceed further back toward the event described in the Gospel by looking at the presumed written sources used by Matthew, such as Mark's account. (This assumes that Mark was the first Gospel written and that Matthew used Mark. If the reverse were true, we would investigate Matthew's account as the earliest, then proceed to the investigation of the oral materials.)

Next, the investigator would seek to understand how Mark interpreted the oral account of the resurrection he used and remove any of his literary or theological contributions from it. This again involves redaction criticism, but here the purpose is not to understand what Mark sought to teach by his contributions to the account but to eliminate the material he has added.

Having done this, he or she would be able to investigate this account as it circulated during the period in which the Gospel materials were passed on orally. That involves the period between the death of Jesus and the writing of the first Gospel. What was the "form" of this account? Why was it preserved in the life of the early church? What were the needs that it met? What was the earliest form of this account? This kind of study is called *form criticism*. The next question the historian can raise at this point involves how the oral tradition originated. The answer is that this oral account of the resurrection arose from the faith of the earliest disciples.

Up to this point the historical-critical method raises no theoretical difficulty. The issue of the supernatural has not yet come into play. In practice, there will be all sorts of problems (such as the role of the eye-witnesses in all this). In theory, however, the historical investigation sketched above encounters no philosophical roadblock. Much of the best investigation of the resurrection accounts has been done by those who hold to this methodology. Both those holding a presupposition of open-ness to the supernatural and those denying the possibility of the super-natural can investigate and debate with one another the areas described so far. At this point, however, the presuppositions one brings to the study predetermines the conclusion to the question "How did the resur-rection faith of the disciples arise?"

If a person accepts an unqualified version of the principle of analogy as taught by Troeltsch and incorporated in the historical-critical method, he or she must conclude that whatever gave rise to the faith of the disciples, it cannot be the miracle of the resurrection. Although never stating it quite so bluntly, an investigator of Matthew's resurrection account using the historical-critical method is essentially saying, "Let's investigate what we can learn about the history of this account, but we must of course agree at the start that Jesus did not rise from the dead!"

In recognition of the historical-critical method's inability to deal with the historical dimension of the miracles, a distinctive vocabulary has been coined. This vocabulary originated in Germany, where several different words were available to describe historical investigation. An account is called *historisch* when it involves historical events that can be investigated by the historical-critical method. These involve such accounts as the crucifixion, Jesus' baptism and his association with the outcasts of Israel, which do not involve the supernatural. Sometimes the English word *historical* is used as an equivalent. An account is called *geschichtlich*, however, when the historical-critical method does not suffice—that is, when it involves the miraculous. Events such as the virginal conception, the resurrection and Jesus' miracles are *geschichtlich* because they involve the supernatural. The English words *kerygmatic* and *historic* are sometimes used to translate this second German term.

Some confusion has arisen over the use of the terms *geschichtlich*, *kerygmatic* and *historic*, however. Sometimes these terms are used to refer to an event which cannot be dealt with by the historical-critical method. Since by the principle of analogy the historical-critical method cannot deal with miracles, they are *geschichtlich*. By this reasoning, calling something *geschichtlich*, or "historic," is simply a matter of definition. The material, in other words, deals with the miraculous.

Some scholars, however, use these terms in a different sense. They do not admit that the historical-critical method is limited in scope and cannot deal with events that claim to be supernatural. They do not use this term as a description of the kind of events being discussed but rather as a historical judgment. In this sense, an event that is *geschichtlich* did not happen because it could not. Here, without any investigation of the evidence, a historical judgment has been made on the basis of a prior faith commitment that miracles cannot happen. In such instances, people's use of the language and categories of historical investigation has resulted in the conclusion that the discipline's inability to deal with events outside their own uniform experience of reality has now determined what could or could not have happened in real life.

Several attempts have been made to coin another name to describe a method of historical research which is equally concerned with interpreting events in their historical context but is open to the supernatural. One of the names suggested is *grammatico-historical method*. Other suggestions have been *historical-theological method* and *biblical-historical method*. These suggestions view the term *critical* as the villain that denies the supernatural. Yet the term *critical* is not so much concerned with a judgment concerning the possibility of the supernatural occurring in history as with the care, exactness and analytical nature of such investigation. It is the term *historical* and the baggage associated with it that causes the problem. For many scholars this term implies that history is closed to the supernatural and that the historical-critical method must assume this. Thus the "offensive" term that needs removing is *historical*. Since, however, scholars who maintain an openness to the supernatural also use *historical-critical method* as an expression to describe their methodology, we must recognize that this expression means different things for different people. Consequently it may be best to retain this expression and define exactly what one means by it.

In light of the importance of presuppositions about the supernatural on the outcome of one's work, authors should make clear from the start the position they take on this matter. It is misleading to say that "due to their investigation of the accounts" authors conclude that Jesus was not born of a virgin, that the miracles are later myths created by the church, that the faith of the early church gave rise to the accounts of the resurrection and not the other way around, and so on. All these conclusions were predetermined before any investigation began. It should come as no surprise that when one starts with the view that miracles cannot happen, the conclusion is that the miracles investigated did not happen.

Conclusion

The issue of whether the miracles associated with the life of Jesus truly occurred in history should not be resolved on the basis of an arbitrary decision that eliminates God from acting in history. On the contrary, whether Jesus worked miracles should be decided on the basis of the evidence. A more "liberal" approach to the life of Jesus, which does not predetermine the results, is to be open to the possibility that the miracles attributed to Jesus in the Gospels really did take place in history. Whether they did or not should be decided by the evidence.

For the evangelical Christian such evidence is strong: the nature of the written accounts in which these miracles are found (over the centuries the Christian church has seen the Gospels as different from other books, as inspired Scripture); the fact that the miracles occurred in public, were acknowledged by Jesus' opponents and were performed over a period of time and in a variety of circumstances; the character of the eyewitnesses, whose veracity is seldom denied. The miracle traditions are found in all the Gospel strata (Mark, Q, M, L and John) and in a multitude of different literary forms (sayings, miracle stories, summaries, controversy stories, stories about Jesus and the passion narrative). As a result, the evidence in favor of certain miracles, such as the resurrection, is weighty and convincing indeed.

A study of the life of Jesus that excludes the miraculous is destined from the start to produce a Jesus who is an aberration. He will be a stranger both to his opponents, who acknowledged his miracles (compare Mk 3:22; *b. Sanhedrin* 43a), and to his followers, who will no longer be able to identify him as the object of their faith. There is a certain wholeness about the Jesus who preached the arrival of the kingdom of God, who ate with tax collectors and sinners, who healed the sick and raised the dead, who died sacrificially on the cross and rose triumphantly from the dead. This wholeness produces an overall portrayal of Jesus of Nazareth that is convincing to a sympathetic reader of the Gospels. Attempts to strip the supernatural from Jesus' life can only produce a Jesus so radically different that he is unrecognizable and his impact on history unexplainable.

References

Blackburn, Barry L. "Miracles and Miracle Stories." In *Dictionary of Jesus and the Gospels*, edited by Joel B. Green, Scot McKnight and I. Howard Marshall, pp. 549-60. Downers Grove, Ill.: InterVarsity Press, 1992.

Brown, Colin. *Miracles and the Critical Mind.* Grand Rapids, Mich.: Eerdmans, 1984.

Davis, Stephen T. *Risen Indeed: Making Sense of the Resurrection.* Grand Rapids, Mich.: Eerdmans, 1993.

Evans, C. Stephen. *The Historical Christ and the Jesus of Faith: The Incarnational Narrative as History.* Oxford: Clarendon, 1996.

Fitzmyer, Joseph A. "Historical Criticism: Its Role in Biblical Interpretation and Church Life." *Theological Studies* 50 (1989): 244-59.

Hofius, Otfried. "Miracle, Wonder, Sign." In *New International Dictionary of New Testament Theology,* edited by Colin Brown, 2:620-35. Grand Rapids, Mich.: Zondervan, 1976.

Kee, Howard Clark. *Miracle in the Early Christian World: A Study in Sociohistorical Method.* New Haven, Conn.: Yale University Press, 1983.

Latourelle, René. *The Miracles of Jesus and the Theology of Miracles.* New York: Paulist, 1988.

Meier, John P. *A Marginal Jew: Rethinking the Historical Jesus,* 2:509-970. New York: Doubleday, 1994.

Sanders, E. P. *The Historical Figure of Jesus,* pp. 132-68. New York: Penguin, 1993.

Theissen, Gerd. *The Miracles Stories of the Early Christian Tradition.* Philadelphia: Fortress, 1983.

Wenham, David, and Craig Blomberg, eds. *The Miracles of Jesus.* Vol. 6 of *Gospel Perspectives.* Sheffield, U.K.: JSOT, 1986.

2

WHERE CAN WE GO?

Sources for Studying
the Life of Jesus

HAVING ESTABLISHED THE METHODOLOGY FOR STUDYING THE LIFE of Jesus (an openness to the supernatural), we must now delimit the sources that are available for such a study. The primary sources can be divided into the following categories: non-Christian sources, which subdivide into pagan and Jewish; and Christian sources, which divide into extrabiblical and biblical.

Non-Christian Sources

Pagan sources. The term *pagan* is traditionally used to define those sources whose origin is neither Jewish nor Christian. It does not carry any moral connotation but simply designates those early Greek and Roman authors who refer to Jesus but who are not part of the Judeo-Christian tradition. The number of such authors is few and for the most part late. That is not surprising, for one would not expect such writers to refer to a small and, in their eyes, insignificant sect and its founder. As time passed, however, and the members and influence of the Christian movement

grew, greater attention was paid them. Thus at the beginning of the
second century pagan writers begin to refer to Christians and their founder, Jesus of Nazareth. The main pagan sources available for studying the
life of Jesus are Pliny the Younger, Tacitus and Suetonius; sources of less
importance are Mara bar Serapion and Julius Africanus.

1. Pliny the Younger *Epistles* 10.96. The name Pliny "the Younger" (c.
A.D. 62-113) distinguishes this writer from his more famous uncle, Pliny
the Elder, who earlier wrote his great work *Natural History*. As governor
of the Roman province of Bithynia, Pliny the Younger wrote this letter
(c. 112) to the emperor Trajan concerning the trial of Christians under
his jurisdiction. He mentions that he allowed opportunity for these
Christians to abandon their faith by calling upon the pagan gods, showing reverence to the emperor's image and cursing Christ, and he released
those who did so. His reason for doing this, he explains, was that he had
been informed that those who are really Christians cannot be forced to
do any of these acts. Those, however, who were obstinate and stubborn
he put to death unless they were Roman citizens. The latter he sent to
Rome (compare Acts 25—28). From his questioning of Christians Pliny
learned that

> they were in the habit of meeting on a certain fixed day before it was
> light [Sunday], when they sang in alternate verses a hymn to Christ,
> as to a god, and bound themselves by a solemn oath, not to any wicked
> deeds, but never to commit any fraud, theft or adultery, never to
> falsify their word, nor deny a trust when they should be called upon
> to deliver it up; after which it was their custom to separate, and then
> reassemble to partake of food—but food of an ordinary and innocent
> kind.

2. Tacitus *Annals* 15.44. Tacitus was a Roman historian (c. A.D. 60-120)
who wrote a history of the Roman Empire that covered the years A.D.
14-68. We are missing some of the books that make up the *Annals*, and
unfortunately one of the gaps occurs between the years 29 and 32. Thus
the most important years with respect to the life of Jesus are missing.
Jesus, however, is mentioned by Tacitus in his reference to the burning
of Rome (A.D. 64) during the reign of Nero. He writes that, in order to
squelch the rumor that it was Nero himself who had ordered the fire that
ravaged Rome, the emperor placed the blame on the Christians and per-
secuted them. In the midst of describing Nero's murder and torture of

Christians, Tacitus states (c. 115),

Christus, the founder of the name, had undergone the death penalty in the reign of Tiberius, by sentence of the procurator Pontius Pilatus, and the pernicious superstition was checked for a moment, only to break out once more, not merely in Judaea, the home of the disease, but in the capital itself, where all things horrible or shameful in the world collect and find a vogue.

3. Suetonius *Life of Claudius* 25.4. About A.D. 120 the Roman historian Suetonius (c. A.D. 75-160) compiled a series of biographies of the first twelve emperors, beginning with Julius Caesar. In the section titled *Lives of the Twelve Caesars*, in which he discusses the emperor Claudius, he states, "Since the Jews constantly made disturbances at the instigation of Chrestus, he expelled them from Rome." Most historians believe that Suetonius has both misspelled the name "Chrestus" and misunderstood the event. The man involved was not "Chrestus" (a common misspelling) but "Christus," and the disturbance was not caused *by* "Christus" directly but was *over* "Jesus Christus." Apparently during the reign of Claudius, Christian and non-Christian Jews were involved in a riot over the preaching of the gospel (compare Acts 13:49-51; 14:19-20). If this is how Suetonius's account should be understood, it agrees with what Luke says in Acts 18:2: "There [Paul] found a Jew named Aquila, a native of Pontus, who had recently come from Italy with his wife Priscilla, because Claudius had ordered all Jews to leave Rome."

4. Mara bar Serapion. In a seventh-century Syriac manuscript found in the British Museum is preserved a letter dating from the second or third century written by a man named Mara ben Serapion to his son. He refers to the martyrdom of Socrates, Pythagoras and Christ. The Athenians experienced famine and judgment for putting Socrates to death. The people of Samos were overwhelmed by the sea for burning Pythagoras. The Jews in "executing their wise King" were "ruined and driven from their land [and now] live in complete dispersion. . . . Nor did the wise King die for good; he lived on in the teaching which he had given" (Bruce, *Jesus and Christian Origins Outside the New Testament*, p. 31).

5. Julius Africanus *Chronology* 18. In this work written in the early part of the third century, the author refers to the time of Jesus' crucifixion:

This darkness Thallus, in the third book of his *History*, calls, as appears to me without reason, an eclipse of the sun. For the Hebrews celebrate the passover on the 14th day according to the moon, and the passion of our Saviour falls on the day before the passover; but an eclipse of the sun takes place only when the moon comes under the sun. *(The Ante-Nicene Fathers)*

Pagan sources for the life of Jesus are few in number and secondary in nature. Rather than providing eyewitness accounts or reports, these sources give information that has been acquired from contact with Christians at least two or three generations removed from the actual events. Thus they are more valuable for studying the history of the early church than the life of Jesus.

Two other accounts worth mentioning in this regard are *Against Celsus* by Origen and *The Passing of Peregrinus* by Lucian of Samosata. Origen defends Christianity against the attacks of Celsus, and Lucian ridicules Christianity by telling of the huckster Peregrinus, who feigned conversion in order to reap benefits from naive and sympathetic Christians. In both works mention is made of the life of Jesus, but as in the case of Pliny and Suetonius this information is obtained secondhand from Christians removed by some time from the actual events.

In the case of Tacitus, however, his information concerning Jesus' being sentenced and put to death by Pontius Pilate during the reign of Tiberius may be based on the official records in Rome. Regular dispatches were sent to Rome from the provinces reporting major events that had taken place. It is possible that a report of Jesus' trial and crucifixion could have been sent to Rome. (Justin Martyr in his *First Apology* 35.7-9 and 48.3 states that the crucifixion of Jesus is recorded in the official Roman records entitled the "Acts of Pilate." The apocryphal nature of the Acts of Pilate, however, disallows our taking this claim too seriously.)

Jewish sources. Among Jewish writers the two main sources of information concerning the life of Jesus are Josephus and the rabbinic writings.

1. Josephus *The Antiquities of the Jewish People* (18.3.3 [18.63-64] and 20.9.1 [20.200-203]). Joseph the son of Matthias was born into a priestly family in A.D. 37. Precocious as a child, he studied the beliefs of all the main Jewish sects and later became a Pharisee. During the Jewish revolt against Rome, he was placed in charge of the defense of Galilee despite his being only twenty-nine years of age. In Galilee he prepared the defenses and raised up troops for the inevitable Roman attack. By 67 the

only Jewish fortress left in Galilee was Jotapata. After a forty-seven-day siege it also fell, and Josephus fled the city. Hiding in a cave with some forty other Jews, he was discovered. Although the group decided on suicide as the honorable thing to do, Josephus escaped the mass suicide by trickery. He and the only other survivor then surrendered to the Romans (*War* 3.8-9 [3.392-403]).

Upon being brought before Vespasian, the Roman general, Josephus greeted him as "Caesar" and predicted that both he and his son, Titus, would become emperors of Rome. Nero was succeeded in A.D. 68 by Galba, Otho and Vitellius, whose combined reigns lasted a little more than a year. Because of the chaos in Rome, Vespasian's legions proclaimed him emperor, and he and his son after him became emperors of Rome. Thus Josephus experienced a radical change in fortune. He was freed, became a ward of the court and was renamed Flavius (after the family name of Vespasian and Titus) Josephus. During the siege of Jerusalem, Josephus served Titus as a translator and interpreter and became an apologist for Rome.

After the war Josephus went with Titus to Rome and there wrote various works. His two most famous are *The History of the Jewish War* (c. 77) and the even more important *The Antiquities of the Jews* (c. 93). (He also wrote *The Life of Josephus*, a defense of his behavior during the Jewish revolt, and *Against Apion*, a defense of the Jewish religion.) Within the *Antiquities* are two important references to Jesus. The most famous is called the "Testimonium Flavianum":

> About this time there lived Jesus, a wise man, if indeed one ought to call him a man. For he was one who wrought surprising feats and was a teacher of such people as accept the truth gladly. He won over many Jews and many of the Greeks. He was the Messiah. When Pilate, upon hearing him accused by men of the highest standing amongst us, had condemned him to be crucified, those who had in the first place come to love him did not give up their affection for him. On the third day he appeared to them restored to life, for the prophets of God had prophesied these and countless other marvellous things about him. And the tribe of Christians, so called after him, has still to this day not disappeared. (18.3.3 [18.63-64])

At first glance this testimony to Jesus is most impressive. Upon reflection, however, numerous questions arise. Only one other reference to

Jesus occurs in this massive work, when Josephus introduces James just prior to James's martyrdom in A.D. 62:

> Possessed of such a character, Ananus [the high priest] thought that he had a favourable opportunity because Festus was dead and Albinus was still on the way. [Festus and Albinus were Roman governors.] And so he convened the judges of the Sanhedrin and brought before them a man named James, the brother of Jesus who was called the Christ, and certain others. (20.9.1 [20.200-203])

This latter reference to Jesus raises the question whether an author who refers affirmatively to Jesus' being the Messiah and rising from the dead would now refer to him as the "Jesus who was called the Christ."

Other problems also rise. We know from Origen (*Contra Celsum* 1.47) that Josephus was not a Christian. If that is true, why do we find here so strong a witness to Jesus' being the Messiah and rising from the dead? It is also interesting to note that the early church fathers do not quote the Testimonium Flavianum in their apologetic works. That would be strange if they knew that the famous historian Josephus had written so powerful an endorsement of Jesus and affirmed his resurrection. The earliest Christian writer to refer to the Testimonium is Eusebius in the fourth century.

Another problem with the authenticity of this passage is that it breaks the continuity of Josephus's argument. The previous narrative ends with the words "Thus ended the uprising." The following passage begins, "About this same time another outrage threw the Jews into an uproar." Thus, whereas the omission of the Testimonium permits the passage to read smoothly, its presence breaks the continuity and makes one wonder if the testimony is a foreign insertion. Despite the fact that all the oldest Greek manuscripts (eleventh century) of the *Antiquities* contain this witness to Jesus, its authenticity is greatly disputed.

Three positions are possible with respect to the Testimonium Flavianum. One is to accept it at face value as written by Josephus. If true, we have a most important historical reference to Jesus by a Jewish historian of the first century. Few scholars, however, hold this view. A second alternative is to view it as a foreign insertion by a Christian scribe who placed this testimony to Jesus upon the pen of Josephus. The third alternative is to see the present, positive form of the testimony as being an emended version of an earlier, negative or neutral statement by Josephus.

The fact that the works of Josephus were preserved and copied primarily by Christians lends support to the last two positions, but scholars are divided between them. The majority of scholars are united in rejecting the present form of the Testimonium Flavianum as authentic. Those who hold the second view reject it entirely as a legitimate source for the study of the life of Jesus.

2. The rabbinic writings. The most important rabbinic writing is the Talmud. It contains two parts: the Mishna and the Gemara. The Mishna consists of the oral traditions that circulated in Judaism from about 200 B.C. to A.D. 200 (compare Mk 7:1-13). They were, according to tradition, written down in Hebrew by Rabbi Judah. (Additional traditions, which did not find their way into the Mishna, were later incorporated into a work called the Tosefta.) Around these traditions arose various commentaries called Gemara, which were written in Aramaic. Together the Mishna and Gemara make up the Talmud.

The Gemara, which arose in Palestine, was combined with the Mishna sometime between A.D. 350 and 400 and make up what is known as the Palestinian (or Jerusalem) Talmud (PT). In Babylon a Gemara was added to the Mishna approximately A.D. 500. Together they make up the better-known and much larger Babylonian Talmud (BT). The Talmud consists of sixty-three "Tractates" arranged in six "Orders." The main problem involved in evaluating the Talmudic materials is to separate later accretions from the earlier materials. All too often it appears that the Talmudic materials witness not to what actually took place in a previous period but to an idealized rendering of how things should have taken place if the later rabbinic understanding of the law had been in force.

The Talmud contains several references to Jesus. The most famous is found in *b. Sanhedrin* 43a (BT):

> On the eve of the Passover Yeshu was hanged. For forty days before the execution took place, a herald went forth and cried, "He is going forth to be stoned because he has practised sorcery and enticed Israel to apostasy. Any one who can say anything in his favour, let him come forward and plead on his behalf." But since nothing was brought forward in his favour he was hanged on the eve of the Passover!—Ulla retorted: Do you suppose that he was one for whom a defence could be made? Was he not a *Mesith* [enticer], concerning whom Scripture says, *Neither shalt thou spare, neither shalt thou conceal him?* With Yeshu how-

ever it was different, for he was connected with the government [or royalty, i.e., influential]. Our Rabbis taught: Yeshu had five disciples, Matthai, Nakai, Nezer, Buni, and Todah.

We find a number of parallels between this tradition and the Gospel accounts. Jesus' death is associated with the Passover and occurs on the eve of the Passover (compare Jn 19:31). Indirectly his miracle-working activity is witnessed to by the claim that he worked sorcery (compare Mk 3:22, where Jesus' miracles are attributed to a demonic source). He is accused of apostasy, and although the penalty for this is "stoning," Jesus was not stoned but "hanged," that is, crucified. No mention is made of the Roman part in the trial of Jesus. But that is not surprising in that the concern of the Mishna is to explain the Jewish law, and in this respect the role of Rome was irrelevant. There is present an acknowledgment that the leadership of Israel was involved in Jesus' death. Mention is made of Jesus' having had disciples, but only five are listed, and their names do not make a great deal of sense (Matthai = Matthew; Nakai = Nicodemus?; Nezer = Nazarene?; Buni = Boanerges, the Sons of Thunder?; Todah = Thaddaeus?).

The question must be raised whether this material comes from oral traditions of those who were themselves eyewitnesses of the trial or who had access to eyewitness reports of what took place. If so, these traditions would be extremely valuable. Most of the material, however, arose from later Jewish-Christian debates and appears to be apologetic in nature. For instance, the statement that for forty days a search was made for witnesses on Jesus' behalf looks like an apologetic on the part of rabbinic Judaism against the Christian claim that Jesus did not receive a fair trial. Thus we find that whereas this material is most helpful in the investigation of Judaism and the early church during the second through fifth centuries, it is less valuable for the study of the life of Jesus.

Several other references in the Talmud have been seen as referring to Jesus. But they are for the most part problematic in that they do not mention Jesus directly. The Jewish avoidance of using the name of heretics could explain this. The following passages may be counterapologetics to the Christian claim of the virginal conception:

Balaam also the son of Beor, the soothsayer, [did the children of Israel slay with the sword]. A soothsayer? But he was a prophet!—R. Johanan said: At first he was a prophet, but subsequently a soothsayer. R. Papa observed:

This is what men say, "She who was the descendant of princes and governors, played the harlot with carpenters." (b. Sanhedrin 106a; compare also 106b)

> Said R. Simeon B. 'Azzai: I found a roll of genealogical records in Jerusalem, and therein was written, "so-and-so is a bastard [having been born] from [a forbidden union with] a married woman," which confirms the view of R. Joshua. (b. Yebamot 49a)

This also brings to mind the claim of a man named Celsus as recorded in Origen (c. 248): "Let us return, however, to the words put into the mouth of the Jew, where the mother of Jesus is described as having been turned out by the carpenter who was betrothed to her, as she had been convicted of adultery and had a child by a certain soldier named Panthera" (Contra Celsum 1.32). It is evident that this reference is an apologetic by the neo-Platonist Celsus against the Christian claim that Mary, the mother of Jesus, was a virgin when she conceived him. There may even be a pun here. Whereas Christians claimed that Jesus was conceived and born of a virgin (parthenos, the Greek term for virgin), opponents said, "No, not of a parthenos but of Panthera." By a simple reversal of the r and n they "discovered" the real father of Jesus and argued that Jesus was illegitimate.

The references given above from the Tractates Sanhedrin and Yebamot may very well represent a similar attack on the Christian claim. Several arguments favor this interpretation. For one, although the name of the woman and child are not given, it is assumed that people would know to whom these sayings referred. Jesus would certainly have been a prime candidate in people's minds. Second, the reference to a carpenter fits well the fact that Joseph and Jesus were carpenters, even though it is not the husband of Mary but the adulterer who is so described. It may also be that the reference to Mary's being a descendant of princes and governors may be an allusion to the Gospel genealogies in which we find such royal figures as David, Solomon and Zerubbabel (Mt 1:1-17; Lk 3:23-37). It has also been argued that the name Balaam was seen by Jews as a type for Jesus. If so, the above passages are probably references to Jesus created as counterpropaganda against Christian claims. They are, however, secondary in nature and the result of later Jewish-Christian debate rather than contemporary, eyewitness reports.

Several passages dealing with the treatment of heresy have also been suggested as possible allusions to Jesus even though his name is not present.

☐ *b. Berakot* 17b: "May our company not be like that of Elisha, from which issued Gehazi. *In our broad places:* may we produce no son or pupil who disgraces himself in public." One manuscript (M) adds to the end of this saying "like the Nazarene."

☐ *b. Sanhedrin* 103a: "Another interpretation: *'There shall no evil befall thee'*— thou wilt not be affrighted by nightmares and dread thoughts; *'neither shall any plague come nigh thy dwelling'*—thou will not have a son or a disciple who publicly burns his food." The expression "to burn food" refers to accepting or propounding heresy.

Other possible allusions to Jesus or his teachings may be found in *b. Šabbat* 116b (a possible reference to Mt 5:17) and *b. Sanhedrin* 107b, where one manuscript tradition refers to "Jesus the Nazarene [who] practised magic and led Israel astray."

The key question that arises involves the origin of these rabbinic references. The value of these passages would be greatly enhanced if they originated from contemporaries of Jesus who were eyewitnesses of the events they were reporting. This would be true even though they presented the side of Jesus' opponents. On several occasions, however, aspects of these accounts seem to be due less to eyewitness reports than to later Jewish interaction with the teachings and claims of the early church. This is especially true with respect to such matters as the claim that a forty-day search for witnesses on Jesus' behalf preceded his trial and, if the accounts refer to Jesus, to his birth being due not to a virginal conception but to adultery on the part of his mother. As a result, the rabbinic materials are primarily valuable for providing information concerning second-, third- and fourth-century Judaism, and even here they must be read critically. Like the pagan sources, however, they provide little information for the historian seeking to construct a life of Jesus.

Christian Sources

Extrabiblical sources. It is evident that not everything Jesus said or did is recorded in the four canonical Gospels. This is explicitly stated in John 21:25: "But there are also many other things that Jesus did; if every one of them were written down, I suppose that the world itself could not contain the books that would be written." It is probable that traditions concerning Jesus were remembered and were passed on orally even after the Gospels were written. Some of these may later have been recorded. Papias, an early church father, stated (c. 130) that he actually preferred to investigate some of these oral traditions.

> For unlike most I did not rejoice in them who say much, but in them who teach the truth, nor in them who recount the commandments of others, but in them who repeated those given to the faith by the Lord and derived from truth itself; but if ever anyone came who had followed the presbyters, I inquired into the words of the presbyters, what Andrew or Peter or Philip or Thomas or James or John or Matthew, or any other of the Lord's disciples, had said, and what Aristion and the presbyter John, the Lord's disciples, were saying. For I did not suppose that information from books would help me so much as the word of a living and surviving voice. (quoted in Eusebius *Eccl. Hist.* 3.39.4)

Where can one go to find such traditions? The main possibilities are (1) the apocryphal Gospels, especially the *Gospel of Thomas,* (2) various hypothetical manuscripts such as Q, the *Secret Gospel of Mark* and a "Cross Gospel," (3) quotations found in the early church fathers and (4) textual variants found in various Gospel manuscripts.

During the middle of the second century a number of works began to appear called apocryphal Gospels. Many of them claim, falsely to be sure, apostolic authorship and bear such names as *Infancy Gospel of Thomas, Gospel of Peter, Gospel of Nicodemus, Gospel of Philip, Gospel of Barnabas, Gospel of Mary, Gospel of Thomas* and *Gospel of the Twelve Apostles.* Some bear such names as *Gospel of Truth, Gospel of the Ebionites, Gospel of the Egyptians, Gospel of the Hebrews, Gospel of the Nazareans, Protevangelium of James* and *Secret Gospel of Mark.* Others even bear the names of heretics: *Gospel of Cerinthus, Gospel of Basilides, Gospel of Marcion, Gospel of Apelles, Gospel of Mani* and so on. We also possess papyrus fragments of other apocryphal-like Gospels.

In character these works range from orthodox to semiorthodox, from heterodox to heretical in nature. Some we possess in complete form; others are fragmentary in nature; some are known only because they are mentioned in other works. The value of these works for the study of the early church in the second through fourth centuries is evident, but their value for the study of the life of Jesus is debated. Some works, such as the *Gospel of Truth* (which is little more than a Gnostic theological treatise of the second century), are of no real value:

> The gospel of truth is joy for those who have received from the Father
> of truth the grace of knowing him, through the power of the Word
> that came forth from the pleroma, the one who is in the thought and
> the mind of the Father, that is, the one who is addressed as the Savior,
> (that) being the name of the work he is to perform for the redemption
> of those who were ignorant of the Father, while in the name [of] the
> gospel is the proclamation of hope, being discovery for those who
> search for him. (1.3; *The Nag Hammadi Library in English* [San Francisco:
> Harper, 1988])

Some works are imaginary stories by orthodox Christians about periods
of Jesus' life not discussed in the canonical Gospels. A well-known example is found in the *Infancy Gospel of Thomas:*

> When this boy Jesus was five years old he was playing at the crossing
> of a stream, and he gathered together into pools the running water,
> and instantly made it clean, and gave his command with a single word.
> Having made soft clay he moulded from it twelve sparrows. And it was
> the sabbath when he did these things. And there were also many other
> children playing with him. When a certain Jew saw what Jesus was
> doing while playing on the sabbath, he at once went and told his father
> Joseph, "See, your child is at the stream, and he took clay and moulded
> twelve birds and has profaned the sabbath." And when Joseph came
> to the place and looked, he cried out to him, saying, "Why do you do
> on the sabbath things which it is not lawful to do?" But Jesus clapped
> his hands and cried out to the sparrows and said to them, "Be gone!"
> And the sparrows took flight and went away chirping. The Jews were
> amazed when they saw this, and went away and told their leaders
> what they had seen Jesus do. (2.1-5; *ANT*, pp. 75-76)

The *Infancy Gospel of Thomas* goes on to tell how a Jewish boy fell down dead
when he broke up the pool of water that Jesus had made. Another boy
who ran and accidentally knocked into Jesus also fell down dead. It is easy
to see that these stories lack any historical basis in Jesus' life. John 2:11
explicitly states that the wedding miracle at Cana was Jesus' first sign,
or miracle. No doubt what we have here is the reading back into Jesus'
childhood what pious (or impious) Christians thought the Son of God
must have been like during his early years.

Of the apocryphal Gospels, the *Gospel of Thomas* stands out above all others in importance. This Coptic work was discovered in 1945 among the numerous manuscripts found at Nag Hammadi in Egypt. Some Greek papyri fragments (*Oxyrhynchus Papyrus* 1, 654, 655) discovered earlier in 1897 and 1904 now appear to be parts of three different copies of this work. The date of the *Gospel of Thomas* is greatly debated. Some have argued that its original form dates to the middle of the first century and is earlier than any of the canonical Gospels. The present Coptic manuscript dates to c. 400, whereas the Greek papyri fragments date to c. 200. The present form probably is to be dated c. 150, although it contains sayings that go back to the first century. Whether there was an earlier written form of this gospel is a matter of debate.

The *Gospel of Thomas* consists of a collection of 114 sayings. Some of them repeat almost verbatim the sayings found in our Gospels; some are similar to our Gospel sayings but have an interesting twist or addition. Others are quite strange and betray a clear Gnostic bent:

Jesus said: If they say to you, Whence have you come? say to them, We have come from the light, (from) the place where the light came into existence through itself alone; it has . . . and it has revealed itself in their image. (50)

His disciples [*mathētēs*] said to him: Twenty-four prophets [*prophētēs*] spoke in Israel and all of them spoke concerning [literally, in] you. He said to them: You have forsaken the Living One who is in your presence and have spoken about the dead. (52)

Jesus said: I am the light which is over everything. I am the All; the All came forth from me and the All has reached to me. Split the wood; I am there. Lift up the stone, and you will find me there. (77)

Jesus said: The images [*eikōn*] are manifest to man, and the light which is within them is hidden in the image [*eikōn*] of the light of the Father. He will be revealed, and his image [*eikōn*] is concealed by his light. Jesus said: The days (when) you see your likeness, you rejoice. But when [*hotan de*] you see your images [*eikōn*] which came into being before you—which neither [*oute*] die nor [*oute*] are manifested—how much will you bear! (83-84)

Other sayings are not necessarily Gnostic but are nonetheless strange.

The disciples [*mathētēs*] said to Jesus: We know that you will go away from us. Who is it that will (then) be great over us? Jesus said to them: In the place to which you have come, you will go to James the Just [dikaios], for whose sake heaven and earth came into existence. (12)

Jesus said: The kingdom is like a shepherd who had a hundred sheep. One of them went astray; it was the largest. He left the ninety-nine (and) sought for the one until he found it. After he had exerted himself, he said to the sheep, I love you more than [para] the ninety-nine. (107)

What makes the *Gospel of Thomas* valuable, however, are the sayings that are similar or nearly identical to those in the four Gospels. Most scholars do not believe that these sayings were obtained from the canonical Gospels but come from separate traditions, either oral or written. If so, we have in these places an independent witness to the Gospel traditions. In those instances, when it sides with the form of one Gospel saying over against another, it gives support in favor of the authenticity of the one with which it agrees.

An example is found in the parable of the Great Supper. In Luke's form of the parable (Lk 14:15-24) the servants are sent out twice to seek replacement guests, and in so doing the Evangelist alludes to the Gentile mission of his day. But in both Matthew's form (Mt 22:1-14) and the *Gospel of Thomas* (64) there is only a single sending out of servants to seek replacement guests. This suggests that the second sending out is Luke's addition. Other sayings in the *Gospel of Thomas* that are similar to those in our Gospels are numbers 26, 31 and 47:

Jesus said: You see the speck that is in your brother's eye, but [de] you do not see the log which is in your own eye. When [hotan] you take the log out of your own eye, then [tote] you will see to take out the speck from your brother's eye. (26)

Jesus said: No prophet [prophētēs] is acceptable in his village; no physician works cures [therapeuein] on those who know him. (31)

Jesus said: It is impossible for a man to ride two horses (and) to stretch two bows, and it is impossible for a servant to serve two masters; either [ē] he will honor [timan] the one and despise [hybrizein] the other. (47)

Recently extravagant claims have been made with respect to the historical value of three hypothetical documents: Q, a Cross Gospel and the *Secret Gospel of Mark*. Q is a hypothetical reconstruction of a source used by Matthew and Luke (a compilation of the common material found in Matthew and Luke but not in Mark). The existence of Q is based on the view that Mark was the first written Gospel and that Matthew and Luke made use of Mark in the writing of their Gospels. This is the assumption of most New Testament scholars. If so, the next question is why there is so much common material in these two Gospels (about 235 verses) not found in Mark. Where did this material come from if not from Mark? Closely related to this is the question of whether Luke and Matthew knew each other—did Luke make use of Matthew when he wrote his Gospel or vice versa? There are numerous reasons for concluding that Matthew and Luke did not know each other. Thus Matthew and Luke must have used a common source besides Mark. (Probably the designation "Q" comes from the first letter of the German word *Quelle*, which means "source.") This is the belief of most New Testament scholars.

Some remarkably imaginary reconstructions and conclusions are based on this theory. Up to three separate editions in the history of Q have been suggested, and the kind of community that gave birth to this source and the struggles that caused the new editions are confidently described. All one needs to do, however, is to note the probability of all this being true to realize that it is clearly building a foundation on sandy soil. Notice the presuppositions:

1. Mark was the first Gospel written (quite probable, but a theory, not an axiom or proof).

2. Matthew and Luke did not know each other (probable, but again a theory, not an axiom or proof).

3. Q was written (more questionable in that a common oral tradition could explain many of the agreements between Matthew and Luke).

4. Q was a single written document (more questionable still in that the order of the material in Matthew and Luke do not demonstrate their having used a single written document).

5. Q reveals the basic theology of a particular community that created this document (highly questionable). Most literature is the product of individuals. Does Luke reveal the theology of a Lukan community or of Luke the author? Does Mark reveal the theology of a community or of Mark the author? Does Galatians reveal the theology of the Galatian church or of Paul, who wanted to change the theology of the Galatian church to his? Can we assume that the recipients or creators of a New Testament work believed only what is contained in that work? If so, the Pauline churches believed very little about the historical Jesus, as did the

church represented in Hebrews, 1 and 2 Peter, James and 1, 2 and 3 John.

6. Even if we believe that we can determine the final form of Q used by Matthew and Luke, assuming that Q was a single written document, it is incredible to think that we could arrive at the form of an earlier edition.

7. It is even more incredible to think that we could reconstruct the form of the earliest edition of this hypothetical work.

8. Finally, to assume that we could then determine the struggles that supposedly led to these new editions is simply impossible.

The probability of the last presupposition being true is the probability of all these presuppositions multiplied together. In other words, if the probability of the first five hypotheses were (1) 90 percent, (2) 80 percent, (3) 60 percent, (4) 50 percent, (5) 40 percent, the possibility of the fifth being true is $.90 \times .80 \times .60 \times .50 \times .40$, *or a little more than 8 percent!* Some of the hypothetical percentages given above are generous, and we have not even multiplied into our equation the small likelihood of the sixth, seventh and eighth presuppositions. It becomes evident that historical research has switched to the writing of fiction in such a procedure.

The existence of the Cross Gospel and the *Secret Gospel of Mark* is even more debatable. The Cross Gospel is a hypothetical work reconstructed from a late second-century apocryphal Gospel called the *Gospel of Peter*. The so-called *Secret Gospel of Mark* was discovered in 1958 by Morton Smith, but it was not published by him until 1973. The text claims to be a letter of Clement of Alexandria (c. 150-215). It is contained in a handwritten note found in a seventeenth-century edition of the works of Ignatius of Antioch at the monastery of Mar Saba, located between Bethlehem and the Dead Sea. This addition was written by an eighteenth-century hand on the last three pages of this printed work of Ignatius. No one has seen the original manuscript except for Morton Smith, who produced photographs of the material. Whether the handwritten material is a forgery or actually a letter written by Clement of Alexandria is debated. According to some scholars, who assume that this material is an actual fragment of an authentic letter of Clement, this letter contains material from a *Secret Gospel of Mark* that predates the Mark in our Bible and was actually the basis for an early form of a Mark-like Gospel. This Mark-like Gospel was made into a heretical Carpocratian version of Mark, which was then reworked into our Mark. To build such a complicated system upon an eighteenth-century addition to a printed work that no one but the discoverer has actually seen is building a great deal on an exceptionally weak foundation. Furthermore, several scholars have argued convincingly that the material in the *Secret Gospel* is not the basis of the material in our canonical Mark. On the contrary, it presupposes Mark.

The argument for a Cross Gospel is even less convincing. Those who hold this view argue that behind the later second-century *Gospel of Peter* stands a Cross Gospel, which is the sole source for the passion narrative in our Gospels. This Cross Gospel was written in the middle of the first century and was Mark's only source for the passion narrative. Mark's account was then used by Matthew, Luke and John, who also knew the Cross Gospel. However, as in the case of the *Secret Gospel of Mark*, the Cross Gospel has been shown to bear telltale marks of dependence on the canonical Gospels. Thus it provides no independent access to early traditions about the Jesus of history.

Our survey of the noncanonical Christian sources ultimately turns out to be rather negative. This is evident to anyone who reads the apocryphal Gospels. Not only were they written significantly later, but they almost always witness to views and situations far removed from the first-century Israel of Jesus of Nazareth. Only in the *Gospel of Thomas* do we find possible help in understanding the historical Jesus. Even this work, however, is permeated with second-century Gnostic ideas and teachings. Nevertheless, it may bear witness at times to some first-century traditions concerning the teachings of Jesus.

If these traditions were not dependent on our canonical Gospels—and this is quite possible—they can serve at times to support the authenticity of the material found in one canonical Gospel over another. If we, for instance, have two versions of a saying or parable in Matthew and Luke, the witness of the *Gospel of Thomas* in favor of one of these versions supports the authenticity of that version. There are serious problems, however, in arguing that a saying found only in the *Gospel of Thomas* is authentic.

Biblical sources: Acts through Revelation. Within the New Testament, if we exclude the Gospels, we find less information about Jesus of Nazareth than we might expect. For the most part we learn several things regarding his birth, his character, events in his life, his crucifixion and his teachings.

Concerning his birth: he was a descendant of David (Rom 1:3); he was raised as a Jew under the law (Gal 4:4); he was truly a man (that is, there was a real incarnation; 1 Jn 1:1-3; 4:1-3); he was poor (2 Cor 8:9). Although this last verse refers primarily to Jesus' kenosis (his self-emptying in becoming a man), it probably also refers to his economic status as a child.

Concerning his character: he was gentle and meek (2 Cor 10:1); he was righteous (1 Pet 3:18; compare Acts 7:52); he was sinless (2 Cor 5:21; Heb 4:15; 1 Pet 2:22); he was humble (Phil 2:6-8); he was tempted (Heb 2:18; 4:15).

Concerning certain events in his life: the Lord's Supper (1 Cor 11:23-26), the transfiguration (2 Pet 1:16-18), a possible reference to Gethsemane (Heb 5:7).

Concerning his crucifixion: he experienced hostility (Heb 12:3; Rom 15:3); he was betrayed (1 Cor 11:23; compare Acts 1:15-20); the Jews present at his trial chose Barabbas over him (Acts 3:14); the Jewish leadership bore responsibility in his crucifixion (1 Thess 2:14-15; Acts 2:23, 36; 7:52); he suffered without resisting (1 Pet 2:21-23); he was crucified (for example, 1 Cor 1:23); he rose from the dead (for example, 1 Cor 15); he ascended into heaven (Acts 1:9-11; Eph 4:8-10).

Concerning certain of his teachings: compare Romans 12:14 with Matthew 5:44; Romans 12:17 with Matthew 5:39; Romans 13:7 with Mark 12:17; Romans 13:8-10 with Mark 12:31; Romans 14:10 with Matthew 7:1.

Apart from the Gospels we would be entirely ignorant about many things: the birth of Jesus, his baptism, his ministry to the outcasts, the events of Caesarea Philippi, the events surrounding his trial and crucifixion, his miracles, such teachings as his parables, the beatitudes and the Lord's Prayer. It is clear that the writers of Acts through Revelation did not intend to supply their readers with information about Jesus of Nazareth. They all probably assumed, as Luke did with respect to the readers of Luke-Acts, that they already possessed such information (compare Lk 1:4).

Another source of information concerning the life of Christ is the agrapha. The term *agrapha* combines *grapha*, which means "writings," and *a*. The negating effect of *a* can be seen in such words as *theistic (atheistic), moral (amoral)* and *typical (atypical)*. In Gospel studies this expression refers to the unwritten sayings of Jesus—authentic sayings of Jesus not found in the canonical Gospels. Sayings of the risen Christ (Rev 1:8, 11, 17—3:22; compare Acts 9:4-6, 11-12, 15-16) are excluded. This material has been sought in several places: the New Testament apart from the Gospels (Acts 20:35; Rom 14:14; 1 Cor 7:10; 9:14; 11:23-26; 1 Thess 4:15-17[?]), manuscript variants of the Gospels (Lk 6:5 in Codex D; Jn 7:53—8:11), the apocryphal Gospels, especially the *Gospel of Thomas,* writings of the early church fathers (see, for example, the supposed letter of Jesus to King Abgar in Eusebius *Eccl. Hist.* 1.13.4-10) and such miscellaneous sources as the Talmud and even the Qur'an.

It is difficult to demonstrate that an alleged agrapha in a work such as the *Gospel of Thomas* was actually said by Jesus. For example, is *Gospel of Thomas* 19 ("Jesus said: Blessed is he who was before he became . . .") an agrapha? It is highly improbable, for it is too unlike what we find in the Gospels and too much like what we find in second-century Gnosticism. What about *Gospel of Thomas* 47: "Jesus said: It is impossible for a person to ride two horses (and) to stretch two bows, and it is impossible for a servant to serve two masters; either he will honor the one and despise the other . . ."? The latter part of this saying agrees with what we find in Matthew 6:24 and Luke 16:13, and many would therefore be comfortable with accepting it. But what about the first part? It does not conflict with what we believe Jesus said elsewhere, but is it authentic? Perhaps. What about "Jesus said: It is impossible for a man to ride two chariots and it is impossible for a man to ride two motorcycles"? Clearly the latter is not authentic because it is anachronistic—it conflicts with what we know of the times of Jesus. But what about the former? It would fit, but it was created by the present author. No doubt the reader could also create similar sayings that would fit the day and age of Jesus and the general tenor of his teachings.

The problem with the agrapha is simply this: whereas we may eliminate possible agrapha that Jesus could not have said ("No one can ride two motorcycles"), it is impossible to prove which ones he might have said. The primary evidence that argues in favor of the authenticity of such sayings involves the value we give to its witnesses. If we give little credence to the apocryphal Gospels, to later scribes who added such sayings to various manuscripts and to church fathers removed in time from the actual events, then it is difficult to give credence to the reported alleged sayings of Jesus. If we give a higher credibility to the New Testament, then it is more likely that we will accept such a saying as "It is more blessed to give than to receive" (Acts 20:35) because of our positive view concerning the witness of the New Testament. In so doing, we must acknowledge our prejudice. We give credence to the New Testament over other books because we consider the New Testament to be unique and under divine guidance in a way that we do not acknowledge in these other materials. Apart from such credence, it is difficult, if not impossible, to accept as true agrapha those sayings found in the apocryphal Gospels and other nonbiblical sources.

Biblical sources: the Gospels. With respect to the canonical Gospels it has always been apparent that three of them (Matthew, Mark, Luke) bear a great resemblance to each other, whereas one is quite different (John). The look-alike quality of the first three Gospels in the New Testament has resulted in their being called the "Synoptic Gospels"—Gospels that are to be viewed side by side. Why these Gospels resemble each other and what their relationship is to one another has been called the "Synoptic problem." This relationship was discussed early in the history of the church. The general solution and what the situation was before the Gospel traditions were written is as follows.

Before the traditions of Jesus were ever written down in the form of our Gospels, Christians passed on this material orally. Thus in the first decades of the early church, people learned about Jesus through preaching and teaching. Exactly how these traditions of Jesus were passed on is much debated. Although there are some difficulties with the analogy, probably the best available pattern for how this process was carried out is the method of memorization used by rabbis and their students described in the rabbinic writings.

Whatever the exact method, Luke argues that this all took place under the supervision and care of the apostolic eyewitnesses (Lk 1:1-4). Luke by writing his Gospel sought to demonstrate the reliability of those oral traditions that his reader, Theophilus, had been taught. This indicates that there must be a close continuity between the oral traditions with which his reader(s) was familiar and the accounts in Luke's Gospel and the other two Gospels that look like his (Matthew and Mark). A radical discontinuity between the oral traditions known by Theophilus and the accounts in the Gospel of Luke would lead to doubt, not certainty (Lk 1:4).

As time progressed, collections of the oral traditions began to be written down. These consisted of similar kinds of material: collections of parables, miracle stories and controversy stories, the passion narrative and so on. Most scholars believe that the first written Gospel was what we call the Gospel of Mark. Tradition states that it was written by John Mark in association with Peter sometime between A.D. 65 and 70. Matthew and Luke in writing their Gospels used Mark, a collection of various sayings of Jesus not found in Mark (the Q material, along with their own unique collection of traditions), M (the traditions of Jesus found only in Matthew) and L (the traditions of Jesus found only in Luke). M and L may have been written or oral, two single sources or several different sources. The general dates given for when they were written is 75-90. John, according to tradition, was written late, c. 90-95, and whereas the apostle John is associated in the tradition with this Gospel, it is clear that the last chapter of the Gospel was written by his disciples (see Jn 21:24—"We [the writers of chapter 21] know that his [the beloved disciple's] testimony is true").

Tradition has not attributed apostolic authorship to either Mark or Luke. The fact that this goes so contrary to the church's tendency to name Gospels after apostles (Matthew, John and the apocryphal Gospels of Peter, Paul, Thomas and so on) suggests that such testimony should receive serious attention. The attribution of the second Gospel to John Mark found in the Anti-Marcionite Prologue (c. 150-180) ought to be carefully considered because of the negative description it gives to him as "stumpfinger." The "we sections" of Acts (Acts 16:10-17; 20:5—21:18; 27:1—28:16) fit very well with Luke's authorship, and that a nonapostle is named as the author should be taken seriously.

Tradition is united with respect to Matthew's authorship of the first Gospel, but tradition is also united in saying that he wrote it in the Hebrew (probably Aramaic) language. This causes great difficulty because Matthew cannot be easily translated from its present Greek into Aramaic, which one would expect if it were indeed a translation from Aramaic. The Greek origin of the present form of Matthew is also supported by its dependence on the Greek Gospel of Mark. Thus the question of authorship by the apostle Matthew is a difficult one. One of the most important considerations in this regard involves one's view of tradition. Someone who takes the tradition seriously will probably want to see somewhere in the formation of the sources of Matthew or in a proto-Matthew the hand of the apostle.

The tradition is also clear with respect to the apostolic authorship of John, and again the issue must be raised as to how one views the tradition. Another factor that plays an important role with respect to the claim of apostolic authorship (Matthew and John) or close ties with apostles (Mark with Peter and Luke with Paul) involves one's presuppositions. Although seldom if ever mentioned, one's view toward the supernatural plays an extremely important role with respect to the claim of apostolic authorship of Matthew and John and the tie with apostles in Mark and Luke. If one denies the supernatural and the possibility of miracles and if the Gospels report numerous such miracles, how could the Gospels have been written by eyewitnesses? (The same holds true for Acts, whose author claims to be an eyewitness in the "we sections.") How could eyewitnesses, whose intelligence and historical competency have been questioned but not their integrity, because they truly believed the contents of their Gospels, write Gospel accounts containing miracles? Thus, if the authors believed what they wrote (and they did), they must be removed from the actual events. It is evident, therefore, that one's presuppositions concerning the historical-critical method and whether miracles are by definition excluded from history play a major role in the issue of authorship.

Criteria for the Authenticity of Jesus' Sayings

How can one be sure if an alleged saying of Jesus in the Gospels is authentic—that Jesus actually said it? Are the sayings in our Greek Gospels accurate translations of what Jesus said and taught during his ministry?

Attempts have been made to establish certain criteria to judge the probable authenticity of particular sayings and teachings of Jesus. Some of them are more valuable than others. Some are of doubtful value. Yet if a teaching of Jesus fits these criteria, the likelihood of its being authentic is increased, and the more criteria that it meets, the more likely is its authenticity. There are six *positive* criteria: multiple attestation; multiple forms; Aramaic linguistic phenomena; Palestinian environmental phenomena; dissimilarity; divergent patterns from the developing tradition. The primarily *negative* criteria number three: the tendencies of the developing tradition, environmental contradiction and contradiction of authentic sayings.

1. The criterion of multiple attestation. This has also been called "the Cross-Section Approach." It argues that if the various sources we find in our Gospels (Mark, Q, M, L and John) witness to a teaching of Jesus, then it is likely to be authentic. An example is that in Mark (Mk 2:21-22), Q (Luke 11:20), M (Mt 5:17), L (Lk 17:20-21) and John (Jn 12:31) we find teachings concerning the kingdom of God having become a present reality in Jesus' ministry.

2. The criterion of multiple forms. Like the previous one, this seeks multiple witnesses, but it finds them in the various forms of the Gospel material rather than in the various sources. Here we find, for example, Jesus' teaching that the kingdom of God had already arrived in pronouncement stories (Mk 2:18-20), miracle stories (Lk 7:11-17), stories about Jesus (Lk 4:16-30), parables (Lk 14:15-24) and sayings (Mt 5:17).

3. The criterion of Aramaic linguistic phenomena. This criterion argues that since Jesus' native tongue and the language in which he taught was Aramaic, if we find in the Gospels Aramaic linguistic characteristics, that brings us closer to the situation of Jesus and makes it more likely that such teachings came from him. An example is found in Matthew 23:24, which when translated into Aramaic is a pun (gnat = *galma;* camel = *gamla*).

4. The criterion of Palestinian environmental phenomena. This is much like the preceding one, but, instead of looking for linguistic phenomena that reflect the situation of Jesus (Aramaic), it looks for sociological, geographical, religious or cultural aspects of the tradition that betray Jesus' Palestinian environment. This again increases the likelihood that the tradition comes from Jesus. Examples can be found in the parables of the sower and the seed (Mk 4:2-20), the Pharisee and the tax collector (Lk 18:9-14), the great net (Mt 13:47-50), the laborers in the vineyard (Mt 20:1-16) and the wise and foolish maidens (Mt 25:1-13).

5. The criterion of dissimilarity. This criterion has received the most attention and weight. It argues that if a tradition could not have arisen out of the environment of the early church or of first-century Judaism, then it must have come from Jesus. The title "Son of Man" fits this criterion. This criterion was greeted initially with great enthusiasm by scholars, but its use is now seen as quite limited. One should not expect that the vast majority of Jesus' teachings would be dissimilar to both

those of first-century Judaism and those of the early church any more than one would expect that most of Martin Luther's teachings would be dissimilar to those of sixteenth-century Roman Catholicism and Lutheranism. By this criterion we are able to arrive at pieces of authentic tradition. By definition, however, it can reveal to us only what is distinctive about Jesus' teachings and not what is most characteristic. The latter would have much in common with the teachings of the early church or the Judaism of the first century.

6. The criterion of divergent patterns from the developing tradition. If one were to find in a Gospel a saying of Jesus or an incident that does not serve the emphasis of the Evangelist or may even conflict with it, this witnesses to the antiquity of the material and ultimately to its authenticity. That is because the only reason the Evangelist would have included the tradition is that it was well established and had been around for a long time. This brings the tradition back closer to the time of Jesus and argues in favor of its authenticity. A saying such as Matthew 11:13 ("For all the prophets and the law prophesied until John came") fits this criterion in that it does not support the Matthean emphasis on the abiding significance of the law.

7. The criterion of the tendencies of the developing tradition. If we were able to establish how oral traditions developed as they were passed on, we could work backward and eliminate from the tradition those tendencies. The problem with this criterion is that the oral traditions were not governed by "laws." We discover that sometimes traditions became more detailed, sometimes less detailed. Sometimes they tended to give names to unnamed characters; sometimes they omitted them. As a result, the whole question of what tendencies, if any, existed in the passing on of such tradition is greatly debated.

8. The criterion of environmental contradiction. According to this criterion, if a saying or activity of Jesus presupposes a situation in his life that was impossible, the saying or activity is inauthentic. It has been suggested that the saying about a wife divorcing her husband (Mk 10:12) could not be authentic because Jewish women could not divorce their husbands. It should be noted, however, that the tetrarch of Galilee was criticized by John the Baptist for marrying a woman who had just done this (Mk 6:17-18). That example should warn us about the danger of using this criterion uncritically. It is difficult to be certain as to what Jesus

could or could not have said or done. The saying concerning a wife divorcing her husband in Mark 10:12 may or may not be authentic, but to say that Jesus could not have said this is wrong.

9. The criterion of contradiction of authentic sayings. This criterion argues that if one comes across a saying in the Gospels that contradicts known authentic material, this saying must be inauthentic. There is a problem with this, however, in that we must be certain that such material is truly contradictory. Jesus' lavish use of exaggeration, figurative language and hyperbole makes such certainty difficult at times.

There is a danger when using such criteria to assume that the burden of proof rests on those who believe that a Gospel tradition is authentic. Such a burden of proof is both unfair and prejudiced. Even as a person is innocent until proven guilty, so the Gospel traditions should be assumed authentic unless proven inauthentic. The criteria listed above are rather limited in scope. We are unable to apply these criteria to numerous sayings of Jesus. Nevertheless, they do serve a purpose. If we demonstrate that the authenticity of various sayings and teachings of Jesus is supported by these criteria (and we can), this gives confidence as to the authenticity of other sayings and teachings that cannot be tested by the criteria.

Conclusion

It is evident that we do not learn a great deal about Jesus of Nazareth from sources outside the New Testament. The non-Christian sources establish beyond reasonable doubt the following minimum: (1) Jesus was truly a historical person. This may seem silly to stress, but through the years some have denied that Jesus ever lived. The nonbiblical sources put such nonsense to rest. (2) Jesus lived in Palestine in the first century of our era. (3) The Jewish leadership was involved in the death of Jesus. (4) Jesus was crucified by the Romans under the governorship of Pontius Pilate. (5) Jesus' ministry was associated with wonders/sorcery. Much more than this we cannot learn.

From the nonbiblical Christian sources we find little of which we can be certain. The *Gospel of Thomas* may contain various agrapha, but that cannot be demonstrated. Its main value lies in supporting one canonical Gospel over another with respect to the form of a particular saying. Other apocryphal Gospels are virtually of no value. In the New Testament apart from the Gospels we do find information about Jesus, and this has been listed. The amount of material, however, is small. It has been evident from the earliest days of the church that anyone wanting to learn about Jesus has to go to the Gospels of Matthew, Mark, Luke and John.

References

Birdsall, J. Neville. "The Continuing Enigma of Josephus' Testimony about Jesus." *Bulletin of the John Rylands University Library of Manchester* 67 (1984): 609-22.

Bruce, F. F. *Jesus and Christian Origins Outside the New Testament.* Grand Rapids, Mich.: Eerdmans, 1974.

Cameron, Ron, ed. *The Other Gospels: Non-canonical Gospel Texts.* Philadelphia: Westminster Press, 1982.

Elliott, J. K. *The Apocryphal New Testament.* Oxford: Clarendon, 1993.

Evans, Craig A. "Jesus in Non-Christian Sources." In *Dictionary of Jesus and the Gospels,* edited by Joel B. Green, Scot McKnight and I. Howard Marshall, pp. 364-68. Downers Grove, Ill.: InterVarsity Press, 1992.

Hofius, Otfried. "Unknown Sayings of Jesus." In *The Gospel and the Gospels,* edited by Peter Stuhlmacher, pp. 336-60. Grand Rapids, Mich.: Eerdmans, 1991.

Jeremias, Joachim. *Unknown Sayings of Jesus.* London: S.P.C.K., 1958.

Meier, John P. *A Marginal Jew: Rethinking the Historical Jesus,* Vol. 1. New York: Doubleday, 1991.

Schneemelcher, Wilhelm, ed. *New Testament Apocrypha.* Louisville, Ky.: Westminster Press, 1991.

Stein, Robert H. *The Synoptic Problem.* Grand Rapids, Mich.: Baker Book House, 1987.

Stroker, William D. *Extracanonical Sayings of Jesus.* Atlanta: Scholars, 1989.

Wenham, David, and Craig Blomberg, eds. *The Jesus Tradition Outside the Gospels.* Vol. 5 of *Gospel Perspectives.* Sheffield, U.K.: JSOT, 1985.

3

WHEN DID ALL THIS TAKE PLACE?

The Problem of Chronology

T HE GOSPEL WRITERS WERE FOR THE MOST PART NOT INTERESTED IN the "when" of the various events in Jesus' life. This can be seen even in a superficial survey of the Gospels. Mark is written around a simple geographical framework. The first part deals with events that took place in Galilee and its environs (Mark 1—9), followed by events that took place in Judea (Mark 10—16). Consequently any event that occurred in Galilee must appear in the early chapters, whereas any event that occurred in Judea must appear in the later ones. (By contrast, in the Gospel of John Jesus moves back and forth between Galilee and Judea.) Matthew follows Mark and keeps this same Galilee-Jerusalem framework but alternates his account between series of events (Mt 1—4, 8—9, 11—12, 14—17, 19—22, 26—28) and sayings (Mt 5—7, 10, 13, 18, 23—25; compare 7:28-29; 11:1; 13:53; 19:1; 26:1). Luke, on the other hand, has placed the majority of Jesus' teachings in two sections of his Gospel (6:20—8:3 and 9:51—18:14). All this does not mean that the attempt to arrive at a chronology of the life of Jesus is illegitimate or of no value. It does warn us, however, against trying to interpret the Gospels as modern-day diaries of Jesus' life.

The Birth of Jesus

The death of Herod. Since Jesus was born "in the time of King Herod" (Mt 2:1; compare Lk 1:5) and since we know with reasonable certainty the year of Herod's death, we are able to arrive at the latest possible date (the *terminus ad quem*) of Jesus' birth. In 40 B.C. Herod was proclaimed king of Judea by the Roman Senate. After three years of fighting and with the help of Rome, Herod overcame his opponents and began to reign as king in 37 B.C. According to Josephus he died in the thirty-fourth year of his reign (*Ant.* 17.8.1 [17.191]; *War* 1.33.8 [1.665]). This was, according to the Roman calendar, 750 A.U.C. (*ab urbe condita*—from the foundation of the city [of Rome]). Translated into our present-day calendar it is 4 B.C. (Our present calendar is the work of a sixth-century Scythian monk named Dionysius Exiguus, who obviously erred by at least four years.) Josephus states that an eclipse of the moon took place shortly before Herod the Great died (*Ant.* 17.6.4 [17.167]). This eclipse took place on March 12-13, 4 B.C. Josephus also tells us that the Passover that year (April 11) occurred after Herod's death (*Ant.* 17.9.3.[17.213]; *War* 2.1.3 [2.10]). Consequently Herod's death can be dated fairly precisely some time between March 12 and April 11. Thus Jesus must have been born no later than between March 12 and April 11 in 4 B.C.

But how long before Herod's death was Jesus born? Herod reigned for thirty-four years! If we had only this information, Jesus could have been born anywhere between 37 and 4 B.C. Fortunately we do have more data. According to Luke we know that Jesus was circumcised on the eighth day after his birth (Lk 2:21; compare 1:59; Phil 3:5; Lev 12:3). On the forty-first day Mary underwent her purification rite and Jesus was "presented" to the Lord. The latter rite was a symbolic reliving of the exodus Passover, when the firstborn sons of Israel were protected by the blood of the Passover sacrifice and were not slain by the destroying angel (Ex 12:1-30). The redemption of Jesus in this rite involved a small sum of money (five shekels according to Num 3:47-48). Mary's purification involved the giving of a pair of doves or two young pigeons (Lk 2:24).

This sacrifice has clear implications with respect to the economic status of Jesus' parents. According to Leviticus 12:6 the normal sacrifice for a woman's purification was a lamb and a dove or young pigeon. However, if the couple were poor they could give two doves or two pigeons (Lev 12:8). Thus forty-one days after Jesus' birth his parents were so poor that they could not give the normal sacrifice for purification. It would appear from this that the wise men had not yet arrived with their gifts of gold, frankincense and myrrh. Thus we can date Jesus' birth at least forty-one days earlier than Herod's death, assuming that the wise men came to Herod on the day of his death. It is unlikely, however, that one can fit the visit of the wise men to Herod, their visit to Jesus in Bethlehem, and Herod's discovery of his having been tricked (Mt 2:1-12) into a single day. Thus we must add additional time to the forty-one days.

Matthew 2:16, 19-20 suggests that we must date Jesus' birth earlier still, perhaps as much as two years before Herod's death. Matthew takes care in his account to point out that Herod carefully inquired from the wise men as to the "exact time when the star had appeared" (Mt 2:7) and that the slaughter of the innocents of Bethlehem involved all "who were two years old or under, according to the time that [Herod] had learned from the wise men" (Mt 2:16). By this Matthew indicates that Jesus could have been up to two years old at the time of the wise men's visit. Also, the fact that the wise men found Jesus in a "house" (Mt 2:11) rather than a "manger" (Lk 2:16), makes clear that their coming was some time after the visit of the shepherds. Thus sometime during the years 7-5 B.C. is as good a guess as possible with respect to the date of Jesus' birth.

Luke's dating. According to Luke 2:1 Jesus was born during the days of Caesar Augustus, who reigned from 44 B.C. to A.D. 14, when Quirinius was governor of Syria (Lk 2:2). The reference to Quirinius (Cyrenius in the KJV) is the most difficult problem involved in the dating of Jesus' birth. We know most of the dates of the governors of Syria for this period: M. Titius (10 B.C.), C. Sentius Saturninus (9-7/6 B.C.), P. Quinctilius Varus (7/6-4 B.C.), Gaius Caesar (1 B.C.-A.D. 4), L. Volusius Saturninus (A.D. 4-5), P. Sulpicius Quirinius (A.D. 6-7). (We do not know who was governor from 3 to 2 B.C., but this is not critical, for it is too late for the birth of Jesus.)

Josephus (*Ant.* 17.13.5 [17.355] and 18.1.1 [18.1]) knows of Quirinius's being governor of Syria only in A.D. 6. Is Luke's mention of Quirinius as governor at Jesus' birth therefore wrong? Tertullian, an early church father writing around A.D. 210, apparently thought so (*Adv. Marc.* 4.19).

He maintained that C. Sentius Saturninus was governor when Jesus was born. There is, however, no textual support at all for reading C. Sentius Saturninus instead of Quirinius in Luke 2:2. Numerous attempts have been made to explain this historical difficulty.

One suggests that the term *first (prōtos)* in Luke 2:2 should not be translated as an adjective (*first* census) but as an adverb (this census was *before* the census made by Quirinius). *Prōtos* can be translated in these two ways, but "before" is an unlikely way to translate the term here. (The genitive absolute "while Quirinius was governor" argues against it.) All the major Bible translations translate it "first."

Another explanation that has been suggested is that the census mentioned in Luke 2:2 and the one in Acts 5:37 are two aspects of the same census. Luke 2:2 refers to the *apographē* (registration) that took place in 7 B.C. under Saturninus. This was completed fourteen years later under Quirinius in A.D. 6-7 by the *apotimēsis* (actual tax assessment). Thus Luke in referring to Quirinius in Luke 2:2 was referring to the more famous governor who completed this census. There are several problems with this attempted solution. One is that it is far from certain that these two words were technical terms referring to two parts of a single census. Josephus (*Ant.* 18.1.1 [18.1]) uses them interchangeably. It should also be observed that Luke uses *apographē* in both Luke 2:2 and Acts 5:37. It appears therefore that Luke 2:2 and Acts 5:37 refer to two different censuses.

Another attempt to explain this difficulty is the argument that Quirinius was governor of Syria on two separate occasions. The latter occasion was in A.D. 6. The former was as special legate sometime between 12 and 6 B.C., when he was charged by the Roman Senate to quell the Homonadensian revolt in southeast Turkey, which was then part of Syria (see Strabo *Geography* 12.6.5, and Tacitus *Annals* 3.48). At that time, it is argued, he was given an extraordinary command and possessed a kind of co-governorship with C. Sentius Saturninus. Support for this is seen in a damaged inscription (called the Lapis Tiburtinus [*CIL* XIV, 3613]) found in Tivoli in 1764 and now located in the Vatican Museum. This inscription speaks of an unnamed Roman citizen who was a legate on two separate occasions and, at least the second time, was legate or governor of Syria. It has been suggested that this refers to Quirinius and that the first time he was legate he was also legate in Syria. Thus Quirinius was legate of Syria not only in A.D. 6-7 (all accept this) but also in 7-6 B.C. This thesis suffers the weakness of having to assume that the inscription refers to Quirinius and that he was legate of Syria on both those occasions.

From our discussion it is evident that there are a number of problems concerning the reference to the census of Quirinius in Luke 2:1-2. Has Luke committed a colossal historical blunder? The way one answers this question is determined to a great extent by the overall impression of Luke as a historian. If we believe that Luke had indeed investigated "everything carefully from the very first" (Lk 1:3) and that he anticipated that the reading of his Gospel would give Theophilus certainty with respect to the things that he had been taught (Lk 1:4), we become more cautious about saying that Luke made a mistake. Because he was aware of the later census in A.D. 6-7 under Quirinius (Acts 5:37) and because of the overall accuracy of the material in Acts, we should hesitate to attribute such a blunder to Luke. Thus even apart from the question of divine inspiration, it is probably wisest at this point to acknowledge the difficulty of what Luke says but to hold off calling this a clear error. Perhaps in the future additional evidence may become available that will explain the present difficulty.

The visit of the wise men. Closely associated with the birth of Jesus is the appearance of the "star" of Bethlehem (Mt 2:1-12). The appearing of the star has been made famous in Christian art and music, and the account of the wise men is inconceivable without it. The ancients' interest in the stars is well documented. Perhaps less known is the ability of ancient astronomers and astrologers to predict the orbits and conjunctions of planets and their careful recording of astronomical phenomena. Matthew's account of the visit of the wise men (Mt 2:1-12) has raised questions about the star that is said to have led them.

As early as 1606 the astronomer Johannes Kepler sought to explain this by a triple conjunction of the planets Saturn and Jupiter in May/June, September/October and December of 7 B.C. Shortly thereafter Mars passed by in conjunction with these two planets. This latter threefold conjunction, which occurs only once every 805 years, Kepler argued was the "star" of Bethlehem. Thus he concluded that Jesus was born in 7/6 B.C. Kepler's thesis is made even more interesting by the fact that in those days Jupiter was understood as a star of kings and Saturn was associated with the sabbath and with the Jews. This conjunction would fit well with the suggestion that Jesus was probably born around 7-5 B.C.

Another suggestion is that what the wise men saw was a nova or supernova. These involve the explosion of a star that produces an unusual amount of light for several weeks. The former frequently involves a star too faint to be seen by the eye but whose brightness increases up to 100,000 times. The latter is more spectacular still, for during this explosion the light increases millions and even billions of times. Such an explanation is not impossible, but it is an unprovable theory. Not many such occurrences are recorded in history.

It has even been suggested that the star might be Halley's comet, which would have been visible in 12/11 B.C. This appears, however, to be too early. Chinese records refer to comets or supernovas being sighted in 5 and 4 B.C. On the other hand, if the star was not a normal conjunction of planets or other astronomical occurrence but a "miracle" star, all attempts to explain or date it are misguided.

Astronomy/astrology enjoyed considerable popularity in the Ancient East. The appearance of a star in those days would have been seen by many people as foretelling an important event. It would be reckless to be dogmatic about the star of Bethlehem. People such as the wise men would, however, have observed such an occurrence and speculated over its meaning. If we allow the use of figurative language in Matthew 2:9, the conjunction of the planets Jupiter and Saturn might well have been associated with the birth of a Jewish "king." This is especially so if, as Suetonius (*Vespasian* 4) and Tacitus (*Histories* 5:13) suggest, there existed an expectation of a world ruler arising out of Judaism.

The Beginning of Jesus' Ministry

At first glance it appears that we have a very clear chronological reference to the beginning of Jesus' ministry in Luke 3:1-2:

> In the fifteenth year of the reign of Emperor Tiberius, when Pontius Pilate was governor of Judea, and Herod was ruler [tetrarch] of Galilee, and his brother Philip ruler [tetrarch] of the region of Ituraea and Trachonitis, and Lysanias ruler [tetrarch] of Abilene, during the high priesthood of Annas and Caiaphas, the word of God came to John son of Zechariah in the wilderness.

Except for the reference to the "fifteenth year," the other temporal references mentioned by Luke cover a broad period of time. Pilate was governor of Judea from A.D. 26 to 36; Herod was tetrarch of Galilee from 4 B.C. to A.D. 39; Philip was tetrarch of Iturea and Trachonitis from 4 B.C. to A.D. 34; Caiaphas was high priest from about 18 to 36; and Annas, the father-in-law of Caiaphas, was high priest from about 6 to 14, retaining the title in a ceremonial capacity until his death, whose date is uncertain; Lysanias's rule as tetrarch of Abilene cannot be dated accurately. It is evident, therefore, that there is a considerable overlap in time with respect to the reigns of the people mentioned by Luke.

Unfortunately even the reference to the fifteenth year of the reign of Tiberius Caesar is not as clear as we would like. Does Luke refer to the fifteenth year after the death of Caesar Augustus on August 19, A.D. 14, or the fifteenth year after Tiberius became coemperor with Augustus in A.D. 11/12? If Luke refers to the former, then the fifteenth year would be 28/29; if the latter, it would be 25/26. Several other factors make the issue even more complicated. Did Luke distinguish between the accession year of Tiberius and the regnal years, or did he consider the first partial accession year (the time between when he began to reign and the official beginning of the Roman year of rule, that is, the regnal year) as the first regnal year? And what calendar was he using? Was it the Julian, or Roman, calendar? the Jewish? the Syrian-Macedonian? the Egyptian? If, as is more likely, Luke in writing to a Greek used the Julian calendar, we have the following possibilities: the fifteenth year of corule not using an accession year—25/26; the fifteenth year of corule using an accession year—26/27; the fifteenth year of sole rule not using an accession year—28; and the fifteenth year of sole rule using an accession year—29.

One other piece of evidence in seeking to date the beginning of Jesus' ministry is found in John 2:20. The statement that the temple rebuilding program was in its forty-sixth year appears to have been made in the early part of Jesus' ministry. According to Josephus (*Ant.* 15.11.1 [15.380]) the reconstruction of the temple began in the eighteenth year of the reign of Herod the Great, or about 20-19 B.C. Josephus gives a different date, the fifteenth year, elsewhere (*War* 1.21.1 [1.401]), but this may refer to the inception and initial planning of the rebuilding program. If we accept the more likely reference to the eighteenth year, then the forty-sixth year would be about A.D. 28.

Finally it should be noted that Luke is referring in 3:1-2 to the beginning of John the Baptist's ministry. How much time intervened between the start of his ministry and the baptism of Jesus? Was it a matter of months or of years? Probably the former is more likely. In light of all the considerations mentioned above, most scholars believe that Jesus began his ministry in approximately A.D. 28.

The Age of Jesus

According to Luke 3:23 Jesus "was about thirty years old" when he began his ministry. It may be that Luke knew the exact age of Jesus when he began his ministry and used the round number thirty in order to parallel David's beginning his kingship at that age (2 Sam 5:3-4; compare also Joseph [Gen 41:46], Ezekiel [Ezek 1:1] and CD 17.5-6, where one had to be thirty in order to serve in a position of leadership in the Qumran community). Most probably by this statement the Evangelist was admitting that he did not know the exact age. For Luke, whether Jesus was twenty-five, thirty, thirty-five or some age in between did not affect his teaching or work in any way. If Jesus was born 7-5 B.C. and began his ministry about A.D. 28, that would make him about thirty-three years old when he began his ministry.

One additional reference to the age of Jesus is found in John 8:57: "Then the Jews said to him, 'You are not yet fifty years old, and have you seen Abraham?' " This should not be taken as an exact reference by Jesus' opponents to his actual age. The statement seeks rather to emphasize the difference between Jesus' age and the time of Abraham more than fifteen centuries earlier. How could Jesus and Abraham have known each other, as Jesus claimed (Jn 8:56)? Fifty years is most probably a generous exaggeration of Jesus' age for the sake of argument. Even if Jesus was attributed an age older than he really was, the Jews argued that he could not have seen Abraham.

The Length of Jesus' Ministry

The Synoptic Gospels seem to indicate that the ministry of Jesus lasted a little more than a year. No yearly event such as a Passover is mentioned twice. Attempts have been made to establish an order of events as follows: Mark 1:9—baptism during a warm period before winter; Mark 2:23—springtime and harvest; Mark 6:39—spring; the events of Mark 6:45—13:37 requiring several months; Mark 14:1—Passover after a summer-fall-winter required in the preceding time period. The problem with such reasoning is that it assumes that Mark arranged his material in a precise chronological order. There are several reasons for doubting this. The fact that his material is arranged into two geographical divisions—Jesus' activities in Galilee (Mk 1—9) and his activities in Judea (10—16)—suggests that the materials are placed where they are primarily for nonchronological reasons.

Usually one turns to John for information concerning the length of Jesus' ministry. In John we have the following: an early ministry (Jn 1:29—2:12), Passover number 1 (Jn 2:13), January/February (Jn 4:35), Passover number 2 (Jn 6:4), the Feast of Tabernacles (Jn 7:2), the Feast of Dedication (Jn 10:22) and Passover number 3 (Jn 11:55). Added to this is a reference to "a festival of the Jews" (Jn 5:1), which is ambiguous. If John has arranged his material chronologically and is referring to three distinct Passovers, then we have either a two-year-plus ministry or a three-year-plus ministry, according to how we interpret John 5:1.

The Date of Jesus' Death and Resurrection

Closely related to the previous question concerning the length of Jesus' ministry is the question of the date of the crucifixion. The last possible date for this would be the last year of Pontius Pilate's rule in Judea (36/ 37). A second piece of evidence confirms this as the last possible date: Caiaphas, the ruling high priest at the time of the crucifixion, was deposed as high priest in 37. Fortunately we have an additional piece of evidence in dating the year of Jesus' death and resurrection. Later it will be argued that Jesus died on a Friday, the fourteenth or fifteenth of Nisan, and that this day was followed by a sabbath (Mk 15:42). (See the discussion in chapter fifteen.) Since the Jewish month was determined by a new moon, we can determine through astronomical calculations which years between 27 and 37 the fourteenth or fifteenth of Nisan preceded or involved a sabbath. These are the years 27, 30, 33 and 36. The first possibility is clearly too early, and the last is too late. Thus for all practical purposes we are limited to either 30 or 33 as the date of Jesus' death.

In favor of 33 is the fact that we have little difficulty fitting in a three- or four-year ministry. On the other hand, it is less easy to fit this in with the date of Paul's conversion, which was about A.D. 33, and with Luke 3:23. The A.D. 30 date has less difficulty with respect to these two issues, but we are hard pressed to squeeze in a three-year ministry. All things considered, most scholars have opted for the year 30.

Conclusion

It is evident that whereas we can arrive at approximate dates with respect to the life of Jesus, it is difficult to be certain as to the exact dates of the major events in his life. We will not be far wrong, however, if we affirm the following dates:

Jesus' birth: 7-5 B.C.

Beginning of Jesus' ministry: A.D. 27-28

Length of Jesus' ministry: one and a half to three and a half years

Crucifixion and resurrection of Jesus: A.D. 30 or 33, with the former more likely

References

Brown, Raymond E. *The Birth of the Messiah*. New York: Doubleday, 1979.

Caird, George B. "The Chronology of the NT." In *Interpreter's Dictionary of the Bible*, 1:599-607. New York: Abingdon, 1962.

Donfried, Karl P. "Chronology." In *Anchor Bible Dictionary*, 1:1012-16. New York: Doubleday, 1992.

Finegan, Jack. *Handbook of Biblical Chronology*. Princeton, N.J.: Princeton University Press, 1964.

Fotheringham, J. K. "The Evidence of Astronomy and Technical Chronology for the Date of the Crucifixion." *Journal of Theological Studies* 35 (1934): 146-62.

Hoehner, Harold W. *Chronological Aspects of the Life of Christ*. Grand Rapids, Mich.: Zondervan, 1977.

Meier, John P. *A Marginal Jew: Rethinking the Historical Jesus*, 1:372-433. New York: Doubleday, 1991.

Ogg, George. *The Chronology of the Public Ministry of Jesus*. Cambridge: Cambridge University Press, 1940.

Olmstead, A. T. "The Chronology of Jesus' Life." *Anglican Theological Review* 24 (1942): 1-26.

Part Two
THE LIFE
OF CHRIST

4
CONCEIVED BY THE HOLY SPIRIT, BORN OF THE VIRGIN MARY
How It All Started

THROUGHOUT ITS HISTORY THE CHIRSTIAN CHURCH HAS CONFESSED that Jesus of Nazareth was "conceived by the Holy Spirit, [and] born of the Virgin Mary." This claim stems from the accounts found in Matthew 1:18-25 and Luke 1:26-38, 46-56; 2:1-7. Attempts have been made to see allusions to the virgin birth, or better yet the "virginal conception," in many passages.

Mark 6:3   Jesus is referred to as Mary's rather than Joseph's son.

John 1:13   John supposedly has Jesus' virgin birth in mind when he refers to being born "not of blood or of the will of the flesh."

John 6:41-51   John again supposedly has the virgin birth in mind.

John 7:41-42   Since John apparently knows of Jesus' birth in Bethlehem, it is assumed that he must have known of the virginal conception associated with that birth.

John 8:41	The statement by Jesus' opponents that they are not "illegitimate children" is seen as an attack against the claim of Jesus' virginal conception, which they viewed as really an attempt to cover up his illegitimacy.
Romans 1:3	Jesus is "descended" not "born" of David.
Galatians 4:4	Jesus is begotten *(genomenon)*, not "born of a woman" *(gennōmenon)*.
Philippians 2:7	Jesus took the nature of a slave rather than was "born in[to]."

These alleged references by themselves would never lead to the establishment of a doctrine of the virginal conception. They are at best allusions to such a doctrine established from the clear teaching found in the accounts of Matthew and Luke. Even as allusions, however, they are quite tenuous and could easily be explained differently. For instance, in Galatians 4:4 Paul is not seeking to demonstrate the "otherness" of Jesus but his "likeness" to those he came to redeem. Thus "born of a woman" seeks to establish Jesus' true humanity. (Compare Job 14:1, where the same Greek term is used to describe normal birth.)

Critical Views of the Virginal Conception

Many criticisms have been raised regarding the virginal conception and the accounts associated with this teaching. For some, the very possibility of such a conception and birth is excluded as a logical consequence of the elimination of the supernatural from history (see chapter one). If miracles cannot happen, then by definition there cannot be a virginal conception. Though various reasons are given in support of this view, they are not the cause but are at best additional support for it. The cause is their having eliminated the supernatural from history. For some, however, various historical difficulties associated with the biblical accounts are the cause for doubting the claim of the virginal conception found in Matthew and Luke. As a result, the traditional teaching of the Christian church on this subject must interact with such arguments.

Probably the most frequent argument raised against the virginal conception is that too many other parallels exist in ancient literature to allow us to take the Christian account seriously. According to this view, the accounts in Matthew and Luke arose among Greek Christians who were acquainted with the many myths in paganism that spoke of the virgin births of various Greek gods and superheroes. Consequently Christians in the early church created a similar account of their hero and "Lord." Two of the most frequently repeated analogies are the birth of Perseus, whose mother Danae was loved by Zeus and who was conceived by means of a rain of gold that descended upon her, and the birth of Hercules, who was the child of Zeus and a human mother.

Upon closer investigation, however, all these alleged parallels turn out to be quite different from the New Testament accounts. Almost all the pagan accounts involve a sexual encounter between a god and a human woman. Most times, therefore, the woman had no possible claim to be a virgin, and, if she was a virgin before the encounter, she was certainly not considered a virgin afterward. Even in the case of the birth of Perseus, his conception is clearly due to the adulterous lust of Zeus for his mother. Whereas it is true that there are numerous supernatural births in Greek literature, they always involve a physical generation. Paganism simply does not have accounts of *virgin* births. It possesses no clear analogy that could have given rise to the Gospel accounts.

A strong argument against such an alleged derivation is a careful comparison between pagan myths and the Gospel accounts. The more closely they are compared, the clearer becomes the stark contrast between them. As to supernatural births, paganism offers many examples. Being sexual in nature, however, they offer no real parallel to the Gospel accounts. The asexual nature of the Gospel accounts is clearly seen when one asks such questions as "Did YHWH lust after Mary?" "How did the Holy Spirit impregnate Mary?" The offensiveness of such questions clearly shows how different the Gospel accounts are from what we find in paganism. Suggestions of a mating between the angel Gabriel and the virgin Mary are only slightly less offensive. The early church fathers were well aware of and emphasized the sharp contrast between the biblical accounts of the virginal conception and these alleged pagan parallels (see Tertullian *Apology* 15, 21; Origen *Against Celsus* 1.37).

Perhaps the strongest argument against such attempts to explain the origin of the virgin birth accounts is the Jewish nature of the accounts.

The Gospel accounts of Jesus' birth did not arise among Greek Christians. On the contrary, the account in Luke is the most Jewish part of his entire Gospel. This account did not arise in the Hellenistic church but in a Jewish setting. And where in Judaism would a story of a virginal conception have arisen? Even in a Hellenistic Jewish setting any thought of a sexual dimension between God and Mary would be impossible.

It has been suggested that perhaps the virgin birth accounts arose among Jewish Christians due to the church's interpretation of Isaiah 7:14. Since this is a prophecy concerning a future virgin birth, it is claimed that the church created the virgin birth accounts to fulfill this prophecy. The problem with this explanation is that Isaiah 7:14 was not interpreted in the first century as referring to a virginal conception. The predominant interpretation was that it referred to a young woman (the Hebrew term 'almâh refers primarily to a "young woman" who may or may not be a virgin), and it was interpreted as referring to the birth of Hezekiah, the son and successor to King Ahaz. There is also no evidence that this passage was interpreted in a messianic sense in Judaism. In the Greek translation of the Old Testament, called the Septuagint, the word used is *parthenos* (virgin), but this was understood as referring to one who was presently a virgin and would conceive through a normal birth process. It was not interpreted as referring to a woman who would conceive as a virgin.

Thus whereas the interpretation of Isaiah 7:14 as referring to the virgin birth is understandable in the Christian church due to an already established tradition of the virgin birth, the reverse is not at all likely. It is difficult to believe that the reading of Isaiah 7:14, apart from an already existing tradition of the virgin birth, would give rise to the biblical accounts in Matthew and Luke. It was the story that gave rise to the messianic interpretation of this passage, not the reverse.

A good example of this process is found in Matthew 2:23: "There he made his home in a town called Nazareth, so that what had been spoken through the prophets might be fulfilled, 'He will be called a Nazorean.' " This biblical text could never have given birth to the tradition of Jesus' having been raised in Nazareth. Its use by Matthew stems from the already existing tradition that Jesus' home was Nazareth. Most prophecies involving the birth of Jesus seem to be afterthoughts or reflections on the already existing Gospel traditions. It is hard to see how historical traditions would have arisen from them. Certainly Matthew would have found it hard to say "All this took place to fulfill what had been spoken by the Lord through the prophet" (Mt 1:22) if he had just created the story to fulfill the biblical prophecy. The fact that such explanations appeal to the creation of this material by the "anonymous church" reveals this difficulty. The same problem persists, however, for anyone in the church who would have created such a tradition. Furthermore, most legends created by this kind of midrashic interpretation require a longer period of time than that available between the historical Jesus and the establishment of the traditions underlying the birth accounts in Matthew and Luke.

Within Judaism the virginal conception was denied and an alternative explanation given. The explanation involved the Greek term for "virgin," *parthenos*. Jesus, it was argued, was not born of a virgin but was the illegitimate offspring of Mary and a soldier named Panthera (or Pandira). Thus Jesus was not conceived supernaturally to a virgin *(parthenos)* engaged to Joseph. On the contrary, this whole myth was created to cover up Jesus' illegitimacy resulting from Mary's adultery with Panthera (see chapter two under "Jewish Sources"; see Origen *Against Celsus* 1.28 and 32; *b. Sanhedrin* 106a-b; *b. Yebamot* 49a). This parody based on switching the *r* and the *n* in the Greek term has no historical evidence in its support. It arose from Jewish counterpropaganda directed against the Christian proclamation of the virginal conception.

When all the alleged analogies from paganism and all suggested origins out of Old Testament texts are examined, the fact remains that no adequate example of a virginal conception can be found to explain the origin of the Gospel accounts that Jesus was "conceived by the Holy Ghost [and] born of the Virgin Mary." Rationalistic explanations of the origin of these biblical accounts will always be found wanting due to the lack of any serious analogies that might have caused their creation. There was, furthermore, no need for such a miraculous conception of the Messiah among Jewish Christians. In Jewish thinking the Messiah would be the offspring of a Davidic descendant through a normal physical conception. In a Greek milieu heavily influenced by the dualism of Platonic or Gnostic philosophy, a virginal conception might protect the offspring somewhat from "physical contamination." Within Judaism, however, such an explanation would be quite foreign, for a normal physical birth of the Messiah would not have been thought of negatively. As already pointed out, the virgin birth accounts clearly betray a Jewish, not a Greek, origin.

Historical Difficulties in the Biblical Accounts

Along with the difficulty that the miracle of the virginal conception creates for some, the biblical accounts that speak of the virgin birth contain within them additional historical difficulties. Two of them, the governorship of Quirinius and the appearance of the star of Bethlehem, were discussed in the previous chapter (see under "Luke's Dating" and "The Visit of the Wise Men"). Here we shall look at the historical difficulties created by three phrases: "All the world should be registered" (Lk 2:1); "he was the son (as was thought) of Joseph" (Lk 3:23); and "Rachel weeping for her children" (Mt 2:18).

"All the world should be registered." The claim that there was a universal census at the time of Jesus' birth (Lk 2:1) creates a serious problem. The NIV translates the term *world (oikoumenēn)* as "Roman world." This better captures the thought of Luke than "all the world" as found in the KJV and NRSV. The hyperbolic nature of this term for Luke can be seen in Acts 11:28, where the famine localized around Judea is referred to as occurring "over all the world." In fact, "all" and "entire" are used twenty-three times in Luke 1—2.

During the reign of Caesar Augustus no single census was conducted throughout the entire Roman Empire at the same time. Yet under his rule censuses and various tax assessments were made in a systematic way that eventually involved the "whole" empire (see Tacitus *Annals* 1.11; Dio Cassius 53.30.2). We possess numerous records of them. We even possess records of such censuses in autonomous city-states. We know that in Egypt a Roman census was conducted every fourteen years from A.D. 34 to 258 (Oxyrhynchus Papyrus 2.254-256) and that censuses of Roman citizens were taken in 28 and 8 B.C. and in A.D. 14 (Suetonius *Augustus* 27.5). Likewise in Gaul a census occurred in 27 and 12 B.C. and in A.D. 14-16. Records of censuses in other places are also known. The existence of such a census in Judea is therefore not impossible but quite probable.

That Caesar Augustus issued a decree that "all the world should be registered" need not be interpreted as referring to a single, universal census. It can refer to his having instituted a program in which various censuses at different times and for different places would encompass the entire empire. It may be that Luke used nontechnical terminology to describe only one aspect of the far-ranging census, the one involving Joseph and Mary, that Caesar Augustus instituted.

Objection has also been raised that such censuses did not require traveling to one's birthplace or of bringing one's wife. The latter objection possesses little weight for at least two reasons. Even if Mary was not required to go to Bethlehem, she may have desired to go. The desire to be near her husband at such a time would be quite natural. Also, if Mary pondered over the birth of a son who was to inherit "the throne of his ancestor David" (Lk 1:32), she may have wanted her son to be born in Bethlehem, the "city of David." Second, there are records of certain censuses in which women were required to appear. As to the objection that traveling to one's birthplace or ancestral home was not necessary, there is no proof of such a view. On the contrary, we know of certain censuses where the father of the family was required to register in his ancestral home. In Israel such a census might well have taken into consideration the Jewish attachment to ancestral relationships.

"He was the son (as was thought) of Joseph." Within the Gospels are two separate genealogies involving Jesus: Matthew 1:1-16 and Luke 3:23-38. From earliest times the differences between these accounts were observed and discussed. Some differences caused little or no difficulty. The fact that Matthew's genealogy goes back only to Abraham, whereas Luke's goes back to Adam, was not seen as conflicting but as simply revealing the complementary theological interests of the two Evangelists. Matthew wanted to show his Jewish-Christian readers that Jesus was the fulfillment of all the Jewish hopes and promises. He therefore traced Jesus' lineage back to Abraham, the father of the Jewish people. Luke, on the other hand, wanted to show his Gentile-Christian readers that Jesus was the fulfillment of the hopes of all humanity. Thus he traced his lineage back to Adam, the father of all people. Other differences, such as the diverse locations of the genealogies in the two Gospels and Matthew's arrangement of his genealogy into three groups of fourteen, caused no difficulty.

The main difficulty found in the two genealogies involves the people who make up the list of Jesus' ancestors. Whereas the descendants between Abraham and David are essentially the same in both (compare Mt

1:2-6 and Lk 3:31-34), from David to Jesus we find only three names in common. The descendant of David through whom the lineage of Jesus is traced is different: whereas Matthew follows the line of Solomon, Luke follows the line of Nathan. Thus from David to Jesus we find only three names in common between the two lists: Shealtiel, Zerubbabel and Joseph. A comparison of the most recent ancestors reveals the following: in Matthew 1:14-16, Joseph, Jacob, Matthan, Eleazar, Eliud and Achim; in Luke 3:23-24, Joseph, Heli, Matthat, Levi, Melchi and Jannai. The differences between the genealogies are quite obvious.

It would be incorrect to conclude that these genealogies must be fictional based on the assumption that lengthy records tracing one's lineage did not exist in Jesus' day. On the contrary, Paul knew that he was a Benjaminite (Phil 3:5). Josephus reproduced his own genealogical table in his autobiography (*Life* 1.3), and the great rabbi Hillel was able to trace his lineage back to David. The Babylonian Talmud refers to a rabbi who traced the genealogy of a prospective daughter-in-law back to David (*b. Ketubot* 62b). Thus it is not the possibility of a genealogy of Jesus that is the problem. Rather, it is the differences that exist between the two.

Attempts to resolve this problem go back at least to A.D. 220. Julius Africanus, in his letter to Aristides, refers to an explanation of the differences as due to Matthew's giving the *royal* lineage of Jesus via Joseph through Solomon, whereas Luke gives Jesus' *priestly* lineage also via Joseph but through Nathan. John Calvin, and later J. Gresham Machen, argued for a variation of this view: that Luke gives the physical lineage of Jesus via Joseph. Julius Africanus's own view was that Jacob (Mt 1:15-16) and Heli (Lk 3:23) were half-brothers. After the death of Heli, Jacob assumed the role of husband via a Levirate marriage (Deut 25:5-10) and fathered Joseph. Thus the differences in the genealogies are to be explained by Luke's having referred to the lineage of Joseph's legal father (Heli), whereas Matthew referred to the lineage of Joseph's actual father (Jacob). Common to all these explanations is the view that both genealogies in Matthew and Luke are the genealogies of Joseph.

Another attempted explanation involves the view that the two different genealogies trace the family of Jesus' two different "parents": the genealogy in Matthew is that of Joseph, and the one in Luke is that of Mary. The key issue here is how one should translate Luke 3:23. Most translations interpret the expression "as was supposed" in this verse as parenthetical: "Jesus, when he began his ministry, was about thirty years of age, being the son *(as was supposed)* of Joseph, the son of Heli, the son of . . ." (RSV; italics added). The reader of Luke, of course, knows from what he has already read in Luke 1:1-3:22 (and perhaps due to familiarity with the tradition) that Jesus' conception was of a virgin and that Joseph was only the adoptive father: Joseph in turn was the son of Heli, who was the son of . . . This way of translating the sentence implies that the genealogy that follows is that of Joseph. The text, however, can also be interpreted as follows: "Jesus, when he began his ministry, was about thirty years of age, being the son *(as was supposed of Joseph)* of Heli, the son of . . ." (italics added; compare NASB). By enlarging the parenthetical comment to include "of Joseph," we now have a genealogy of Heli, who according to this interpretation was the father of Mary. That Luke has a special interest in Mary is evident from the amount of space he devotes to her in the first three chapters and by such comments as found in Luke 2:19 ("But Mary treasured all these words and pondered them in her heart") and 51 ("His mother treasured all these things in her heart"). The latter references may even suggest that Mary was the ultimate source of some of the birth narrative traditions.

Although the last explanation of the two different genealogies would resolve the problem nicely, it must be admitted that the more natural interpretation of Luke 3:23 is to exclude "of Joseph" from the parenthetical comment rather than include it. It should also be noted that Luke is interested in the Davidic lineage of Joseph and earlier pointed out that Joseph was "of the house of David" (1:27). As a result one is somewhat predisposed to interpret a genealogy mentioning David (3:31) as referring to Joseph's lineage due to the earlier reference in 1:27. At the present time a satisfactory explanation of this problem has not come forth. On the other hand, it is even more difficult to imagine that one or both of these genealogies are simply creative fictions, because some of the family of Jesus were alive at the time they were written and could have been consulted.

"Rachel weeping for her children." Still another difficulty associated with the birth narratives is the massacre of the innocents in Bethlehem (Mt 2:16-18). There is no record of such a massacre in the histories of the time, and it is alleged that such a horrendous slaughter, if it had occurred, would have been recorded. But this is an argument from silence, and

such arguments are usually inconclusive. Furthermore, we do not have a great many historical records from the first century, and to claim that Josephus would have had to refer to such an event cannot be demonstrated. It is also important to realize that Bethlehem was only a small village and that the number of male children two years old or younger would probably not have been much more than twenty.

On the other hand, the massacre is attributed to Herod the Great. Was his character such that it would be incredible to attribute such a horrendous act to him? Certainly to attribute this kind of act to an Albert Schweitzer or a Francis of Assisi would raise great skepticism and doubt. Such men would never have done so evil a deed. But Herod the Great? Everything we know about this man tells us that he was precisely the kind of person who would have done this sort of thing. He was paranoid concerning his rule. He not only built fortresses such as Antonia in Jerusalem, Sebaste, Caesarea, Gaba, Heshbon, Masada and Herodium for his protection, but he ruthlessly slaughtered anyone he suspected of being involved in political intrigue against him. He drowned Aristobulus III and executed Hyrcanus II, two high priests. He killed his uncle Joseph, his mother-in-law (Alexandra), his sons Alexander and Aristobolus, his favorite wife (Mariamne) and Antipater, the son he had chosen to succeed him, because he thought they were trying to overthrow him. As he was dying in the fortress of Herodium, he had the leading citizens of his kingdom gathered in the amphitheater of Jericho. Then he ordered that upon his death all these citizens be killed so that his death would be mourned! (Fortunately, the order was never carried out.)

Even if no clear extrabiblical document confirms the massacre of the innocents, there is no need to deny the historicity of the event. Some scholars, however, believe that an allusion to this event is found in *Assumption of Moses* 6:2-4. The passage refers to Herod and his slaying of the "old and young." It is impossible to demonstrate that it is an allusion to this incident. Yet it fits well with what we know of the ruthless and paranoid Herod the Great. There was just reason in Rome for the saying "Better Herod's swine [hys] than his son [hyios]." Herod, being half-Jewish, refrained from eating pork. Swine were therefore safe. But pity the son of whom Herod was suspicious. To such a man Matthew attributes the slaughter of the innocents.

The Birth of Jesus

Integral to the account of Jesus' birth is the story of the birth of John the Baptist, a "relative" (the term is vague) of Jesus. To a devout elderly priest named Zechariah and his wife, Elizabeth, who were childless and long past the age of childbearing, an angelic messenger announced the coming of a son (Lk 1:5-22). This supernatural birth, like other births to Old Testament people well past the age of having children (Gen 18, 25, 30; Judg 13; 1 Sam 1), indicated that the one so born would play a special role in God's plan of salvation. In this case, the child would be the forerunner to prepare the people for the coming of the Messiah.

Six months after the angelic visit to Zechariah and Elizabeth (Lk 1:26), the same angel visited a young woman named Mary to announce an even more amazing birth. It would be better to refer to Mary not as a woman but as a young girl. Engagements in Israel frequently took place before puberty, and the normal age for a betrothal was about thirteen. Mary was told that she would experience a most unusual occurrence. She would bear a son who would be the long-desired Messiah (Lk 1:31-33). Being a virgin, Mary questioned how this could happen. She was confused because the angelic message stated that she was to conceive immediately as a virgin rather than later, when she married Joseph. Informed that this would be a miracle worked by the Holy Spirit, she was reassured by the fact that God had already worked a similar, although less spectacular miracle in bringing about the pregnancy of her relative Elizabeth (Lk 1:35-38).

Because Joseph was a righteous person, he sought to divorce her when he became aware of Mary's pregnancy. (The description of Joseph as a righteous man in Matthew 1:19 explains why he sought to divorce Mary, not why he sought to do it quietly.) It would have been wrong according to the law to marry Mary since she had, according to his reasoning, committed adultery. In first-century Judaism an engagement was a legally binding contract between the man and the woman. During this period they were considered husband and wife even though the marriage ceremony and consummation of the marriage had not yet taken place. This marriage contract could be broken only by a formal divorce proceeding. If a woman was unfaithful during this time, she was considered an adulteress. Therefore, believing that Mary had committed adultery, Joseph sought to divorce her. Upon hearing the angelic explanation of Mary's

virginal conception, he took Mary as his wife, but no sexual consummation of this marriage took place until after the birth of Jesus (Mt 1:25).

In obedience to the census of Caesar Augustus, Joseph proceeded from
Nazareth to Bethlehem to be enrolled there because he was a descendant
of David. There is no need to deny the Davidic lineage of Jesus simply
because it is in accord with the messianic expectations of that day. Paul
in Romans 1:3 quotes an early church creedal formula when he refers
to Jesus as "descended from David" (compare also 2 Tim 2:8). Attempts
to argue that in Mark 12:35-37 Jesus denies a Davidic lineage are unconvincing, since both Luke (Lk 20:41-44) and Matthew (Mt 22:41-46) include this account. Certainly they did not believe that their accounts
refuted the Davidic lineage of Jesus that they clearly taught in their
virgin birth accounts (compare also Mk 10:47; Mt 9:27; 12:23; 15:22;
20:30-31; 21:9, 15; Lk 18:38-39; Acts 2:25-31; 13:22-23). Eusebius (*Eccl.
Hist.* 3.20.1-6) supports the Davidic lineage of Jesus when he refers to an
event in which Jesus' relatives were questioned by the emperor Domitian
because they were descendants of David. It should furthermore be remembered that the Jews of Jesus' day consisted for the most part of two
and one-half tribes: Judah, from which David came; Benjamin; and half
the tribe of Levi. It should not be surprising that there would be numerous Davidic descendants alive in the first century.

Because of his Davidic lineage, Joseph went to Bethlehem to be enrolled in the census. He took Mary with him. The distance between
Nazareth and Bethlehem is eighty-five to ninety miles, and such a trip
would have been on foot, averaging fifteen to eighteen miles a day. After
a trip of perhaps five or six days, they arrived in Bethlehem. During their
stay Jesus was born. It is uncertain how soon after their arrival this took
place. Although the birth of Jesus is usually portrayed as taking place
immediately after they arrived in Bethlehem, an apocryphal tradition
indicates that it took place a short time *before* the arrival in Bethlehem
(*Protevangelium of James* 17.3). The biblical account simply states that it took
place "while they were there" (Lk 2:6).

The birth is located by Luke in a place with a "manger" (a feeding
trough for animals), for there was no room for them in the "inn." We
should not read into this the notion of a motel or hotel with a "no
vacancy" sign. The term *inn* could refer to a public caravansary (a crude
place for caravans passing through), a primitive kind of inn (compare Ex

4:27; 1 Sam 1:18; however, Luke uses a different word for such an inn in Lk 10:34), a guest room in a home or an unspecified place of lodging (Sirach 14:25). Although the "innkeeper" has been the object of ridicule and much maligned over the centuries for not having given the holy couple a room, what Luke may mean in 2:7 is that the guest room did not have sufficient space ("room" or *topos* may mean "space," as in Lk 14:22) for Mary to give birth and for the baby to stay. As a result, the baby was born in a stall and placed in a manger found in the stall.

The traditional site of Jesus' birth is a cave located today in the Church of the Nativity. It is difficult to know exactly how to treat such traditions. One must resist, on the one hand, an unquestioning acceptance of all the "holy" sites in Israel as authentic and, on the other hand, the danger of rejecting all the sites as having no basis in history. In favor of the traditional site is the reference to a cave in *Protevangelium of James* 18:1 and by Justin Martyr and Origen, as well as the early dating of this site. (The tradition concerning the present site was so well established that in A.D. 325 a church was built to mark it. Jerome, who lived in the area for some time, remarked that since A.D. 135 the site was honored by Christians.)

At the birth of Jesus an angelic announcement of this joyous occasion was made to shepherds who were in the fields with their sheep (Lk 2:8-20). Tending sheep in the fields usually took place between March and November. In the winter months the sheep were penned up. We should not romanticize this scene as being a pronouncement to hardworking and respected "ranchers." Shepherds were generally considered dishonest (*b. Sanhedrin* 25b). They were unclean according to the law. Their presence at the birth of Jesus was recorded by Luke to show his readers that the good news of the gospel is for the poor, for sinners, for outcasts, for people like these shepherds.

Following the angelic announcement they found the holy couple and baby Jesus. He is described as wrapped in "bands of cloth" (Lk 2:12) or "swaddling cloths" (RSV). These were strips of cloth wrapped around the limbs to keep them straight (Ezek 17:4; Wisdom 7:4). The irony in this scene should not be lost. It was not the kings and nobles of the day who were present at the birth of the Son of God but the outcast, despised shepherds. They came not into a palace or a temple of great beauty but found the King of Israel lying in a trough used for feeding animals. With the coming of the Son of God the values and thinking of this world were turned on their head. God deemed foolish the world's wisdom and thinking (1 Cor 1:20).

Three Jewish rituals involving the birth of Jesus are described by Luke. The first involves Jesus' circumcision on the eighth day (compare Lk 1:59; Phil 3:5; and for the Old Testament background Gen 17:12-14; 21:4; Lev 12:3). At that time he was given the name Jesus, which the angel had announced (compare Lk 2:21 with 1:31). This name is the shortened form of Joshua or Jeshua. It was a popular Jewish name until the second century, when its association with Jesus Christ caused it to lose somewhat its appeal among Jews. Josephus refers to some twenty individuals with this name, and about half of them were contemporaries of Jesus of Nazareth. The description "of Nazareth" was necessary to distinguish this Jesus from other people so named. Jesus' name was given him to describe what he would do. Jesus means "YHWH is salvation," and Jesus of Nazareth would "save his people from their sins" (Mt 1:21).

Thirty-three days after Jesus' circumcision we read of the second ritual—Mary's purification. (Luke 2:22 actually refers to "their" purification, but the rite was for the woman only. "Their" may be used by Luke in that Joseph and Mary went together as a couple, as the union of one flesh, and did this together.) According to the law, after the birth of a son a woman would undergo a rite of purification, which involved the sacrificial giving of a lamb and a pigeon or dove (Lev 12:1-8). A poor family, however, could instead give two pigeons, and that is what Mary and Joseph did (Lk 2:24), indicating that they were poor. Obviously the wise men had not yet appeared on the scene to give their precious gifts (Mt 2:11).

Closely associated with Mary's purification was a third ritual involving the presentation, or "redemption," of Jesus (Lk 2:22-23; compare 1 Sam 1:22-24). This ritual involving the firstborn son in a family was a symbolic reliving of the Passover. The sparing of the firstborn from the angel of death by the sacrifice of a Passover lamb was now relived by the symbolic consecration of the firstborn to God (Ex 13:2, 12). It involved the payment of five shekels (Num 3:47-48; 18:15-16). The latter two rituals were performed in the Jerusalem temple, located five miles north of Bethlehem.

At the time of Mary's purification and Jesus' presentation Luke records an incident involving a priest named Simeon and a prophetess named

Anna (Lk 2:25-38). (Luke is fond of placing side by side events involving a male and a female: Zechariah and Mary [Lk 1:5-38]; the healing of a man with an unclean spirit and Simon's mother-in-law [Lk 4:38-39]; the healing of the centurion's servant and the raising of the widow of Nain's son [Lk 7:1-17]; the healing of the Gerasene demoniac and the hemorrhaging woman [Lk 8:26-56]; and the pairing of parables involving a man and a woman [Lk 13:18-21 and 15:4-10; this pairing is obscured in the NRSV].) Upon seeing Jesus, Simeon gave thanks that he had lived long enough to see the salvation promised long ago and now realized in the coming of the Messiah, but he made a veiled reference to a sword piercing Mary's soul (Lk 2:35) and thus to a dark side in all this. Anna also rejoiced in having seen the redemption that God was now bringing about for the sake of his people.

Matthew tells of wise men coming from the East some time after this to see the king of the Jews (Mt 2:1-12). Although popular folklore places three wise men at the manger alongside the shepherds at the time of Jesus' birth, Matthew points out that "they" (the number is ambiguous) found Jesus in a "house" (Mt 2:11), not in a stall with a manger (Lk 2:7, 12). Matthew's reference to the time of the star (Mt 2:7) and the subsequent slaughter of the children two years old and younger (Mt 2:16) indicates that he understood Jesus as being up to two years of age at the time of the wise men's visit. The reference to the wise men fits well with Matthew's understanding of the universal nature of the good news, for at the very beginning of the gospel story Gentiles are present. It does not, however, require that the story of the wise men be considered a fictional creation by him. Rather, it is better to see here a selection by Matthew of a tradition he included in his Gospel because it served well his theological purpose.

Warned in a dream not to return to Jerusalem, the wise men returned home a different way. Joseph also received via a dream a similar warning concerning the evil designs of Herod and fled with Mary and Jesus to Egypt. Their flight saved them, but the jealous fury of Herod was unleashed against the innocent children of Bethlehem. Nothing is said in the Bible about the time spent in Egypt, although some apocryphal Gospels delight in creating stories about the trip and sojourn there. Doubtless living in a foreign land would have been difficult for the Holy Family. Joseph's trade was useful, but it was a trade that at best earned only an adequate living. Perhaps during this time it was the gifts of the wise men that sustained them. When Herod died in 4 B.C., Joseph returned with his family to Nazareth (Mt 2:19-23).

As with the virginal conception, critics have argued against the historicity of Matthew's accounts of the wise men, the flight to Egypt and the slaughter of the innocents. It is true that Luke does not refer to them, but to argue from this that they are therefore fictional is unwarranted. Such an argument from silence possesses the weakness of having to assume (1) that Luke must have known about such traditions if they had occurred and (2) that he would have recorded these traditions if he had known them. That is impossible to demonstrate. Furthermore, even if Luke was unaware of these traditions, this would not prove that they are not historical.

At times critics have argued that such traditions were created to fulfill messianic prophecies and expectations. In Matthew 2:15 the Evangelist states that the stay in Egypt and subsequent return constituted a fulfillment of the prophecy in Hosea 11:1 ("out of Egypt I called my son"). It is difficult to believe that the tradition of the stay in Egypt and the return to Nazareth was created by someone who thought that Hosea 11:1 was a messianic prophecy that required such a tradition to "fulfill it." The reverse is far more likely—the tradition of the stay in Egypt and return to Galilee caused someone to see Hosea 11:1 as a prophecy that predicted this. In similar fashion, it is more likely that the tradition of Jesus' birth in Bethlehem resulted in the church's seeing in this the fulfillment of the messianic prophecy in Micah 5:2 rather than the reverse. The very difficulty that Christians have had in seeing how events in the Gospel traditions fulfilled various Old Testament prophecies (consider Mt 2:15, 18; 4:15-16; and so on) argues in favor of the traditions' being historical and leading the church to see various Old Testament passages as predictions of these events.

The Theological Importance of the Virginal Conception

During the late nineteenth and early twentieth centuries in response to the denial of various biblical teachings, a twelve-volume work entitled *The Fundamentals* was written. One of the five "fundamentals" listed in this work was the virgin birth. (The others were the inerrancy of Scripture, the deity of Christ, the substitutionary atonement, and the bodily resurrection and imminent bodily second coming of the Lord.) In the mid-twentieth century a leading theologian argued that the virgin birth accounts were impertinent attempts by the early church to explain the incarnation. What was crucial in the biblical story was that the Word became flesh (Jn 1:14). No attempt, he argued, should be made to explain how this took place.

The latter criticism should be taken seriously. The essence of the Christmas story is not that Mary conceived as a virgin. Nor is the Christmas story a sentimental ode to motherhood. The essence of Christmas is that God's Son came into the world in human form and dwelt among us. It is the "fact" of the incarnation that is the key to Christmas, not the "how" by which this was brought about. It would be presumptuous to claim that the omnipotent God of all creation could not have brought about the incarnation in any other way.

Some have argued that a virginal conception was necessary to keep the Son of God from inheriting the corruption and sin of Adam. (Sometimes people who argue this way bring with them a negative view of the sexual act, which comes from a Platonic-like dualism rather than from a biblical understanding that within the God-ordained plan such an act is "good" [Gen 1:28-31].) Yet the person who thinks this way must somehow protect the Son of God from inheriting such sin and corruption via Mary. It is not surprising therefore that a logical consequence to this kind of thinking was to argue for the immaculate conception of Mary. Now the Son of God could truly be protected from such sin, since he could not have inherited sin from his mother. The New Testament does not enter into such speculations. Luke simply says that the Holy Spirit came upon Mary and overshadowed her through all this. Through his protection the offspring would be holy, the Son of God (Lk 1:35).

The incarnation, not the virginal conception, is the essence of the Christmas story. For orthodox Christianity that is self-evident. The Son of God did not come into existence through a virginal conception. The Son of God was, is and always will be. Long before the virginal conception, the birth of Mary, the entire genealogy of Luke 3:23-38 and the creation of the world, the Son was. The virginal conception was simply the means by which God brought about the incarnation of his Son.

Nevertheless, the Bible does say that the incarnation was through a virginal conception. If that was God's way of bringing this about, we can do nothing but acknowledge it. The importance of confessing or denying the virginal conception lies not in its christological consequences. The virginal conception and birth did not make Jesus the Son of God. It was not required to keep him holy and undefiled. What is at stake involves not a doctrine of Christ but of Scripture. The virgin birth served for the authors of *The Fundamentals* as a kind of litmus text concerning one's view of the Bible. To deny it was obviously to reject the Bible as an infallible rule of faith. In this respect the question "Do you believe the virgin birth?" served as a kind of twentieth-century shibboleth (Judg 12:6) testing a person's view of the Bible.

Conclusion

You will conceive . . . and bear a son, and . . . name him Jesus. He will be great, and will be called the Son of the Most High, and the Lord God will give to him the throne of his ancestor David. He will reign over the house of Jacob forever, and of his kingdom there will be no end. . . . Therefore the child to be born will be holy; he will be called Son of God. (Lk 1:31-35)

She will bear a son, and you are to name him Jesus, for he will save his people from their sins. (Mt 1:21)

And the Word became flesh and lived among us. (Jn 1:14)

References

Brown, Raymond E. *The Birth of the Messiah*. New York: Doubleday, 1979.

Cranfield, C. E. B. "Some Reflections on the Subject of the Virgin Birth." *Scottish Journal of Theology* 41 (1988): 177-89.

Johnson, Marshall D. *The Purpose of the Biblical Genealogies*. Cambridge: Cambridge University Press, 1988.

Machen, J. Gresham. *The Virgin Birth of Christ*. New York: Harper, 1930.

Maier, Paul L. *First Christmas*. New York: Harper, 1971.

Meier, John P. *A Marginal Jew: Rethinking the Historical Jesus*, 1:205-52. New York: Doubleday, 1991.

Miguens, Manuel. *The Virgin Birth*. Westminster, Md.: Christian Classics, 1975.

Nolland, John. *Luke*, 1:13-135. Word Biblical Commentary. Dallas: Word, 1989.

Witherington, Ben, III. "Birth of Jesus." In *Dictionary of Jesus and the Gospels*, edited by Joel B. Green, Scot McKnight and I. Howard Marshall, pp. 60-74. Downers Grove, Ill.: InterVarsity Press, 1992.

5
WHAT WAS THE BOY
JESUS REALLY LIKE?
The Silent Years

THE CANONICAL GOSPELS RECORD ONLY ONE EVENT BETWEEN THE infancy and baptism of Jesus. Luke 2:41-52 is an account in which Jesus, when he was twelve years old, accompanied his parents to Jerusalem to celebrate the Passover. It was apparently the custom of his family to do this each year (v. 41). The event was recorded by Luke because of its unusual nature. He wanted his readers to know that already at the age of twelve Jesus sensed a unique relationship to God: the temple was his "Father's house" (v. 49). Returning home with a caravan of pilgrims, Joseph and Mary assumed that Jesus was with the other children. When they discovered that he was not, they returned to Jerusalem. There they found Jesus in the temple manifesting his unique wisdom among the religious leaders. His parents' surprise (vv. 48-49) reveals that despite the miraculous events surrounding his birth, the subsequent years had been quite normal—so much so that the uniqueness of their son and his divine calling had faded from their memory.

The Normalcy of Jesus' Silent Years
Along with the surprise of Joseph and Mary over Jesus' behavior during

this incident there is additional evidence that the silent years of Jesus were normal. The fact that this is the only incident recorded in the Gospels during this period suggests that no other traditions involving this period of Jesus' life were christologically significant. The Gospel writers were unaware of any other unusual or miraculous events that occurred during this time. John explicitly states this after recounting Jesus' miracle of turning the water to wine: "Jesus did this, the first of his signs, in Cana of Galilee" (Jn 2:11).

Still another factor that argues for the normalcy of these silent years is the unbelief of Jesus' family and community. Unlike the stories found in the *Infancy Gospel of Thomas* (see chapter two under "Extrabiblical Sources"), there was no cemetery in Nazareth devoted to the victims of Jesus and no major sparrow problem that would have led his family (Jn 7:5) or community (Mk 6:4) to believe in his unique divine calling and relationship to God.

It might be argued that if the biblical teaching about the person of Jesus is correct, his silent years must have been unique. The confession that Jesus was without sin would, of course, make him unique and most unusual (2 Cor 5:21; Heb 4:15; 9:14; 1 Pet 2:22; 1 Jn 3:5; compare also Lk 1:35; Jn 8:46). Yet would the sinlessness of Jesus be something that others would have seen? Leaving aside the portrayal in medieval art of the boy Jesus with a halo over his head, would his sinlessness really have been observable? No doubt his piety and goodness would have been noticed. Such things as his obedience to his parents (Lk 2:51), honesty, truthfulness and integrity would have been observable. But would his sinless character? To claim that Jesus was sinless would require that a person witness his behavior twenty-four hours a day, every day of his life. And even then one could not be sure because of the inability to judge his thoughts and the motives of his heart. Jesus' sinlessness was something known to God alone. It was not something about which his family and community were aware.

The Brothers and Sisters of Jesus

The New Testament mentions the brothers and sisters of Jesus in several places (Mk 3:31-35; 6:3; Jn 2:12; 7:3-5, 10; Acts 1:14; 1 Cor 9:5; Gal 1:19). Within the early church these references were interpreted in three main ways. (1) According to Helvidius (fourth century), they were Jesus' younger brothers and sisters, born to Joseph and Mary in later years. (2) Epiphanius (fourth century) argued that they were the sons and daughters of Joseph by a previous marriage. Joseph, according to this view, was a widower when he married Mary and brought with him into their marriage at least four sons and two daughters (Mk 6:3). (3) Jerome (fourth century), whose Latin name was Hieronymus, maintained that Jesus' siblings were not true brothers and sisters at all. They were actually cousins. The expression "brothers and sisters," he argued, should be understood as referring to a looser relationship, much like when the New Testament refers to fellow believers as "brothers and sisters."

The close association of the brothers and sisters with Jesus' mother in Mark 6:3 suggests that they were not mere nephews and nieces or relatives. This is even clearer in the Matthew parallel, where the Evangelist refers to "his mother and his brothers" (Mt 12:46). These verses raise a serious objection to the Hieronymian interpretation. That Mark 6:3 ties Jesus' brothers and sisters to Jesus' mother rather than to his father also raises a serious problem for the Epiphanian view. Were it not for the doctrine of the perpetual virginity of Mary held in some parts of the Christian church, there would be no need for the Epiphanian and Hieronymian explanations. (The doctrine of the perpetual virginity of Mary is not only a Roman Catholic teaching. Eastern Orthodoxy holds this view, and John Calvin left this question open.) Some biblical support for the Hieronymian view is found in John 19:26-27, where Jesus entrusted the care of his mother into the hands of the disciple John.

The most natural way of interpreting the references to the brothers and sisters of Jesus is to understand them as referring to the sons and daughters of Joseph and Mary. Along with the grammatical argument that it is the most natural way of interpreting this expression, additional support in favor of this view is found in Matthew 1:24-25: "When Joseph awoke from sleep, he did as the angel of the Lord commanded him; he took [Mary] as his wife, but had no marital relations with her until she had borne a son; and he named him Jesus." The term *until* is only one way of interpreting the Greek expression *heōs hou*. It can also be interpreted as meaning that from the time of the angelic announcement to the time of Jesus' birth Joseph did not have marital relations with Mary ("know" in KJV, RSV), without implying that afterward he did. However, the best way by far of interpreting the Greek expression in this passage is "until," with the implication that after the birth of Jesus, Joseph and Mary lived in a normal marital relationship and that this relationship was blessed with at least four sons and two daughters. (The reference to Jesus as the "firstborn son" in Lk 2:7 should be interpreted in light of Ex 13:2 and Num 3:12-13; 18:15-16 as a technical term that need not imply the birth of subsequent brothers. An ancient funeral marker refers to a woman who died giving birth to her "firstborn son.")

The Family Life of Jesus

That Jesus was born into a poor family is evident from the sacrifice offered for Mary's purification (see chapter four; Lk 2:24; compare Lev 12:8). Paul suggests this when he says, "For you know the generous act of our Lord Jesus Christ, that though he was rich, yet for your sakes he became poor, so that by his poverty you might become rich" (2 Cor 8:9). Although Paul is primarily thinking of the Son's emptying himself (Phil 2:7) in taking the form of a human, the sharp contrast in this verse would be lost if he had been born into wealth. The disdain shown Jesus by the leaders of his day (Mk 11:27-28; Lk 4:22; compare Jn 1:46; 7:41-42, 52), his ease with and concern for the poor (Lk 4:18-19; 14:13, 21) and his burial in another man's tomb (Mk 15:42-47) also suggest this.

Jesus was a carpenter by occupation (Mk 6:3). (There is absolutely no evidence that Jesus was a peasant farmer.) This term can refer not only to a worker of wood but also to a craftsman who worked with stone or metal. Justin Martyr in the second century (*Dialogue with Trypho* 88) referred to Jesus' having made plows and yokes. Whether he had additional information for saying this or inferred it from the biblical reference is impossible to determine. As carpenters Jesus and his father, Joseph, were part of the working poor, although it would be incorrect to describe them as destitute. Jesus' occupation required of him physical labor, so the later art of the church that tended to portray Jesus as skinny and weak is clearly in error.

Whereas we read of Mary (Mk 3:31-35; 6:3; 15:40; Acts 1:14) during the ministry of Jesus, we never read of Joseph. The reference to Jesus as "the son of Mary" in Mark 6:3 is difficult to understand even if Joseph was dead, because usually a man was referred to as the son of his father. If Joseph were alive, however, such a reference would be virtually impossible to imagine. The fact that Mark 3:35 mentions Jesus' "brother[s]," "sister[s]" and "mother" but no mention is made of his "father" also suggests that Joseph was no longer living at the time. It appears that sometime between the incident of the twelve-year-old Jesus in the temple and the beginning of Jesus' ministry, Joseph died.

Speculations as to how his father's death affected Jesus are simply that—speculations. Those who speak of his death as the turning point in Jesus' life, of the crushing blow that this caused Jesus due to his "father fixation," are writing creative fiction. Such fictionalized conjectures will always appear to the devout as irrelevant and often irreverent speculations that reveal more about the writers than about Jesus. The only thing we really know is that with the death of Joseph the responsibilities of caring for the mother and family fell on the oldest son—Jesus. (Note the concern of Jesus for his mother in Jn 19:27.) Thus for the period after Joseph's death to the time of his ministry, Jesus was the active bread-winner and responsible head of the family.

The Personal Life of Jesus
Attempts have been made to discover the physical appearance of Jesus. Some have sought to argue from Isaiah 53:2 ("He had no form or majesty that we should look at him, nothing in his appearance that we should desire him") that Jesus must have been quite unattractive in appearance. Such a view, however, misinterprets the poetic language of this passage. On the other hand, it has also been argued that since the rabbis of Jesus' day had high standards regarding the outward appearance of Jewish teachers, Jesus must not have had any major physical impairment because they never criticized him for his appearance.

It is impossible to demonstrate or refute either of these views. In the divine wisdom and providence virtually nothing has been preserved concerning the outward form in which the Lord's Anointed appeared. All we can say is that Jesus was a first-century Jewish male. Probably he was average in size and weight, but that cannot be proven. Clearly the Gospel writers were far more concerned with *who* Jesus was and *what* he did than with *how he appeared*. It would be wise for us to have a similar concern.

Sensational claims have been made that Jesus was married. Some have even written tabloidlike works claiming that Jesus was married to Mary Magdalene or Salome. The strongest argument made for the view that Jesus was married is that it was normal for Jewish men to marry and that it was expected that teachers should marry and be an example in this area. In discussing whether or not Jesus was married we must be careful to recognize that a decision on this subject should not be based on whether or not one believes that celibacy is more noble than marriage.

That there is no reference in the New Testament to a wife of Jesus and that there is nothing whatsoever in the New Testament that suggests that Jesus was married argues strongly (if not conclusively) against such a view. It should also be mentioned that certain groups in Israel refrained from marriage and advocated celibacy. The Essenes held such a view (Josephus *War* 2.8.2 [2.120-21]; *Ant.* 18.1.5 [18.18-22]; Pliny the Elder *Natural History* 5.15.73; Philo in Eusebius *Preparation for the Gospel* 8.11), as did the Therapeutae, a group of ascetics who lived in lower Egypt. The argument that Jesus would have been unusual if he did not marry also confronts the objection that Jesus was in fact most unusual. The concern for his mother (Jn 19:27) but lack of any concern for an alleged wife also raises powerful objections. There is in reality no evidence whatever that Jesus was married.

The Languages of Jesus

In the time of Jesus three languages figured prominently in the life of the people. Although the life and teachings of Jesus have been preserved in the New Testament in the Greek language, the native language of Jesus was Aramaic. We have some of the Aramaic words and expressions he used preserved in the Gospels: *Talitha cum* ("Little girl, get up!"; Mk 5:41), *Eloi, Eloi lema sabachthani* ("My God, my God, why have you forsaken me?" Mk 15:34), *Abba* ("Father"; Mk 14:36; Gal 4:6; Rom 8:15), *Cephas* ("Peter"; Jn 1:42), *Mammon* ("wealth"; Mt 6:24 RSV), *Raca* ("fool"; Mt 5:22 RSV) and so on. It is possible to be even more specific and say that Jesus spoke a Galilean version of "western Aramaic," differing from that spoken in Jerusalem (Mt 26:73; compare Acts 2:7).

It appears that Jesus could read and speak Hebrew. Although it was once thought that Hebrew was essentially a dead language in the first century, the discovery of the Dead Sea Scrolls has revealed that Hebrew was still used quite extensively in certain circles. Jesus' ability to read Hebrew is evident from Luke 4:16-20, where Jesus read the Hebrew Scripture lesson in the synagogue of Nazareth. A few Hebrew words are also preserved in the Gospels: *Ephphatha* ("Be opened"; Mk 7:34), *amen*

("amen"; Mt 5:26; Mk 14:30 RSV).

The third major language spoken in Palestine was Greek. The impact of Alexander the Great's conquests in the fourth century B.C. resulted in the Mediterranean's being a "Greek sea" in Jesus' day. In the third century Jews in Egypt could no longer read the Scriptures in Hebrew, so they began to translate them into Greek. This famous translation became known as the Septuagint (LXX). Jesus, who was reared in "Galilee of the Gentiles," lived only three or four miles from the thriving Greek city of Sepphoris. There may even have been times when he and his father worked in this rapidly growing metropolitan city, which served as the capital city of Herod Antipas until A.D. 26, when he moved the capital to Tiberias.

The existence of the "Hellenists" in the early church (Acts 6:1-6) suggests that from the beginning there were Jewish Christians in the Jerusalem church whose native tongue was Greek. (It is best to understand the expression "Hellenists" as primarily revealing their language rather than their cultural and philosophical outlook.) Two of Jesus' disciples were even known by their Greek names: Andrew and Philip. In addition, there are several incidents in Jesus' ministry when he spoke to people who knew neither Aramaic nor Hebrew. Thus unless a translator was present (though none is ever mentioned), their conversation probably took place in the Greek language. Probably Jesus spoke Greek during the following occasions: the visit to Tyre, Sidon and the Decapolis (Mk 7:31ff.), the conversation with the Syrophoenician woman (Mk 7:24-30; compare especially 7:26) and the trial before Pontius Pilate (Mk 15:2-15; compare also Jesus' conversation with the "Greeks" in Jn 12:20-36).

It would appear, then, that Jews lived in a trilingual environment. Thus although Jesus' native language was Aramaic, he could probably also converse in Hebrew and Greek. It may even be that he was familiar with certain Latin terms due to the influence of Rome, its legions and its administrative officials. Nevertheless it would be more accurate to say that although Jesus was a trilingual Jew, he was not a trilingual teacher.

To what extent was Jesus an educated man? Although education is highly valued in the Talmudic literature, Jewish education was not broadly based in the first century. Being the oldest son, Jesus was the most likely of the children to have received formal education. Yet John quotes Jesus' opponents with apparent approval: "How does this man have such learning, when he has never been taught?" (Jn 7:15). That Jesus could read is evident from Luke 4:16-21, where he read the Scriptures at sabbath worship in Nazareth. The later noncanonical passage found in John 7:53—8:11 suggests that he could write (Jn 8:6), but one must judge this scribal addition most critically. That Jesus was a learned man goes without saying. He engaged in debates with the intellectual leaders (Mk 2:23-28; 3:1-6; 7:1-23; 10:2-12; 12:13-17, 18-27, 28-34; Lk 11:14-23); he was called "Rabbi" (Mt 26:25; Mk 9:5; 11:21; 14:45; Jn 1:38, 49; 3:2) and "Teacher" (Mk 4:38; 9:17, 38; 10:17, 20, 35, 12:14); and most important, he taught in the synagogues (Mt 4:23; 9:35; Mk 1:21, 39; 6:2; Lk 4:15, 28, 33, 44; 6:6; 13:10; Jn 6:59; 18:20). So whereas we do not know how Jesus received his training and education, the fact remains that his ability to read, to debate the Scriptures and to answer exegetical questions reveals that he was an educated man.

Conclusion

The silent years of Jesus do not play an important role in the Evangelists' reporting of "the good news of Jesus Christ, the Son of God" (Mk 1:1). Except for the one incident in the temple involving the twelve-year-old Jesus, the traditions available to them did not refer to this period of his life. This stands in sharp contrast with such apocryphal Gospels as the *Infancy Gospel of Thomas* and the *Protevangelium of James*, which take great delight in reading back into this period of Jesus' life imaginary speculations of what the divine Son of God must have been like.

The silence of our Gospels reveals that this period in Jesus' life was essentially normal and like that of any other Jewish child, boy, young man and man. No teachings of Jesus are preserved from this period, and only one incident was recorded. And that was preserved due to its christological significance. Even at the age of twelve Jesus of Nazareth had a unique awareness of his sonship. For Jesus the temple in Jerusalem was "my [not our] Father's house" (Lk 2:49). Thus Luke indicates that Jesus' sonship revealed at the annunciation to Mary (Lk 1:32, 35) was affirmed during the silent years. Its ultimate manifestation, however, awaited the baptism and subsequent ministry. The Gospels do not describe a developmental process in which the baby Jesus gradually came to realize his sonship and unique relationship with God. They are silent about any psychological or religious development. What they tell us clearly is that already at the age of twelve such a consciousness was present.

Despite the silence in our Gospels concerning this time in Jesus' life, the significance of this period for the believing community is nonetheless great. The writer of Hebrews argues that because of Jesus' experiences during this time, as well as during his ministry, he is able "to sympathize with our weaknesses" because "in every respect [he] has been tested as we are" (Heb 4:15). Thus his followers are invited to come boldly to him in their time of temptation and need. Because he shared in our humanity (Heb 2:14), we can come to Jesus knowing that he truly understands our temptations and weaknesses:

> Since, then, we have a great high priest who has passed through the heavens, Jesus, the Son of God, let us hold fast to our confession. For we do not have a high priest who is unable to sympathize with our weaknesses, but we have one who in every respect has been tested as we are, yet without sin. Let us therefore approach the throne of grace with boldness, so that we may receive mercy and find grace to help in time of need. (Heb 4:14-16; compare also 2:14-18)

References

Barr, James. "Which Language Did Jesus Speak? Some Remarks of a Semitist." *Bulletin of the John Rylands University Library of Manchester* 53 (1970): 9-29.

Brown, Raymond E., et al., eds. *Mary in the New Testament.* Philadelphia: Fortress, 1978.

Fitzmyer, Joseph A. "The Languages of Palestine in the First Century A.D." *Catholic Biblical Quarterly* 32 (1970): 501-31.

Harrison, Everett F. *A Short Life of Christ,* pp. 51-65. Grand Rapids, Mich.: Eerdmans, 1968.

Meier, John P. *A Marginal Jew: Rethinking the Historical Jesus,* 1:253-371. New York: Doubleday, 1991.

6
THE BAPTISM
OF JESUS
The Anointing
of the Anointed

W E KNOW LITTLE ABOUT JESUS BETWEEN HIS VISIT TO JERUSALEM and his baptism. Almost certainly Joseph died during this period, and Jesus, as the oldest son, assumed the leadership role of the family. During this period the Jewish people were once again ruled by a foreign power. Except for a short period of independence from 142-63 B.C., the years following the fall of Jerusalem in 587 B.C. were spent in bondage to other nations. Domination by Nebuchadnezzar's Babylon was followed by domination by Persia, then Greece, then Ptolemaic Egypt, then Seleucidan Syria. The brief hiatus of independence under the Maccabees and their descendants came to an end in 63 B.C., when Pompey led the Roman legions into Jerusalem.

Rome granted numerous concessions to the Jewish people due to early treaties established between the Maccabees and Rome and subsequent acts by various emperors: they did not have to attend pagan religious rites; they were able to qualify the divine titles given to the emperor; they swore loyalty to the emperor using their own religious oaths; they sacrificed to God in their own temple on Caesar's behalf rather than to Caesar in a pagan temple; they did not have to adore images of the emperor; they were exempt from military service, which involved profaning the sabbath and idolatrous acts; they were permitted to use their own calendar; they were able to ask for welfare distribution in cash in case it was being given in a form forbidden by their law; they were able to collect welfare distribution on another day if it was distributed on the sabbath or a Jewish holiday; they were exempt from having to appear in court on the sabbath; they were able to collect a temple tax from Jewish males throughout the Roman Empire. And there were more.

Rome had additional reasons for granting such concessions. The Roman leaders wanted to live peaceably with the Jewish people. Their number, estimated at between three to eight million, made them a significant minority. Approximately one out of every fourteen people in the empire (about 7 percent) was Jewish. Nevertheless, despite such concessions, many Jews in Palestine seethed in discontent. For them a "gracious bondage" was still a bondage, and poor Roman rule often aggravated the problem. As a result, in A.D. 66 this discontent led to an open revolt and the subsequent destruction of Jerusalem.

The Coming of John the Baptist

In A.D. 27 or 28 a strangely dressed man appeared near the southern end of the Jordan River. Ascetic in diet and lifestyle (Mt 11:18; Mk 1:6), his appearance caused a great deal of excitement among the Jewish people. This was due both to his dress and to his preaching. He "was clothed with camel's hair, with a leather belt around his waist" (Mk 1:6), the very kind of clothing worn by the famous prophet Elijah (2 Kings 1:8). The similarity of dress raised an important question: Since it was prophesied that one day Elijah would return (Mal 4:5; compare Mk 9:11-13), was it possible that this man was the returning Elijah?

His preaching strengthened these speculations even further, for his powerful message was of repentance and judgment, like the Old Testament prophets: "You brood of vipers! Who warned you to flee from the wrath to come? Bear fruit worthy of repentance. . . . Even now the ax is lying at the root of the trees; every tree therefore that does not bear good fruit is cut down and thrown into the fire" (Mt 3:7-8, 10). In Jesus' understanding John the Baptist fulfilled the role of the returning Elijah

(Mk 9:11-13). Of course, when asked whether he was actually the prophet Elijah raised from the dead, John had to deny it (Jn 1:21).

At the time John was baptizing, similar rites of washing existed within the Jewish community. Among the sectarians at Qumran a ritual washing was associated with repentance (1QS 3:4-9; 5:13-14; 6:14-23), and among the Jewish people there was the practice of proselyte baptism. The exact date when the latter began is uncertain. Whereas it appears that such a baptism existed at the end of the first century, there is no clear evidence that it existed as early as the ministry of John. There are some clear and distinct differences, however, between the baptism of John and these other two rites.

For one, the other rites were self-administered. In other words, the participants were not baptized by another party but by themselves. As for the Qumran washings, they, unlike John's and proselyte baptism, were repeated on a regular basis. A major difference between John's baptism and Jewish proselyte baptism is that the latter was exclusively for Gentiles—it was for non-Jews who sought to become Jews. Along with circumcision and the offering of a sacrifice, baptism was part of the conversion experience. In contrast, John's message of repentance was addressed primarily to Jews: "Do not begin to say to yourselves, 'We have Abraham as our ancestor'; for I tell you, God is able from these stones to raise up children to Abraham" (Lk 3:8). John clearly rejected the notion that one could enter the coming messianic kingdom simply because of one's ancestry. Race was not sufficient. Only the repentant of Israel would enter the kingdom.

John's message was not simply one of doom. Along with his eschatological pronouncement of judgment came the announced arrival of the awaited messianic kingdom: "The one who is more powerful than I is coming after me; I am not worthy to stoop down and untie the thong of his sandals. I have baptized you with water; but he will baptize you with the Holy Spirit" (Mk 1:7-8). The "more powerful" one John spoke of was not God but the Messiah. Stooping down and untying the thong of God's sandal would make no sense. Called "the Baptist" because of his practice of baptizing, John saw himself as the forerunner of the Messiah and sought to prepare the people for him: "I am the voice of one crying out in the wilderness, 'Make straight the way of the Lord' " (Jn 1:23; compare Mk 1:2-3). (Despite the fact that the "wilderness" in the experience of Israel was associated with murmuring and disobedience, it was also a place of revelation and unique providential care. Consequently the blessings of the coming messianic age were frequently seen as a returning to the "wilderness" [Is 40:3; 48:20-22; Hos 2:14-15; 12:9; 1QS 8:12-14]. To what extent John was influenced by such thinking is unclear. What is clear is that he saw himself as called to prepare people for the one who was to come. Thus in accordance with Isaiah 40:3 he preached in the wilderness.)

In preparing the way for the Coming One, John baptized a repentant people. The exact relationship between this repentance and baptism is not discussed in the biblical texts. The question of whether they could be separated from each other never entered the minds of the biblical writers. The association between the two was so intimate that they were considered part of the same experience. A repentance separated from baptism or a baptism separated from repentance was inconceivable. John's baptism was essentially "ecclesiastical" in nature. It was not primarily a personal experience performed in splendid isolation for the individual but a corporate rite that involved becoming part of a community awaiting the promised Messiah. Thus the experience of repentance and the rite of baptism were inseparable.

The impression made by John the Baptist was heightened even more because in the minds of most Jews the prophetic voice had been silent for nearly four hundred years. The prophets and the presence of the Spirit were a matter of the past:

> Know that our fathers in former times and former generations had helpers, righteous prophets and holy men. . . . We were also in our country, and they helped us when we sinned, and they intervened for us with him who has created us since they trusted in their works. And the Mighty One heard them and purged us from our sins. But now, the righteous have been assembled, and the prophets are sleeping. Also we have left our land, and Zion has been taken away from us, and we have nothing now apart from the Mighty One and His Law. (2 Baruch 85:1-3)

> When the latter prophets died, that is, Haggai, Zechariah, and Malachi, then the Holy Spirit came to an end in Israel. (Tosefta Sota 13:3; compare also 1 Macc 4:46; 9:27; 14:41; Josephus *Against Apion* 1.41)

Some at this time wrote under the names of prophets and saints of early times, when the Spirit was active. In doing so they hoped to gain a greater hearing. Consequently a large number of pseudepigraphic works were written during this period.

Yet whereas the voice of prophecy was associated with the past, it was also associated with the future. For many Jews the Spirit and the prophets would one day return. In that day God would visit his people and bring the "consolation of Israel" (Lk 2:25) and the "redemption of Jerusalem" (Lk 2:38). A time was coming when God would manifest himself in a new and even greater way to his people. The promises made to the patriarchs, David and the prophets would one day be fulfilled. For many Jews this involved the coming of the Lord's Anointed. When this Messiah came, the Holy Spirit would once again be present. John told his hearers that whereas he baptized them with a baptism of repentance in preparation for that time, the coming Messiah would baptize "with the Holy Spirit and fire" (Mt 3:11).

When the Messiah came, it was expected that he would both judge the wicked and deliver the righteous. The reference to "fire" in John's message is best understood as involving a negative judgment upon the unbelieving. Matthew and Luke appear to interpret it in this manner in that a reference to a judgment of fire precedes this saying (Mt 3:10) and follows it (Mt 3:12). Many Jews understood the coming messianic judgment as involving both the destruction of their enemies and the restoration of Israel to greatness. His coming involved both retribution and redemption, damnation and deliverance, judgment and justice. For the repentant the Messiah's baptism was associated with the gift of the Spirit; for the unrepentant his coming would bring a baptism of fiery judgment. When this took place, all roads would lead not to Rome but to Jerusalem.

Jesus did not believe, however, that his ministry would bring the immediate judgment of the nations. Nor would Israel be restored to her former greatness, as in the time of David and Solomon. For Jesus, the judgment of the world would certainly take place, but not at the present time. Such a judgment furthermore would involve not just the Gentiles (Mt 25:31-46) but Israel as well. A more immediate judgment, however, faced Israel (Mk 12:1-12; Lk 11:45-52; 19:41-44).

The sheep would be distinguished from the goats on the basis of their attitude toward Jesus. A clearer delineation of the believing remnant would take place based on the people's response to Jesus. Other groups in Israel spoke of such a separation, but this involved the separation of the righteous remnant from the "accursed people who knew not the law" (the view of certain Pharisees) or of the children of light from the children of darkness (the members of the Essene sect). Yet the coming of Jesus would bring about a more radical separation than this. In his understanding, the "first [would be] last, and the last [would] be first" (Mk 10:31; compare Mt 20:16; Jn 9:39). Through his ministry the tax collectors and sinners entered the kingdom, whereas those who thought they possessed a preferential standing in the kingdom did not (Lk 14:15-24). Since the kingdom belonged to the "poor in spirit" (Mt 5:3), those who considered themselves "first" and were satisfied with their own righteousness excluded themselves from the believing remnant; sinners who acknowledged their unworthiness sought the grace and mercy of God and entered (Lk 7:36-50).

For most Jews, the time preceding the appearance of John the Baptist was marked by the absence of God's prophets and his Spirit. Now once again a prophet was present in Israel. And he spoke of the coming Spirit. In light of all this it is not surprising that his appearance created great excitement. Was this man the returning Elijah? Was God visiting his people? Was the messianic age about to begin? Were those present living in the "last days"?

Less than ten miles away from the region in which John baptized lay a community near the northwest corner of the Dead Sea. This community of Qumran possessed some striking parallels with John the Baptist and his preaching. Both John and Qumran were priestly in descent, stressed the need of repentance, had a similar though not identical "baptism," proclaimed a similar judgment on the Pharisees, were ascetic in their lifestyle and lived in the wilderness. Even more striking, however, was that they both had the same biblical passage as their theme verse: "A voice cries out: 'In the wilderness prepare the way of the LORD, make straight in the desert a highway for our God' " (Is 40:3; compare Mk 1:3 and 1QS 8:12-14). Among the Essenes of Qumran (it has not been proven that the Qumran community were Essenes, but it is probable), there was also a sense that the Spirit was active among them.

These similarities have resulted in a great deal of speculation. Was John the Baptist originally a member of the Qumran community? Had his elderly parents given him up to be raised by the community? Did he become disenchanted with the community's view that Isaiah 40:3 would best be fulfilled by their living apart from the corrupting influences of society and by the study of the law? Writers of fiction revel in such speculations. Historians, however, must confess that they know nothing concerning this. Their proximity to one another makes it reasonable to assume that they knew of each other, but the present state of the evidence does not permit us to say anything more.

The Baptism of Jesus

At the pinnacle of John's career a candidate came forward for baptism who was different from the rest. Jesus' baptism by John is one of the most certain events in the life of Jesus. It is witnessed to in Mark and the common source used by Matthew and Luke (Q), as well as by John. Furthermore, the very difficulty that this event created for the church witnesses to its historicity. Who in the early church would have created an account in which Jesus submitted himself to a baptism of repentance?

Why Jesus experienced John's baptism is indeed puzzling. Was it because he, too, needed to repent of his sins like the rest who came for John's baptism? There is no mention or even hint in the Gospel accounts that Jesus came to John out of a sense of guilt. The *Gospel of the Nazareans*, written in the first half of the second century, contains another attempt at an explanation:

> Behold, the mother of the Lord and his brothers said to him, "John the Baptist baptizes for the remission of sins; let us go and be baptized by him." But he said, "What have I committed, that I should be baptized of him, unless it be that in saying this I am in ignorance?" (*ANT*, p. 13)

Here Jesus is represented as submitting to John's baptism due to the possibility that he might have sinned in ignorance.

Matthew refers to John's hesitancy in baptizing Jesus: "John would have prevented him, saying, 'I need to be baptized by you, and do you come to me?' But Jesus answered him, 'Let it be so now; for it is proper for us in this way to fulfill all righteousness.' Then he consented" (Mt 3:14-15). For others, submission to the baptism of John involved repentance and a decisive break with sin in order to become part of the kingdom of God. Matthew, however, understood Jesus' baptism as involving the fulfilling of "all righteousness." Exactly what Matthew meant by that is not clear. It clearly did not mean for him that Jesus was repenting of sin. Probably it meant following in the path God had revealed to be his will. In Jesus' case this involved identifying with the messianic community John had founded by submitting to its rite of initiation. Convinced that the ministry and baptism of John were divinely ordained, he sought to identify himself with this "righteous" movement.

The uniqueness of Jesus' baptism is such that even though all who follow him are commanded to be baptized (Mt 28:19), nowhere in the New Testament are believers told that in so doing they are following in the footsteps of Jesus. Unlike later teachers who speak of "following Jesus in baptism," the New Testament writers never refer to following Jesus in this way.

John's baptism involved a conversion that required a radical break with the past by repenting and becoming part of the messianic community. For Jesus, baptism involved a "conversion" in the sense of a decisive break with his past and positively associating himself with the kingdom community. It meant leaving the quietness of the carpenter's shop to assume his messianic task. The "silent years" had come to an end. The time had now come to fulfill the mission for which he had been born.

This commitment to his Father's work was total. Later, he would refer to his sacrificial dedication unto death as a baptism. Having been asked by James and John for special privileges in the kingdom of God, Jesus replied,

> "Are you able to drink the cup that I drink, or be baptized with the baptism that I am baptized with?" They replied, "We are able." Then Jesus said to them, "The cup that I drink you will drink; and with the baptism with which I am baptized, you will be baptized; but to sit at my right hand or at my left is not mine to grant." (Mk 10:38-40; compare Lk 12:50)

Whether this implies that Jesus already knew at his baptism that his messianic task involved the cross is uncertain. What is certain is that in his baptism Jesus committed himself to the will of God even if it involved death. Jesus knew what had happened to the Old Testament prophets. He knew that the denunciation of sin and the call to repentance would not be well received by the rich and religious elite. Thus at his baptism Jesus committed himself to a path that inevitably led to conflict and persecution (compare Mt 5:12; 23:29-36; Lk 13:33-34). He who later would invite people to take up a cross and follow him (Mk 8:34) made just such a commitment at his baptism.

The Gospel accounts associate three unusual events with the baptism of Jesus. The first involves the heavens being "torn apart" (Mk 1:10). Second, we read of the Spirit "descending like a dove" on Jesus (v. 10). Third, a voice from heaven was heard (v. 11).

Whether Mark understood the heavens being torn apart as a physical event, as indicating a theological reality, or both, is unclear. At the very least, it was for him the theological reality that Jesus possessed a direct access to God. The Evangelist uses this same term in only one other place—Mark 15:38. There he writes that at the death of Jesus "the curtain of the temple was torn in two, from top to bottom." In so doing he may be indicating to his readers that through the death of Jesus they, too, now have a similar direct access to God.

When we read of the Spirit descending on Jesus "like" a dove, the expressed comparison does not require that an actual dove was present. One of the gifts that the messianic age was expected to bring was the coming of the Spirit. John the Baptist had even proclaimed that whereas he baptized people with a baptism of repentance, the one who was coming after him, the one for whom he was preparing the way, was bringing a baptism associated with the Spirit (Mk 1:8). Yet before the Anointed One would bestow the Spirit on his followers, he must himself be anointed by the Spirit. (It should be remembered that *Messiah, Christ* and *Anointed* are simply Hebrew, Greek and English ways of saying the same thing.)

The epochal importance of this anointing for Jesus and his awareness of how this experience led to a new period in his life is evident from his first sermon in Nazareth. There, opening the scroll of Isaiah, he selected the following passage from Isaiah 61:1-2:

The Spirit of the Lord is upon me,
> because he has anointed me to bring good news to the poor.

He has sent me to proclaim release to the captives
> and recovery of sight to the blind,
> to let the oppressed go free,
> to proclaim the year of the Lord's favor. (Lk 4:18-19; compare Acts 10:38)

Upon returning the scroll to one of the officers of the synagogue, Jesus said, "Today this scripture has been fulfilled in your hearing" (Lk 4:21). At his baptism Jesus was aware that he had been anointed for a divine task. Serving God quietly as a carpenter in Nazareth was a thing of the past. The Spirit had anointed him, and his messianic mission had begun. (Notice that in quoting Isaiah 61:1-2 Jesus excluded "the day of vengeance of our God." He did not understand his present mission as involving this. That day, when he returned as the Son of Man to judge the world, was still future.)

The third thing that took place at Jesus' baptism was a voice from heaven: "You are my Son, the Beloved; with you I am well pleased" (Mk 1:11). (In Mt 3:17 the divine message is reported from the viewpoint of the readers of the Gospel: "This is my Son, the Beloved, with whom I am well pleased.") Attempts have been made to interpret this as the moment in which God adopted Jesus as his Son. Yet that is clearly not how the Evangelists understood this voice. For John, Jesus was/is the Son even before his incarnation (Jn 1:1-4 predates 1:14). For Luke and Matthew, Jesus was the Son of God already at the time of the virginal conception (Lk 1:35, 42-45; Mt 1:20-25). Similarly for Mark these words do not indicate a change in Jesus' status before God. He is not "promoted" at his baptism. Rather, the voice is an affirmation of who Jesus was and a commendation that God was pleased with the silent years. No doubt this commendation brought comfort during the crises and discouragements that Jesus experienced in his ministry.

There has been much speculation as to the relationship of Jesus and John the Baptist. It has been suggested that at the beginning they collaborated with each other and preached a similar message of judgment and baptism (compare Jn 3:22-24; 4:1-2). Some have even argued that Jesus was originally a disciple of John the Baptist. (Attempts to interpret John's reference to one coming "after me" [Mt 3:11; Mk 1:7; Jn 1:15, 27, 30] as "behind me," that is, as my disciple, clearly misinterpret this temporal designation.) As time progressed, however, Jesus supposedly became disillusioned with the doom-and-gloom message of John and began instead to proclaim a positive message of "good news." The break between them was not a hospitable one, and John viewed Jesus as a rebel. Such romanticizing is especially attractive for those who see an evolutionary development in everything. One cannot create history, however.

All the evidence we possess indicates that John the Baptist and Jesus had independent ministries and mutually respected each other (Mt 14:12; Mk 9:11-13; 11:30; Lk 7:24-28; Jn 3:25-30; and especially Mt 11:2-15, in which John during his imprisonment sent disciples to Jesus). For Matthew their message was identical: "In those days John the Baptist appeared in the wilderness of Judea, proclaiming, 'Repent, for the kingdom of heaven has come near' " (Mt 3:1-2; compare 4:17; compare also Mk 1:14-15; Lk 4:18-21, 43). (For other similarities between John the Baptist and Jesus compare Mt 3:7 with 12:34, Mt 3:8 with 7:16-20, Mt 3:9 with 8:11-12, Mt 3:10 with 7:19, Mt 3:12 with 13:30, Lk 3:12-14 with 7:1-10, 29 and Mt 21:31-32.) Thus even though some of the disciples of John (unlike the disciples of Jn 1:35-42) continued as an independent sect for several centuries (Acts 18:24-19:7; Clementine *Recognitions* 1.53-54, 60, 63; *Homilies* 2:23-24; compare also Jn 1:8, 20, 21-23; 3:25-30, which perhaps should be understood as directed against the followers of John the Baptist who were living when the Gospel was written), there is no evidence that anything but respect existed between John and Jesus during their overlapping but independent ministries.

Conclusion

With the coming of John the Baptist the voice of prophecy was once again heard in Israel. The spiritual drought of the past four centuries had come to an end. God was again visiting his people. Yet John's message was not an end in itself. Integral to (and the highlight of) his message was the announcement of the Coming One. A person greater than the greatest of the Old Testament prophets (Mt 11:9-11) was present in John the Baptist, but a far greater one was at hand. John labored to prepare the people for this person, and it was his privilege to baptize him. Whereas John later had questions concerning Jesus' messianic status (Mt 11:2-6), Jesus' reply was apparently satisfactory. At least the Evangelists want us to understand the incident in that way.

At his baptism Jesus began his ministry as the Anointed One, the Christ or Messiah. "Here is my servant, whom I uphold, my chosen, in whom my soul delights; I have put my spirit upon him; he will bring forth justice to the nations" (Is 42:1). Even as prophets (1 Kings 19:16), priests (Ex 29:7, 21) and kings (1 Sam 10:1) were anointed for their tasks, so the Prophet-Priest-King also was anointed for his ministry. The issue of how Jesus would fulfill his divine role and the kind of Messiah he would be now faced him. This would be resolved in the wilderness.

References

Badia, Leonard F. *The Qumran Baptism and John the Baptist's Baptism.* Lanham, Md.: University Press of America, 1980.

Beasley-Murray, G. R. *Baptism in the New Testament.* Grand Rapids, Mich.: Eerdmans, 1962.

————. "Baptism, Wash." In *New International Dictionary of New Testament Theology,* edited by Colin Brown, 1:143-54. Grand Rapids, Mich.: Zondervan, 1975.

Danielou, Jean. *The Work of John the Baptist.* Baltimore: Helicon, 1966.

France, Richard T. "Jesus the Baptist?" In *Jesus of Nazareth: Lord and Christ,* edited by Joel B. Green, pp. 94-111. Grand Rapids, Mich.: Eerdmans, 1994.

Meyer, Ben F. *The Aims of Jesus,* pp. 115-128. London: SCM Press, 1979.

Scobie, Charles H. H. *John the Baptist.* Philadelphia: Fortress, 1964.

Webb, Robert L. "John the Baptist and His Relationship to Jesus." In *Studying the Historical Jesus,* edited by Bruce Chilton and Craig A. Evans, pp. 179-229. Leiden: E. J. Brill, 1994.

Wink, Walter. *John the Baptist in the Gospel Tradition.* Cambridge: Cambridge University Press, 1968.

Witherington, Ben, III. "John the Baptist." In *Dictionary of Jesus and the Gospels,* edited by Joel B. Green, Scot McKnight and I. Howard Marshall, pp. 383-91. Downers Grove, Ill.: InterVarsity Press, 1992.

7
THE TEMPTATION
OF JESUS
The Battle Begun, the Path Decided

INTIMATELY ASSOCIATED WITH JESUS' BAPTISM IS HIS TEMPTATION. MARK connects these two accounts with his characteristic "And immediately" (for example, Mk 1:12 KJV), and Matthew with "Then" (see Mt 4:1). Luke, however, interrupts the sequence with his genealogy of Jesus (Lk 3:23-37). He does this to confirm the divine voice at the baptism ("You are my Son, the Beloved; with you I am well pleased" [Lk 3:22]), showing that Jesus is ultimately the "son of God" (Lk 3:38). The extended accounts of the temptation in Matthew (Mt 4:1-11) and Luke (Lk 4:1-13) contain echoes of Jesus' baptism. In both the opening temptation begins "If you are the Son of God," and in both the temptation to throw himself down from the pinnacle of the temple begins the same way. In all three Gospel accounts the Spirit, who was received at his baptism, leads Jesus into the wilderness.

Apparently even before the Gospels were written the accounts of the baptism and temptation were connected. They were associated together in the tradition, and unless one precludes the supernatural from Jesus' life, there is no necessary reason to deny a historical connection as well. No explanation is given in the accounts as to why the temptation was necessary. Yet the decision as to the kind of Messiah Jesus would be had to be faced early in his ministry. In various religious traditions, initiation (here Jesus' baptism) and temptation often go together: "My child, when you come to serve the Lord, prepare yourself for testing" (Sirach 2:1). An early confrontation with his chief adversary is thus understandable. In order to plunder Satan's kingdom, Jesus would have to defeat him (Mk 3:22-27), and resisting the temptation would be the first of his adversary's defeats (compare Mk 1:21-28, 39; 3:11; 5:1-20; 7:24-30; 9:14-29; and so on).

The nature of Jesus' temptations raises the question of where the Gospel writers obtained this information. It is evident that Matthew and Luke possessed additional information that Mark lacked. Probably this came from their Q source. Yet where did Q, and the church before Q, learn about this? In the account, only Jesus and Satan are present. How then did the church learn of this account?

A possible scenario in which Jesus might have shared this piece of spiritual autobiography would be those times in his ministry when he experienced similar kinds of temptation. On numerous occasions Jesus was confronted with the issue of what kind of Messiah he would be. Peter's suggestion of a crossless mission (Mk 8:31-33), the entrance into Jerusalem (Mk 11:1-11) and the response to some of his miracles, such as the feeding of the five thousand (Jn 6:1-15, especially v. 15—"When Jesus realized that they were about to come and take him by force to make him king, he withdrew again to the mountain by himself"), are a few examples of when Jesus could have shared the vision of his messiahship, which he had hammered out at his temptation (compare also Mt 27:40-43; Mk 12:13-17; Lk 11:16; 16:19-31). The messianic nature of the temptations, which focus upon Jesus' unique sonship, makes it unlikely that the early Christian experience of temptation and testing created this account.

The Nature of the Temptations

The question must be raised as to the exact nature of the temptations Jesus experienced. Were they inward experiences reflecting Jesus' unique struggles over the kind of Messiah he would be? Were they universal temptations that face every human being? Were the temptations primarily psychological or visionary in nature? Were they entirely subjective? To understand the temptations in this manner would not make them in any way less real. Yet the general impression from reading the accounts is that they were objective and involved external events: a real place (the wilderness and the temple in Jerusalem) and real, if symbolic, time (forty days and nights [compare Gen 7:12; Ex 34:28; Deut 9:18; Judg 13:1; 1 Kings 19:8; Ps 95:10]). This argues against seeing the temptations as entirely subjective visions or experiences.

On the other hand, it is clear that at least one of the temptations involved some sort of visionary experience. The third temptation in Matthew (second in Luke) involved Jesus' being taken to a high mountain. There he was shown all the kingdoms and glory of the world. (Compare Moses' seeing from a mountain the Promised Land in Deut 3:27 and 34:1-4.) Needless to say, there is no "place" one could go to see with the unaided eye all the kingdoms of the world. Even apart from the earth's curvature, that would not be humanly possible. In this temptation some kind of visionary experience was involved.

The temptations of Jesus do not fit neatly into the categories of objective or subjective, external or internal. Their real and historical nature does not depend on their fitting such categories. Jesus truly experienced Satan's temptations in the desert. The temptations were real. They truly came from Satan and were truly experienced by Jesus.

The Accounts of the Temptation

Three separate accounts of Jesus' temptation exist. Mark's account is the shortest and consists of a summary of only two verses (Mk 1:12-13). The accounts in Matthew and Luke are considerably longer (eleven and fourteen verses). In contrast to Mark they contain a description of three specific temptations. The similarity between their accounts suggests that they used a common source (Q) for this material. The order of the temptations, however, is different. Both agree about the first temptation—stone to bread—but in Matthew the second and third temptations are the reverse of Luke.

The respective order of the last two temptations fits neatly the theological purposes of the two Evangelists. Matthew's ending the temptations on a high mountain is not surprising. Jesus' first sermon takes place on a mountain. The transfiguration also takes place on a "high mountain" (Mt 17:1-13), and the Gospel ends with the Great Commission being given on a mountain (Mt 28:16-20). But for Luke a mountain is a place of prayer and revelation (Lk 6:12; 9:28; 22:39-40), and his interest in Jerusalem and the temple (Lk 24:49; Acts 1:4; 6:8—7:60; 21:17—22:21) may have caused him to present the temptation on the pinnacle of the temple last for emphasis. Although it is impossible to be dogmatic concerning the original order of the accounts, more scholars favor Matthew's order. This would place the "If you are the Son of God" temptations side by side.

After his baptism Jesus was led by the Spirit into the wilderness. Because the Holy Spirit initiated the temptations, they should be understood not as a defensive struggle but as an offensive attack on the rule of Satan. The kingdom of God had come, and the ruler of this evil age was now challenged. The location of this conflict was the Wilderness of Judah, located on the western side of the Dead Sea. That Jesus went into the wilderness after his baptism would also suggest this region.

What is more difficult to determine is whether the "wilderness" is to be viewed positively or negatively. Is it to be understood negatively as a place of demons (compare 1QM 1) where creation has been cursed (Is 13:19-22; Ezek 34:25; Lk 11:24-28) or positively as a place restored to a new creation by the coming of the messianic age (Is 11:6-9; 32:14-20; 40:3; 65:25; Hos 2:18; compare the pre-Fall paradise of Gen 1:26-28)? Mark's reference to Jesus' being "with the wild beasts" (Mk 1:13) can also be understood either positively or negatively. Does it reflect the evil hostility of the wilderness? (Wild animals and demons are associated together in *Testament of Issachar* 7:7; *T. of Naphtali* 8:4; *T. of Benjamin* 5:2; and wild animals stand opposed to angels in Ps 91:11-13.) Or is this expression meant to reflect the blissful tranquillity of the restored creation in paradise (compare Gen 2:19)?

Most likely the designation "wilderness" and the reference to the "wild beasts" should be interpreted negatively as denoting the fallen nature of the creation now dominated by Satan, the ruler of this age. The temptation of Jesus did not take place in a restored paradise. Such a restoration was still future and awaited his victory in the desert, in his ministry, on the cross and at his glorious return as the Son of Man to conclude history. The temptation took place, rather, in the heart of Satan's domain, an evil wilderness filled with wild animals and demons. Although never explicitly referred to, these accounts recall the failure of Adam.

Whereas the first temptation is located in the wilderness, there is a change of scene for the second and third. The second takes place at the pinnacle of the temple and the third on a high mountain (in Matthew). It is unclear whether a specific mountain is meant or whether this is to be understood as part of the vision. If an actual mountain was involved, neither Matthew nor Luke tell us which one. If they knew of the actual mountain, they considered its name unimportant. If they did not know, Jesus (if this is a piece of autobiography) did not think it important to recount.

The Meaning of the Temptations

"If you are the Son of God, command this stone to become a loaf of bread" (Lk 4:3). In both Matthew 4:2 and Luke 4:2 we learn that after forty days in the wilderness Jesus was hungry. Matthew explains that Jesus was fasting during this period, Luke that Jesus ate nothing. (Compare Moses' fasting of forty days and nights [Ex 34:28; Deut 9:9-18, 25].) Like the original temptation (Gen 3:1-7), this challenge of Satan involves eating. The assumption is that Jesus as the Son of God possessed the ability to perform this miracle. That is evident from both the challenge and Jesus' reply, for the reply assumes that he could do it if he wished.

There is, of course, nothing wrong in seeking to satisfy one's hunger. When satisfying hunger conflicts with what God has ordained, however, it is sin. Jesus, in quoting Deuteronomy 8:3, understood that life involves more than food (Mt 6:25). Life is to be lived in obedience to the will of God as revealed in God's Word. That "word" Jesus understood as being found in the Scriptures. Thus in all three temptations Jesus responded by quoting the Old Testament.

For Jesus, this temptation involved how he would carry out his calling and ministry. It was not a temptation to immorality or sin in the traditional sense. It was rather a testing as to the kind of Messiah Jesus would be. Having been anointed by the Spirit, he possessed a unique authority and power to carry out his messianic mission. Would he use this, however, for his own ends? Would he live by the same requirements of faith and dependence on God as everyone else in the kingdom? Was messiahship an excuse for privileges or a responsibility for serving? How could he call others to follow in obedience, faith and submission to God, if he was not willing to do the same?

The first temptation was, therefore, a test as to whether Jesus would trust his Father to provide for his basic needs. He, who would teach his followers to trust God and pray to him for their "daily bread" (Mt 6:11), proved that he also would trust God during this temptation. Since Jesus came "not to be served but to serve" (Mk 10:45), he must give his life to God in obedience here as well as later. If God wished to provide him manna in the wilderness as he did for the children of Israel (Ex 16:4-21; compare Jn 6:30-31), so be it. Jesus, however, would not usurp God's sovereign rule for his life.

"If you are the Son of God, throw yourself down" (Lk 4:9). The exact intention of this temptation is debated. Some have suggested that it was a temptation to perform a spectacular sign to cause the people of Israel to follow him. We find such a temptation during Jesus' ministry when his brothers challenged him: " 'Leave here and go to Judea so that your disciples also may see the works you are doing; for no one who wants to be widely known acts in secret. If you do these things, show yourself to the world.' (For not even his brothers believed in him.)" (Jn 7:3-5; compare also Jn 6:30 and 1 Cor 1:22).

The problem with this interpretation is that no one is mentioned as being present during the temptation other than Satan and Jesus. If this were a temptation to work a miracle before the people, one would expect mention of them in the account. (This interpretation is also given by some to the first temptation, but the same objection must be raised. No crowds are mentioned there either.)

In support of his challenge Satan picks up Jesus' quotation of the Scriptures in response to the first temptation and quotes from Psalm 91:11-12: "For he will command his angels concerning you to guard you in all your ways. On their hands they will bear you up, so that you will not dash your foot against a stone." Satan quotes the Bible to support his views. He twists its meaning and uses it for his own purpose. (It should be noted that the context and substance of the Old Testament quotation does not involve performing a sign before people in order to gain a hearing.)

The most likely interpretation of this temptation is that it would involve a dare on Jesus' part to make God rescue him. Of all places surely

God would rescue his Son in the temple, where God dwelt so prominently. The diabolical nature of this temptation is that it would dare God on
the basis of "faith" to supernaturally save his Son after he plunged off
the top of the temple. (The exact meaning of "pinnacle," or the highest
point, of the temple is uncertain.)

This temptation has proven to be a common one for those who would
follow Jesus. It is not always clear whether a "leap of faith" is an act of
true faith or putting God to an evil test. That is true even if at times such
a daring of God is called "testing the promises of God." Since Jesus had
spoken of a need to depend on God for his daily bread and not to use
his own messianic powers to provide for himself, Satan now suggested
to Jesus that if he really wanted to depend on God, he should jump from
the temple and "trust" in God's promises of providential care.

Jesus recognized the fine line between trusting God for the needs of
life and challenging him to rescue him from artificially created difficulties. The former would be an act of faith, the latter an evil challenge and
dare placed before God. Jesus again quoted the Scriptures: "Do not put
the LORD your God to the test" (Deut 6:16). Even as God's Son, Jesus
would not dare his heavenly Father. Such an act would not be an act of
faith; it would be, on the contrary, an act of unbelief. The one who has
faith in God's providential care does not have to "prove" this by challenging God. Thus it is precisely because Jesus believed in his Father's care
that he did not need to challenge him. If he lived the life of faith and
obedience that God had assigned him, he could rest in the assurance of
God's loving control of his life.

"If you, then, will worship me, it will all be yours" (Lk 4:7). The last temptation
is visionary in nature. Jesus is transported to a high mountain and shown
all the kingdoms of the world. These Satan would give him if he would
worship him. Since Jesus did not challenge Satan's ability to make such
an offer, it is assumed that Satan, as the prince of this world, had the
power to do this. Thus the question of whether Satan was offering to
Jesus what he was not able to give must be answered negatively. Since
Satan is the ruler of this present age, he could offer these kingdoms to
Jesus. The issue of what would happen in the final judgment with respect
to this authority did not play a role. At the time of the temptation Satan
stated that he could do this, and neither Jesus nor the Evangelists challenged the statement. Thus the biblical writers saw this as a real temp-

tation, not as an attempted deception by Satan to give what he could not.

Although no mention is made in this temptation to Jesus' sonship, that should be assumed because it has been mentioned in the previous two temptations and because Satan does not make this offer to all people but to the Jesus of Matthew 1:1—4:7 and Luke 1:1—4:4, God's Son. This temptation boils down to an offer to win the world without the "cup" God had called him to drink (Mk 10:38). It involves a political solution to the world's problems. If the basic need(s) of the world could be solved by political action, this was the way Jesus should go. With the kingdoms of the world given him he could rid the world of hunger, war, injustice, poverty and so on. A "crossless solution" would resolve such problems, and it would do so with no need of great suffering on his part. On the other hand, if the basic need of the world involved forgiveness, reconciliation with God and salvation from future judgment, then such a "victory" by Jesus would be a shallow one. "For what does it profit a man, to gain the whole world and forfeit his life?" (Mk 8:36 RSV). Jesus saw his mission as saving his people from their sins (Mt 1:21), saving the lost (Mk 10:45) and leading his followers into paradise (Lk 23:43), and he had to follow the path God had ordained for him at his baptism (Mk 10:38-39).

Jesus was well aware that any suggested direction or path for his ministry that denied God would come to naught. He had been taught "I am the LORD your God, who brought you out of the land of Egypt, out of the house of slavery; you shall have no other gods before me" (Ex 20:2-3). As a child he had learned to say, "Hear, O Israel: The LORD is our God, the LORD alone. You shall love the LORD your God with all your heart, and with all your soul, and with all your might" (Deut 6:4-5). His love for God did not permit him to think seriously of such an option. You cannot serve both God and wealth (see Mt 6:24). Thus his only possible reply to this temptation was "Away with you, Satan! for it is written, 'Worship the Lord your God, and serve only him' " (Mt 4:10).

After the last temptation, "the devil left him" (Mt 4:11). Luke adds that "he departed from him until an opportune time" (Lk 4:13). It has been suggested by some that Luke meant by this that Satan did not actually tempt or challenge Jesus again until the time of his arrest, trial and crucifixion (compare Lk 22:3, 31, 53). Yet though such a direct confrontation by Satan did not occur again until that time, he was still active and tempted Jesus during the time leading up to the crucifixion (Lk 8:12; 10:17-18; 11:14-22; 13:11-17; 22:28; compare also Mk 4:15; 8:33). Upon Satan's departure Matthew states that the angels ministered to Jesus. The implication is that they provided him with food (compare 1 Kings 19:4-8).

Conclusion

At his temptation Jesus settled once and for all the kind of Messiah he would be. He would not use his messianic powers for his own ends. Jesus rejected all political concepts of messiahship and especially the path of the Zealots. Instead he would accept the path of the suffering servant that God had ordained for him. He would trust God for his daily needs, even as he taught his followers to trust God. He would experience hunger, hostility, sorrow and frustration like others. As he faced the cross he would not use his messianic powers to rescue himself. Even if twelve legions of angels were at his disposal, he would not call on them (see Mt 26:53). He would trust instead in the providential care of his Father. He would say, like millions who have followed him, "Father, into your hands I commend my spirit" (Lk 23:46). Rejecting the easy road, the author and perfecter of our faith chose instead the small gate and narrow road God had set before him (Mt 7:13-14).

The question has been raised whether Jesus was truly capable of sinning. Usually such questions bring with them a Christology that goes as follows: "Since Jesus was God and since God cannot sin, Jesus was not really able to sin." Even at its best this looks like a theological premise imposed upon the life of Jesus. The Gospel writers give no hint that the "temptation" was simply a matter of play-acting on the part of Jesus. They see the confrontation as a real "temptation." It is impossible to read the accounts of Matthew and Luke and imagine the Evangelists thinking that at any time Jesus could have said, "Bug off, Satan. You know that I can't sin!"

The writer of the book of Hebrews seems to have understood the life of Jesus as one in which sin was a real possibility. He assumes this possibility when he says that "because he himself was tested by what he suffered, he is able to help those who are being tested" (Heb 2:18) and that he "in every respect has been tested as we are, yet without sin" (Heb 4:15).

We must never separate this event in the life of Jesus from his true humanity. It is better to construct a Christology that allows for true temptation and its possibilities than to take away from the biblical accounts the true tempting nature of this event in order to safeguard a preconceived Christology.

References

Bauckham, Richard. "Jesus and the Wild Animals (Mark 1:13): A Christological Image for an Ecological Age." In *Jesus of Nazareth: Lord and Christ*, edited by Joel B. Green, pp. 3-21. Grand Rapids, Mich.: Eerdmans, 1994.

Best, Ernest. *The Temptation and the Passion*. Cambridge: Cambridge University Press, 1990.

Gerhardsson, Birger. *The Testing of God's Son*. Lund, Sweden: CWK Gleerup, 1966.

Harrison, Everett F. *A Short Life of Christ*, pp. 80-93. Grand Rapids, Mich.: Eerdmans, 1968.

Jeremias, Joachim. *New Testament Theology*, pp. 68-75. New York: Scribner's, 1971.

Mauser, Ulrich W. *Christ in the Wilderness*. Naperville, Ill.: Allenson, 1963.

Pokorný, Petr. "The Temptation Stories and Their Intention." *New Testament Studies* 20 (1974): 115-27.

Twelftree, Graham H. "Temptation of Jesus." In *Dictionary of Jesus and the Gospels*, edited by Joel B. Green, Scot McKnight and I. Howard Marshall, pp. 821-27. Downers Grove, Ill.: InterVarsity Press, 1992.

8
THE CALL OF
THE DISCIPLES
You Shall Be
My Witnesses

HAVING BEEN ANOINTED FOR HIS MISSION AT HIS BAPTISM (SEE CHAP-
ter six) and having settled the kind of mission he would undertake at his
temptation (see chapter seven), Jesus began his ministry. No biblical evidence exists that Jesus began his ministry in conjunction with or under
the tutelage of John the Baptist. The Synoptic Gospels (Mk 1:14-20) and
John (Jn 1:35-42) all portray an independent ministry on the part of Jesus.
Most probably their ministries overlapped for a short period of time (Jn
3:22-4:3). If so, then Mark 1:14 ("Now after John was arrested, Jesus
came to Galilee, proclaiming the good news of God"; compare Mt 4:12)
is best understood more as a theological statement than as a chronological one. Mark was aware that John's ministry continued for a time (compare Mk 6:14-29), but he wanted by this statement to tell his readers that
with John the Baptist the old covenant came to a close. He was the last
of the Old Testament prophets. Jesus, on the other hand, inaugurated
the new covenant. John and Jesus belong to two different eras: the time
of prophecy and the time of fulfillment.

The ministry of Jesus is frequently outlined in the following manner:

1. The early Judean ministry. We learn of this primarily from John 2:13—4:43. Because of the geographical scheme by which Mark structures his Gospel (Galilee, Mk 1:14—7:23; outside Galilee, Mk 7:24—9:50; Judea, Mk 10:1—16:8), he and the other Synoptic writers do not speak of an early Judean ministry. Yet there are hints in their accounts that such a ministry existed. Compare Mark 10:46-52; 11:2-6; 14:3-9, 13-16, 49; Luke 13:34.

2. The Galilean ministry. Compare Mark 1:14—7:23 and parallels.

3. The period of travel. Compare Mark 7:24—9:50 and parallels.

4. The journey to Jerusalem and the Judean ministry. Compare Mark 10:1—16:8 and parallels.

These periods are also described as the Year of Obscurity (1), the Year of Public Favor (2) and the Year of Opposition (3 and 4).

There is always a problem in treating the Gospels as if they were strict geographical or chronological accounts of the life of Jesus. Because of his geographical arrangement of the Gospel materials, Mark could not follow a strict chronological scheme, for all the Gospel materials associated with Galilee had to be placed in 1:14—7:23, and all the material associated with Judea and Jerusalem had to be placed in 10:1—16:8. Therefore, no room remained in his Gospel for an early Judean ministry or intervening trips to Judea/Jerusalem.

At times materials are also arranged topically in the Gospels. (Compare Matthew's alternation of stories about Jesus in chapters 1—4, 8—9, 11—12, 14—17, 19—22 and 26—28 with Jesus' sayings in chapters 5—7, 10, 13, 18, 23—25. Note also how the material in Matthew's Sermon on the Mount [chapters 5—7] is scattered throughout Luke 6—16, and how Mark has collections of healing [1:21-45], controversy stories [2:1—3:6], parables [4:1-34] and so on.) As a result, whereas it is probable that Jesus' ministry began with a brief mission in Judea, was followed by a longer Galilean mission and ended with a mission in Judea, one must confess uncertainty as to when and where certain incidents took place and allow room for events that do not fit into this schematic outline.

According to Matthew 4:13 (compare Mt 9:1 and Mk 2:1), Jesus at the start of his ministry left his home town of Nazareth and moved to Capernaum. Although Nazareth, lying only three and a half miles from the major city of Sepphoris, was far from being an isolated rural village, it was less central to the mainstream of Galilean life than Capernaum.

Capernaum was also a much larger city than Nazareth. It was an important trade center lying on an major east-west highway and trade route. Probably Jesus moved to this city because it would serve as a better base for his ministry in Galilee. Whether this move was also due to a less than positive reception to his ministry in Nazareth (compare Mk 6:1-6; Lk 4:16-30) is uncertain.

The Call of the Disciples

One of the first actions of Jesus as he began his ministry was to select twelve disciples. The most famous passage dealing with his calling of the disciples is found in Mark 1:16-20:

> As Jesus passed along the Sea of Galilee, he saw Simon and his brother Andrew casting a net into the sea—for they were fishermen. And Jesus said to them, "Follow me and I will make you fish for people." And immediately they left their nets and followed him. As he went a little farther, he saw James son of Zebedee and his brother John, who were in their boat mending the nets. Immediately he called them; and they left their father Zebedee in the boat with the hired men, and followed him.

The impression received from this passage is that this is the first encounter between Jesus and the four disciples: Simon (Peter) and his brother Andrew, James and his brother John. In John 1:35-51, however, we discover that there had been a previous encounter between Jesus, Peter and Andrew (as well as Nathanael and Philip). Thus the call to leave their occupation and family (Mk 1:17-18) did not come to Peter and Andrew as a bolt out of the blue but was preceded by an earlier encounter and their conviction that Jesus was the Messiah (Jn 1:35-42). There may even have been further contact between them. The response of James and John (Mk 1:19-20) may in turn have been based on the witness of Peter and Andrew.

Jesus called twelve men to be his disciples. The symbolic nature of their number was not accidental. Jesus' audience could not have helped but notice the number. "Twelve" conjured up in the mind of any Jew the twelve tribes of Israel. At the time of Jesus the common conception was that only two and a half tribes remained—the tribes of Judah, Benjamin and half the tribe of Levi. The other nine and a half tribes were lost in 722 B.C. when Samaria fell, and those tribes were scattered in exile among the Gentiles. The time would come, however, when God would visit his people and restore the twelve tribes of Israel. In that day, the day of Israel's salvation, the lost tribes would be reunited and God would establish his kingdom upon the earth (compare Is 11:10-16; 49:6; 56:8; Mic 2:12; Sirach 48:10; and so on).

Jesus' calling of twelve disciples was a symbolic act that demonstrated visually what he proclaimed verbally: "The time is fulfilled, and the kingdom of God has come near" (Mk 1:15). God was visiting the people of Israel. The restoration of the twelve tribes of Israel was taking place. For Jesus, however, this restoration did not involve a political revival of the nation of Israel. It involved, rather, the experience of the divine presence and the arrival of the kingdom of God in a unique way among his people (see chapter nine under "A New Era").

The Names of the Disciples

Within the Gospels we find three listings of the disciples:

Mark 3:13-19	Matthew 10:1-4	Luke 6:12-16
Simon (Peter)	Simon (Peter)	Simon (Peter)
	his brother Andrew	his brother Andrew
James son of Zebedee	James son of Zebedee	James
John (Boanerges, Sons of Thunder)	his brother John	John
Andrew		
Philip	Philip	Philip
Bartholomew	Bartholomew	Bartholomew
Matthew	Thomas	Matthew
Thomas	Matthew the tax collector	Thomas

James son of Alphaeus	James son of Alphaeus	James son of Alphaeus
Thaddaeus	Thaddaeus	
Simon the Cananaean	Simon the Cananaean	Simon the Zealot
		Judas son of James
Judas Iscariot	Judas Iscariot	Judas Iscariot

(There is a fourth listing of the disciples in Acts 1:13, and, although the order is somewhat different, there is no difference in the names.) All four lists of disciples consist of three groups of four names in which the first name of each group is the same (Simon [Peter], Philip, James son of Alphaeus). It is speculation to conclude from this, however, that during Jesus' ministry the Twelve were organized into three groups of four led by these men.

A number of problems arise from these parallel lists. Matthew and Mark refer in their lists to Simon the "Cananaean," whereas Luke refers to Simon the Zealot. This difference is easy to explain: *Cananaean* is the Aramaic word for "Zealot." Whereas Mark and Matthew maintain the original Aramaic description, Luke has translated this term into its Greek equivalent. A second difference in the lists is that Matthew and Luke agree against Mark in placing Andrew's name next to his brother's (Peter, Andrew, James, John), whereas Mark places the three most prominent disciples first (Peter, James, John, Andrew). This agreement of Matthew and Luke is perfectly understandable. It makes more sense to keep the two sets of brothers together than to split one of them apart and sandwich the other set in between.

The greatest difficulty we find in these three accounts involves the names Thaddaeus (Mark and Matthew) and "Judas son of James" (Luke). It has been argued that these two names refer to the same person. Just as the first disciple in the list had a Hebrew name (Simon) and a Greek name (Peter), so this disciple was named Judas (Hebrew name) Thaddaeus (Greek name). Before concluding that this is simply a desperate attempt to harmonize the difficulty, it should be observed that five of the names in the list are qualified: Simon (Peter) and Simon the Zealot; James son of Zebedee and James son of Alphaeus; and Judas Iscariot. In the first four names, a qualification (Peter, the Zealot, son of Zebedee, son of Alphaeus) is given to help distinguish one Simon and James from the other. This is not done in the case of John, Andrew, Philip, Bartholomew, Matthew and Thomas because they need not be distinguished from another disciple with the same name.

On the other hand, Judas is always referred to as Judas "Iscariot." Why? If there were no other disciple by that name, there would be no need to do so. He could simply be referred to as Judas. The fact that he is named Judas Iscariot suggests that another Judas (Judas son of James) was a disciple. Possibly this other Judas was referred to by his "last" or surname Thaddaeus by Matthew and Mark because of the stigma associated with the name Judas. (How many Christians today name their sons Judas?)

The twelve disciples consisted of a strange mixture of people. Peter, Andrew, James and John were fishermen (Mk 1:16-20) and apparently business associates (Lk 5:10). There were two sets of brothers (Peter and Andrew, James and John—Mk 1:19; Jn 1:40). Peter, Andrew and Philip appear to have been disciples of John the Baptist (Jn 1:35-42, 43-46; compare 1:28). Matthew, perhaps also called Levi (compare Mk 2:14 with Mt 9:9), was a tax collector. Among the Jews tax collectors were despised, and their testimony was not acceptable in a court of law. They were seen as collaborators who purchased from the Roman oppressors the right to collect taxes from their fellow Jews. Their profit depended on how much tax they collected, and this led to the extortion of their own people.

On the other hand, there was also among the disciples a super patriot, Simon the Zealot. The Zealots longed to overthrow the rule of the hated Romans and looked forward to the day when the Roman yoke would be removed from the necks of the Jewish people. There were no illusions that this could be done peaceably. They expected that it could be accomplished only through revolution and war. Bartholomew is mentioned in all four lists of the disciples, but nothing is known about him. It has been suggested that Bartholomew and Nathanael were names for the same person, but that is impossible to demonstrate. We also know essentially nothing concerning Thomas and James son of Alphaeus.

Although we possess a considerable amount of material concerning the role Judas Iscariot played in the betrayal of Jesus, not much is known about his background. The term *Iscariot* has undergone a great deal of investigation, and interpretations abound as to what it might mean. The very existence of so many interpretations suggests that we do not possess a convincing explanation. Some think that it comes from the term *Sicarii*. These were zealot assassins who with their daggers (*sikarios* is a Greek loanword from the Latin *sica*, or dagger) killed those who opposed their revolutionary aspirations. Others suggest that it may come from a Hebrew word meaning "false one" or another Hebrew word that means "to deliver," thus connecting the term to Judas's act of betrayal. Perhaps the most popular explanation is that Iscariot comes from the Hebrew words *Ish* ("man of") and *Kerioth* ("the city of Kerioth"). Thus Iscariot denotes the place from which Judas came. (A variation of this last interpretation understands *Kerioth* as referring to the city of Jerusalem.) If this last interpretation is correct, then Judas would be the only disciple who came from Judea rather than Galilee.

The makeup of the twelve disciples witnesses to the remarkable influence Jesus had on them. For the vast majority of his ministry these disciples followed Jesus in a most intimate relationship. They ate, worked and slept together. Although there were occasional outbreaks of rivalry or jealousy among them (Mk 9:33-35; 10:35-45), their ability to work together day after day, week and week, month after month testifies to the marvelous transforming power of Jesus' love. The brothers James and John were called "Sons of Thunder" due to their fiery temperament. (Examples of their hot-headed disposition can be seen in Lk 9:51-56 and Mk 9:38-41.) Yet for the most part these "Sons of Thunder" were tamed by Jesus, and one of them even became known as the disciple of love. Also among the disciples were a traitor (the tax collector Matthew) and a Zealot revolutionary (Simon). The fact that they could coexist side by side for an extended period reveals how Jesus can change the hearts of natural enemies and bring reconciliation and peace. Truly Jesus demonstrated through the lives of his disciples that he could break down the walls of hostility.

Why Jesus Chose the Twelve Disciples
One reason Jesus chose the twelve disciples has already been discussed. It involves the symbolism of the number. With his ministry, the long-awaited kingdom of God had come. The "consolation" (Lk 2:25) and

"redemption" (Lk 2:38) of Israel were now taking place. To symbolize the gathering of the ten (literally—nine and a half) lost tribes˙and the reunion of Israel, Jesus chose twelve disciples. Their number and presence during his ministry was a visual proclamation that the kingdom of God had indeed come.

In Mark 3:14-15 we learn of two other reasons Jesus called the twelve disciples. One is that he chose them to "be with him." They were selected to accompany him during his ministry. In so doing they would learn both from him and of him. They were uniquely chosen to witness his actions and deeds and to master his teachings (Jn 19:35; 21:24; Acts 5:32; 10:39-41; and so on). Only by remaining with him would they be able to observe who Jesus was and master the gospel teachings Jesus would entrust to them.

The second reason Jesus chose the Twelve was that they become his apostles, "ones sent out" to preach his message and to assist in his healing ministry. Even during his ministry Jesus sent the disciples out to represent him and to preach that the reign of God had begun (Mk 6:7-13, 30; compare also Lk 10:1-12). The disciples were the foundation on which Jesus would build his church (Eph 2:20; compare Rev 21:14). Through their testimony and witness the church would grow and be established. It would be their responsibility to pass on and preserve the oral testimony of Jesus' teachings and acts (Lk 1:2). It is, of course, true that Jesus himself is the ultimate foundation of the church (1 Cor 3:11), but the New Testament also points out that in a sense the church is founded on the work and writings of the apostles.

The Historicity of the Twelve Disciples

Attacks against the historicity of the twelve disciples have been numerous. Many have argued that the idea of Jesus' having consciously chosen twelve disciples was a creation of the early church read back into the life of Jesus. Textual support for this is seen in the fact that outside the three accounts in the Synoptic Gospels and the one in Acts (written by Luke) we do not find a listing of the disciples anywhere else in the New Testament. In fact, we never read of a number of the disciples—Bartholomew, Simon the Zealot, James son of Alphaeus, and the later Matthias—elsewhere in the New Testament, and Thaddaeus/Judas son of James is mentioned only once more (Jn 14:22). On the other hand, several weighty arguments can be given in favor of the historicity of this group.

For one, we have the threefold witness of Matthew, Mark and Luke. Even though Matthew and Luke are essentially repeating the tradition they found in Mark, their acceptance of the tradition makes it reasonable to assume that this list was not strange to them. It may even be that Luke thought that he was repeating a tradition Theophilus already knew (Lk 1:4).

Furthermore, the expression "the twelve" is found three times elsewhere in the New Testament. In each instance (Acts 6:2; 1 Cor 15:5; Rev 21:14) it is used in a technical sense without explanation. The writers assume that their readers/hearers were familiar with the expression. The reference by Paul in 1 Corinthians is especially significant in that it is found in a pre-Pauline creedal formula. (Notice how Paul "received" this creedal formula and "delivered" it to the Corinthians when he established the church there [1 Cor 15:3-8] in A.D. 49.) Thus the reference to "the twelve" in 1 Corinthians 15:5 is a very early one. (Some scholars have suggested that this formula originated in the late thirties.) The reference to the Twelve sitting on twelve thrones and judging the twelve tribes of Israel in Matthew 19:28/Luke 22:30 also possesses strong claims in favor of its historicity. It is difficult to believe that such a saying would have been created by the early church when the church knew that Judas was one of the Twelve.

Two additional arguments can be raised in support of the historicity of the Twelve. Luke records in Acts that the first act of the early church was to choose a replacement for Judas. The matter-of-fact way in which Luke records this incident and the fact that the man chosen, Matthias, played no important role in the early church argue in favor of the historicity of this event. The most weighty argument supporting the existence of a group called "the twelve" during the ministry of Jesus is the fact that one of them was a traitor. It is difficult to conceive of the early church creating a completely fictitious story of Jesus' choosing twelve disciples and at the same time making one of them a traitor. The existence of the traitor, Judas, is so integrally related to the trial and death of Jesus that his role in this cannot be denied.

Conclusion

Apart from Jesus' death and resurrection, probably no other event in his life possessed greater significance and had more lasting consequences than his choosing of the Twelve. The act itself reveals that Jesus saw in his ministry the fulfillment of the Old Testament promises. Because the kingdom had now arrived and God was visiting his people, the Old Testament promises were being fulfilled. As we will see in the next chapter, Jesus' message involved a realized dimension. Already, not just in the near future, the end of the ages had come. For Jesus "in that day" had moved from the distant future to the present. His choosing of the twelve disciples illustrates that.

The choosing and training of the Twelve also reveal that Jesus saw his work and ministry as having a lasting consequence. According to some scholars, Jesus thought that history was soon to end and that therefore he could not have planned for a "church" and "apostles" to lead it. Yet it would seem wiser to reverse this reasoning and conclude that because Jesus did choose and train twelve disciples he envisioned a period of time before the ultimate consummation of all things. As a result, he trained Peter, Andrew, James, John and the others to lead his followers, the church, during this period.

Much discussion has focused on how Jesus taught his disciples. Did he teach them according to how the Talmud claims that rabbis taught their disciples, using at times rote memory? Such a procedure conflicts radically with the free-spirited individualism of the present day. It has been argued that Jesus' disciples, unlike rabbinic disciples, were not followers of traditions and ideas but of a person. Yet this would certainly not make them less committed to the teachings of that person. If anything, it would make them even more committed to them. Within the ministry of Jesus we even find a situation in which those teachings were proclaimed by the disciples. It is hard to imagine that when Jesus sent out the twelve disciples to preach (Mk 6:7) he told them to say whatever they felt or whatever came into their minds. What kind of disciple would have preferred his own preaching and formulation of the divine message over that of the divine messenger himself? The proclamation of Jesus' message during this mission would have helped fix these teachings forever in their memory.

After the resurrection and ascension of Jesus, the disciples would provide leadership for the early church and be the guarantors of the gospel traditions. For this they had been both called and trained. They were called to preach (Mk 3:14) and to oversee as "eyewitnesses and servants of the word" the passing on of the Jesus traditions (Lk 1:2). There is a very real sense, therefore, that even today the church is built on the founding work of the twelve disciples. That is true not just in the historical sense that the Christian church today is descended from the apostolic church they founded. It is also true because the Gospels that the church today possesses are the result of the preservation and transmission of the gospel traditions by "those who from the beginning were eyewitnesses and servants of the word" (Lk 1:2). Two of our Gospels are associated in the tradition of the church with the Twelve (Matthew and John). The Gospel of Mark is associated in all the early church traditions with the apostle Peter. Luke claims that his Gospel is the result of his having investigated both the written works of other writers and the oral accounts stemming from the apostolic eyewitnesses themselves (Lk 1:1-3). Thus the church today, if it remains true to the Gospel teachings, still rests on "the foundation of the apostles" (Eph 2:20).

References

Best, Ernest. *Disciples and Discipleship: Studies in the Gospel According to Mark.* Edinburgh: T & T Clark, 1986.

Black, C. Clifton. *The Disciples According to Mark: Markan Redaction in Current Debate.* Sheffield, U.K.: JSOT, 1989.

Bruce, Alexander Balmain. *The Training of the Twelve.* Edinburgh: T & T Clark, 1883.

Harrison, Everett F. *A Short Life of Christ,* pp. 136-49. Grand Rapids, Mich.: Eerdmans, 1968.

Hengel, Martin. *The Charismatic Leader and His Followers.* New York: Crossroad, 1981.

Meye, Robert. *Jesus and the Twelve: Discipleship and Revelation in Mark's Gospel.* Grand Rapids, Mich.: Eerdmans, 1968.

Rengstorf, K. H. μαθητής. In *Theological Dictionary of the New Testament,* edited by Gerhard Kittel, 4:415-60. Grand Rapids: Eerdmans, 1967.

Sanders, E. P. *Jesus and Judaism,* pp. 95-106. Philadelphia: Fortress, 1985.

Wilkins, Michael J. "Disciples." In *Dictionary of Jesus and the Gospels,* edited by Joel B. Green, Scot McKnight and I. Howard Marshall, pp. 176-82. Downers Grove, Ill.: InterVarsity Press, 1992.

_____ . *The Concept of Disciple in Matthew's Gospel.* Leiden: E. J. Brill, 1988.

9
THE MESSAGE
OF JESUS
"The Kingdom of God
Has Come to You"

THE GOSPELS INDICATE THAT JESUS WAS AN EXTRAORDINARY TEACH-
er. The term *teacher* is used more than forty times to describe him, and
Jesus even used this title as a self-designation (Mt 10:24-25; 23:8). The
Aramaic title *Rabbi* is also used in the Gospels fourteen times to describe
him. Although Jesus lacked the formal training associated with the latter
title, he did what other rabbis did: taught in the synagogues, proclaimed
the divine law (Mk 12:28-34), gathered disciples, was asked to settle legal
disputes (Mk 12:13-17; Lk 12:13-21), debated with the scribes (Mk 11:27-
33), sat as he taught (Mt 5:1; Mk 4:1), used Scripture to support his
reasoning (Mk 2:25-26; 10:5-9), used literary techniques to help his disciples memorize his teachings. There were, however, a number of significant differences between Jesus and the rabbis. Although Jesus did
teach in the synagogues, much of his teaching occurred in the open fields
and countryside. His audience also included many who were thought to
be unworthy of rabbinic teaching—women, children, tax collectors and
sinners. The content of his teaching was also quite different, as we shall
see.

Jesus was an extraordinary teacher. Without the use of modern-day
technology, he was able to captivate his audience. At times his skills as
a teacher drew such crowds that they created serious problems for him.

He once had to teach in a boat because of the size of the crowd (Mk 4:1). People were so mesmerized that they forgot about the basic necessities of life. The miracles of the feeding of the five thousand (Mk 6:30-44) and four thousand (Mk 8:1-10) were necessary partly due to his great ability as a teacher. In these two instances the reason the crowds came to Jesus was to hear his message. No reference is made to their having come because of his healing ministry or his miracles.

Jesus was a great success as a teacher for several reasons. One was that with him, as well as with his predecessor John the Baptist, the voice of prophecy was heard once again in Israel after four hundred years (see chapter six under "The Coming of John the Baptist"), and this caused great excitement. People were convinced that what Jesus spoke came from God. In contrast to other contemporary teachers, Jesus brought a message not derived from the traditions of the past. In contrast to the practice of quoting the opinions of other teachers, Jesus would say, "Truly I say to you . . ." Still another factor that played a part in Jesus' success as a teacher was his personality. People were attracted to Jesus because of who he was. Another factor, often overlooked, that made Jesus a great teacher was the exciting manner in which he taught. Added to the *what* of his divine message and the *who* of his person was the *how* of his teaching.

In the teachings of Jesus we find numerous literary forms. He used various kinds of poetry. We possess more than two hundred examples of such poetic parallelism in the Gospels: synonymous parallelism (Mt 7:7-8; Mk 3:24-25), antithetical parallelism (Mt 6:22-23; 7:17-18), step parallelism (Mt 5:17; Mk 9:37), chiasmic parallelism (Mt 23:12; Mk 8:35). In addition, he used hyperbole (Mt 5:29-30, 38-42; 7:3-5), puns (Mt 16:18; 23:24), similes (Luke 13:34; 17:6), metaphors (Mt 5:13; Mk 8:15), proverbs (Mt 26:52; Mk 6:4), riddles (Mt 11:11; Mk 14:58), paradox (Mt 23:27-28; Mk 12:41-44), a fortiori (Mt 7:9-11; 10:25), irony (Mt 16:2-3; Lk 12:16-21) and counterquestions (Mk 3:1-4; 11:27-33). He even made use of parabolic or figurative actions in his teaching (Mk 2:15-16; 3:14-19).

The most famous form associated with the teaching ministry of Jesus is the parable. We possess in the Gospels somewhere between fifty-five and seventy-five parables, depending on whether we define certain sayings as metaphors, similes or parables. During the first eighteen centuries of the church, parables were interpreted as allegories in which the individual details of the parable were to be searched for meaning. Today they are more correctly recognized as extended metaphors, to teach a basic point. At times, however, the details of a p. bear allegorical significance (Mt 13:24-30, 36-43; 22:2-10; Mk 12:1-12). The key for detecting valid allegorical details is to ask whether Jesus' original audience would have interpreted these details in such a manner. Asking this question makes evident that the ring (Lk 15:22) and the fatted calf (v. 23) in the parable of the prodigal son could not be references to Christian baptism and the Lord's Supper, although the vineyard mentioned in Mark 12:1-12 would have been interpreted as a reference to Israel (Is 5:1-2).

The parables were particularly useful for Jesus as a teaching device. Parables tend to disarm the listeners, for the meaning of a parable is often driven home before they can resist the point being made. An excellent example is found in Nathan's parable to David (2 Sam 12:1-4). Before David could defend himself against the point of the parable, the arrow had struck his heart—"You are the man!" (2 Sam 12:7). Jesus often used parables in an attempt to break through the hostility of his hearers. The parables of the lost sheep, the lost coin and the prodigal son are good examples (Lk 15:1-32).

Parables were also an effective way for Jesus to introduce potentially dangerous teachings. To talk about the arrival of the kingdom of God naturally raised concerns on the part of Pontius Pilate, the Roman governor. Yet the statements that the kingdom of God is "like a mustard seed" (Lk 13:18-19) or "like yeast" (vv. 20-21) were sufficiently enigmatic that the political authorities judged them harmless. Through his use of parables Jesus could speak about politically sensitive issues. As a result, those outside his circle of followers could "listen, but never understand, . . . look, but never perceive" (Mt 13:14). But to those within the believing community such teachings were explained.

The content of Jesus' teaching centered on the coming of the kingdom of God. Jesus taught that in his ministry the kingdom of God had arrived. Along with the coming of the kingdom also came a new intimacy with God and a new empowering that would enable his followers to live the ethic of the kingdom.

A New Era: The Arrival of the Kingdom of God

Central to the teaching of Jesus is the arrival of the kingdom of God.

Mark gives a summary of Jesus' message: "The time is fulfilled, and the kingdom of God has come near; repent, and believe in the good news" (Mk 1:15; compare Mt 4:23; Lk 4:42-43). The phrases "kingdom of God" found in Mark and Luke and "kingdom of heaven" found in Matthew (the former also found four times in Matthew) occur eighty-seven times in the Gospels. Besides the frequency with which they occur, they are found in such central teachings as the Beatitudes, the Lord's Prayer, the Last Supper and key parables. Despite the important role this expression plays in the message and ministry of Jesus, there is nevertheless great confusion as to what he meant by it.

In the nineteenth century it was popular to interpret the kingdom of God as referring to God's spiritual rule in the lives of believers. It was essentially noneschatological and belonged to this world. The locus of its operation was the human heart. As time passed, however, it became evident that among Jesus' contemporaries and the biblical writers the kingdom of God was never understood as something occurring in the human heart. Such an understanding had little in common with the first century. It was rather a reading into Jesus' teachings of the nineteenth-century liberal agenda.

Another view, which also denied the eschatological element in this teaching, saw the kingdom of God as political in nature. Jesus in announcing the arrival of the kingdom of God was seen as seeking to rally the people of Israel behind him in a revolutionary attempt to overthrow Roman rule. What he was attempting to do was establish a political Jewish government, with Jerusalem as its capital city. If not a Zealot himself, Jesus was at least a Zealot sympathizer. Numerous sayings of Jesus, however, refute such a view. No Zealot would have said, "Blessed are the peacemakers, for they will be called children of God" (Mt 5:9), or "Give to the emperor the things that are the emperor's, and to God the things that are God's" (Mk 12:17). The fact that Jesus' followers were never rounded up and executed but were allowed to remain in Jerusalem and form a community demonstrates that Jesus was not seen by Roman and Jewish authorities as a political revolutionary.

It is impossible to deny the eschatological dimension in Jesus' teaching concerning the kingdom of God. As a result scholars tend to align themselves in camps that emphasize this eschatological element. Some maintain that Jesus taught that with his appearance the kingdom of God was

now "realized." Support for this view comes from several passages:
> The law and the prophets were in effect until John came; since then the good news of the kingdom of God is proclaimed. (Lk 16:16)
>
> No one sews a piece of unshrunk cloth on an old cloak; otherwise, the patch pulls away from it, the new from the old, and a worse tear is made. And no one puts new wine into old wineskins; otherwise, the wine will burst the skins, and the wine is lost, and so are the skins; but one puts new wine into fresh wineskins. (Mk 2:21-22; compare also Lk 11:20; 17:20-21)

In these passages Jesus claimed that the kingdom of God had in some way arrived. It was not just near but already here. It was realized. The covenant God made with Abraham, Isaac and Jacob and their descendants was now "old." The kingdom of God had arrived and with it a "new" covenant.

Along with specific sayings concerning the coming of the kingdom of God are additional sayings and actions of Jesus that reveal that he saw the kingdom as a present reality. One such group of sayings involve Jesus' understanding that with his coming the promises of the Old Testament were being fulfilled. An example is found in Jesus' words to his disciples: "But blessed are your eyes, for they see, and your ears, for they hear. Truly I tell you, many prophets and righteous people longed to see what you see, but did not see it, and to hear what you hear, but did not hear it" (Mt 13:16-17). In the coming of Jesus the Law and the Prophets were being fulfilled (Mt 5:17). Numerous Old Testament promises were being realized. Another example is found in Jesus' reply to John the Baptist as to whether he was truly the Christ: "Go and tell John what you hear and see: the blind receive their sight, the lame walk, the lepers are cleansed, the deaf hear, the dead are raised, and the poor have good news brought to them. And blessed is anyone who takes no offense at me" (Mt 11:4-6; compare Lk 4:18-19).

In fulfillment of the Old Testament promises the time had come for God to visit the outcasts. The lost, the rejected, the sorrowful, tax collectors and sinners were being called. The good news of the kingdom was being proclaimed to "the poor." Jesus revealed this both by his words and by his parabolic actions. Jesus' table fellowship with the outcasts was not accidental. He did so precisely because he consciously sought to fulfill such Old Testament prophecies as Isaiah 61:1-2 (compare also Is 29:18).

Another sign of the coming of the kingdom of God was the healings and exorcisms performed by Jesus. It is generally agreed that Jesus viewed his miracles as expressions and evidence that the kingdom of God had been inaugurated. In his casting out of demons the kingdom was manifesting itself. Jesus' exorcisms were not simply a foreshadowing of the future kingdom but evidence of its arrival. After refuting the absurd view that his miracles were Satanic in origin, Jesus stated, "If it is by the finger of God that I cast out the demons, then the kingdom of God has come to you" (Lk 11:20). The defeat of Satan in such exorcisms (Lk 10:19) must be understood as indicating that the promised reign of God was a present reality.

The miracles of healing and exorcism present in Jesus' ministry (Lk 4:31-41) were also seen by the Gospel writers as intimately associated with the proclamation of the kingdom's arrival (Lk 4:42-44). The healing of the blind was especially associated with the coming of the kingdom (Mk 8:22-26; 10:46-52; compare Is 29:18; 35:5; and 61:1 in the LXX). The feedings of the five thousand and the four thousand were foretastes of breaking bread in the kingdom of God. Later, by his resurrection Jesus would demonstrate even more powerfully that the end of the ages had come (1 Cor 10:11)—the kingdom had arrived.

Closely associated with fulfillment of various Old Testament promises are certain teachings and actions of Jesus involving what some scholars refer to as the "restoration" of Israel. These include several events: the call of the Twelve (see chapter eight under "The Call of the Disciples"), the anticipated offering of salvation to the Gentiles (Mt 8:5-13; Mk 7:24-30; compare Mk 13:10; 14:9), the establishment of a new covenant (see chapter fifteen under "The Interpretation of the Lord's Supper"), the judgment of the temple (see chapter fourteen under "The Meaning of This Event"), the gathering of the outcasts into the kingdom.

We do not find in Jesus' teachings any hint that he thought his present ministry would bring about the fulfilling of Jewish nationalistic or military hopes. If one so defines the arrival of the kingdom of God, which Jesus proclaimed as meaning the "restoration" of Israel, then by definition Jesus taught such a "restoration." Yet this would require a definition of the term *restoration* so different from the understanding of first-century Judaism that it would no longer mean the "restoration" of Israel. Such teachings of Jesus concerning the destruction of the temple and the fall of Jerusalem simply would not make any sense to Jews awaiting the "restoration" or Israel in the first century.

It is also evident that Jesus did not perceive himself as a religious reformer seeking to restore the purity of the Old Testament religion. On occasion he did seek to undo corrupt religious practices (cf. Mk 7:1-23; 10:2-12; Mt 5:21-48), but he did not see his mission as primarily aimed at purifying Israel's worship. With his coming the Old Testament faith, the covenant God made with Israel, was being fulfilled and transcended. The kingdom of God had come. It was not enough to make sure that old cloth should be sown on old cloaks or that old wine be put in old wineskins (Mk 2:21-22). Those days had now come to an end. The kingdom of God had arrived!

It would seem better, therefore, to understand the arrival of the kingdom of God as God's "fulfilling" his promises found in the Old Testament. Whether there are hints in Jesus' teachings that someday in the more distant future there would be a "restoration" of nationalistic Israel is uncertain. The meaning of such passages as Matthew 19:28 and 23:39, which are often given in support of such a view, is far from clear.

On the other hand, there are passages in which Jesus taught that the kingdom of God involved some future event, something that had not yet occurred:

Father, . . . your kingdom come. (Lk 11:2)

Not everyone who says to me, "Lord, Lord," will enter the kingdom of heaven, but only the one who does the will of my Father in heaven. On that day many will say to me, "Lord, Lord, did we not prophesy in your name, and cast out demons in your name, and do many deeds of power in your name?" Then I will declare to them, "I never knew you; go away from me, you evildoers." (Mt 7:21-23; compare also Mt 5:19-20; 8:11-12; 25:31-46; Mk 14:25; Lk 13:22-30; and so on)

In these passages Jesus taught that the kingdom of God was in some way still future—it was "not yet." In some instances the kingdom of God is even a synonym for eternal life (Mk 10:17, 23; Jn 3:3-5, 15-16). The term *consistent* or *thoroughgoing* eschatology is frequently used to describe this understanding.

In Jesus' understanding a number of key events lay in the future. The most important were the resurrection of the dead (Mk 12:18-27) and the final judgment (Lk 10:13-15; 11:31-32). These events would take place when Jesus as the Son of Man returned to judge the world (Mt 13:41-43; Mk 8:38; 13:24-27). On that day the sheep would be separated from the goats (Mt 25:31-46). This meant blessing for the righteous (Lk 6:20-23) but condemnation for the wicked (Mt 7:21-23; Lk 6:24-26). At that time history as we now know it would come to an end, time would become eternity and the kingdom of God would be consummated. As to the exact day when this would take place, Jesus confessed that neither he nor anyone else knew. God alone knew the day (Mk 13:32). Consequently Jesus rebuked all speculation on the subject (compare Acts 1:6-7).

A great deal of confusion has resulted from the figurative nature of the language Jesus used to describe future events. His prediction of Jerusalem's coming judgment is full of metaphorical language that when interpreted literally leads to great confusion. It is not surprising that Jesus used the same kind of language and imagery to describe divinely ordained future events as the Old Testament prophets. Thus even as Isaiah used cosmic terminology (Is 13:9-11) to describe the overthrow of the Babylonian Empire by the Medes (Is 13:1, 17-19; 14:4, 22) and Jeremiah used such terminology (Jer 4:23-28) to describe God's judgment of Jerusalem (Jer 4:3, 5, 10-11, 31), so Jesus used similar language to describe forthcoming events. As a result, it is not always easy to separate Jesus' prophecy about the destruction of Jerusalem (Mt 22:2-10; Mk 13:5-23; Lk 19:41-44) and the temple (Mk 13:2, 14; Luke 13:33-35) in A.D. 70 from the events associated with the consummation of the kingdom at the end of history (Mk 13:24-27; Lk 21:25-36).

At times proponents of the "realized" understanding have denied the authenticity of those passages in the Gospels that teach a "consistent" view, and proponents of the "consistent" understanding have denied the authenticity of the passages teaching the "realized" view. One cannot, however, simply choose to accept one set of passages over another. Both views are present in Jesus' teachings. The confusion caused by the presence of both the "already" and the "not yet" is aggravated by our tendency to understand "kingdom" as a static, spatial entity. If the kingdom of God involves the coming of some sort of territory or realm, how could Jesus claim that it had come in his ministry? On the other hand, if he understood the term *kingdom* dynamically as involving God's "reign," then it could include both a present and a future. This is in fact the way the

Old Testament and New Testament understand this term (compare Mt 6:33; 20:20-21; Lk 10:9; 17:21; 19:12-15; 23:42).

According to Jesus the kingdom/reign of God had now come in a unique way in his ministry. Already the promised Spirit was at work (see chapter six under "The Baptism of Jesus"), and after the resurrection he would "baptize" all Jesus' followers, beginning at Pentecost. Old Testament prophecies were being fulfilled. A new covenant was inaugurated (Mk 14:24); the resurrection of the dead was about to begin (1 Cor 15:20, 23). Yet the final consummation of all things still lay in the future. Faith had not yet turned to sight, and the church's anticipation of sitting at the messianic banquet (Mk 14:25) was still future and passionately prayed for: "Your kingdom come" (Mt 6:10; compare 1 Cor 16:22; Rev 22:20).

Maintaining a balance between the "already" and the "not yet" of the kingdom of God is critical. When the tension between them is lost and one aspect is emphasized at the expense of the other, two major errors arise. To lose sight of the "not yet" leads to a triumphal enthusiasm that is ultimately doomed to disappointment and disillusionment. The fallen character of this world and our sinful nature will see to that. On the other hand, to lose sight of the "already" leads to defeatism and a defensive mentality that thwarts the spreading of the gospel throughout the world. Kept in proper perspective, Jesus' teaching leads to an optimistic and aggressive evangelism as well as an awareness that in this life we are still "strangers and foreigners on the earth" (Heb 11:13).

A New Intimacy: God as *Abba*

In contrast to the names traditionally used to describe or address God (Yahweh, Elohim, Adonai), Jesus chose a different and more intimate expression—the Aramaic term *Abba* ("Father"). The concept of God as a "Father" was not totally unknown to Jesus' contemporaries. It is used in the Old Testament fifteen times (for example, Deut 32:6; Ps 103:13; Is 63:16), in the Apocrypha six times and in the Pseudepigrapha eight times. It is also found in the Dead Sea Scrolls (1QH 9:35ff. and 4Q372). In comparison to this, however, the term *Father* is used more than 165 times in the Gospels and is found in every layer of the Gospel tradition (Mark, Q, M, L, John). So whereas the Old Testament and other Jewish literature use this metaphor occasionally in reference to God, it was Jesus' favorite way of addressing God.

A great deal of debate surrounds the uniqueness of *Abba* as an address for God. As infrequently as the metaphor "Father" is used to describe God in the Jewish literature, it is used even less as a form of address. It is not found once as an address in the Old Testament and appears only five times in the Apocrypha and Pseudepigrapha combined. Whether the term *Abba* was used as an address for God in Jesus' day is uncertain. If so, it was used rarely. As a result, the frequency with which Jesus used the metaphor and his use of the particular term *Abba* was unique. The word *Abba* is used three times in the New Testament:

> He said, "Abba, Father, for you all things are possible; remove this cup from me; yet, not what I want, but what you want." (Mk 14:36)
>
> And because you are children, God has sent the Spirit of his Son into our hearts, crying, "Abba! Father!" (Gal 4:6)
>
> For you did not receive a spirit of slavery to fall back into fear, but you have received a spirit of adoption. When we cry, "Abba! Father!" it is that very Spirit bearing witness with our spirit that we are children of God. (Rom 8:15-16)

The last two examples are especially significant because they indicate that the Greek-speaking church communities in Galatia and Rome (and no doubt elsewhere) continued to address God as *Abba* even though they did not know Aramaic. There can be only one explanation for this: it was the way Jesus taught his followers to address God, and the church prized this way of addressing God so much that they continued the practice even though it was in a foreign language. To be sure they placed alongside it the Greek equivalent, but they prayed as Jesus taught them: "*Abba*, Father [*patēr*]."

This practice received added impetus because Jesus, in response to the disciples' request in Luke 11:1-2, taught them a specific prayer known as the Lord's Prayer that would identify them as his followers. That prayer begins by addressing God as "our Father in heaven" (Mt 6:9). The early church understood the Lord's Prayer as an identifying prayer, for an individual first repeated this prayer on the day of his or her baptism, after sharing for the first time in the Lord's Supper.

The term *Abba* has been understood as a childlike word that can best be translated as "Daddy." But though children could and did address their fathers by this word, grown children also addressed their fathers in this manner. Thus the better translation is "Father." The writers of the New

Testament understood the term in this way. Consequently they used the Greek term *patēr* to translate it.

In his own relationship with God, Jesus used the term *Abba* as his favorite form of address (Mt 11:25-27; 26:42; Mk 14:36; Lk 10:21-22; 23:34, 36; Jn 11:41; 17:1; and so on). The only exception was at his crucifixion, when he cried out, "My God, my God, why have you forsaken me?" (Mk 15:34). In this instance both the circumstance of dying as the servant of the Lord (Mk 10:45) and his quotation of Psalm 22:1 required him to use this different way of addressing God.

Through his ministry and work Jesus enabled his followers to share in a similar intimate relationship with God. Jesus invited his followers to see and experience God not as some "Unmoved Mover," "First Cause" or "The Force" but as a heavenly Father who cared for and loved them (Mt 6:25-34). Jesus was nevertheless aware that a difference existed between his and his disciples' relationship to God. He was God's Son by nature, whereas his followers entered into an adoptive relationship with God as sons and daughters by faith (compare Jn 20:17).

A cardinal tenet of nineteenth-century liberalism was belief in the fatherhood of God. Many people today still believe that Jesus taught a universal fatherhood of God and the accompanying doctrine of the brotherhood of humankind. Support for this is seen in Jesus' frequent use of the metaphor "Father" for God. In the Sermon on the Mount, for example, Jesus uses "your Father" sixteen times. Yet upon closer examination it becomes clear that Jesus did not teach a doctrine of the universal fatherhood of God. His references to God as "your Father" must be understood in light of the fact that Jesus was not teaching the crowds but his disciples (Mt 5:1-2). Similarly, the Lord's Prayer was not given as a general prayer that all people everywhere should pray. Rather, it was a prayer given to his disciples (Lk 11:1-2).

Jesus did not teach a universal fatherhood of God. Never did he base this relationship with God as Father on something that could apply to everyone, such as God's being Creator of all things. Quite the contrary, Jesus even described some people as having the devil as their father (Jn 8:44; compare Mt 12:34). It was only through faith in him that this relationship with God was possible. "Everyone therefore who acknowledges me before others, I also will acknowledge before my Father in heaven; but whoever denies me before others, I also will deny before my

Father in heaven" (Mt 10:32-33; compare also 11:27; Mk 8:38; Jn 14:6).

Recently some people have argued that the use of the metaphor "Father" as a designation for God perpetuates a male-dominated worldview and the oppression of women. They argue that Christians should abstain from using such "sexist" language or, if this term is retained, ensure that female terminology is also used alongside it. Yet few Christians (if any) who have referred to God as "Father" have inferred from this that God possesses male sexual parts. The expression is simply a metaphor for God, who is a Spirit and thus lacks not merely "sexual parts" but anything material.

To refrain from calling God "Father" is to reject *the* way Jesus told his followers to address God. To claim that Jesus today would be sensitive enough to the plight of women not to use this metaphor is to assume what must first be proved. The suggestion not to address God as "Father" rejects the one title we know Jesus told his followers to use in addressing God.

The importance of retaining the expression *Abba* as our most important way of addressing God can be seen by the following. (1) It is *the* way Jesus addressed God and *the* way he taught his followers to address God, so apart from any clear word to the contrary Christians should follow the teachings and example of Jesus in this matter. (2) The importance and value of this metaphor in the life and thinking of the early church are seen in the fact that they continued to call God *Abba* even though this was a foreign word. (3) When the Christian community prays "Our Father . . ." it is joining with fellow Christians from all continents and nations, races and colors, languages and dialects who for two thousand years have witnessed to their faith in Jesus by praying in this way. It would be unfortunate if the Christian church were to surrender this aspect of its heritage.

A New Heart: The Ethics of the Kingdom

The ethical teachings of Jesus begin with a call to decision. That call to decision appears in different forms throughout the Gospels: repent, follow, believe, deny oneself, take up the cross, acknowledge Jesus, keep Jesus' words, take up his yoke, lose one's life, hate one's family, remove one's hand or eye, sell all one has and give it to the poor, and so on. For the tax collectors and sinners (the poor in spirit), the call to decision was seen as gracious. It was not endured but joyously made (Mt 13:44). Jesus, however, encouraged those who would follow him to reflect and consider the cost of such a decision (Lk 9:57-62; 14:28-33), for he did not believe that God's grace and goodness involved a "cheap grace."

The ethical teachings of Jesus appear in some ways as paradoxical. They are in a sense new and yet not new, different and yet the same. Their sameness with the Old Testament is due to the fact that the ethical teachings of the old and new covenants are rooted in the unchanging character of God: "For I the LORD do not change" (Mal 3:6). Yet there is a difference, a newness, in Jesus' ethical teachings as well. He presented, out of a host of ethical teachings and traditions, a brilliant selection of what is most important. In a day when the teachings of the Old Testament were often encrusted with layers of tradition and casuistry, Jesus presented simply and clearly the essence of ethics and morality. Teachings once useful in the earliest years of God's people (the ceremonial aspects of the law) were now superseded because of the arrival of the kingdom. The embodiment of this teaching came in the life of Jesus. If one wanted to know what it meant to love, one needed only look at Jesus.

Along with a new clarity in word and example, there also came the creation of a new heart. Jesus brought the gift of the kingdom. Whereas John the Baptist baptized his followers in anticipation of the new era in which the Spirit would be poured out on all believers, Jesus now brought with him that Spirit. Present in his person and actions during his ministry, the promised Spirit would come upon all believers at Pentecost, resulting in a new creation (2 Cor 5:17).

It is not surprising to find that the ethical teachings of Jesus stand in strong continuity with the Old Testament After all, he said, "Do not think that I have come to abolish the law or the prophets; I have come not to abolish but to fulfill" (Mt 5:17). Jesus also saw the summation of human responsibility as " 'You shall love the Lord your God with all your heart, and with all your soul, and with all your mind, and with all your strength' . . . [and] 'You shall love your neighbor as yourself.' There is no other commandment greater than these" (Mk 12:30-31; compare also Lk 11:42; 15:18, 21; 18:2). Because he was quoting directly from the Old Testament (compare Deut 6:4-5 and Lev 19:18), the frequent "You have heard that it was said . . . But I say to you . . ." in Matthew 5:21-48 should not be understood as a rejection of the Old Testament teachings. Jesus was rather bringing out various implications of those commands. External obedience and fulfillment of the Old Testament commandments must be accompanied by a corresponding internal attitude. It is not enough to be concerned about cleaning the outside of the cup; one must also be concerned with cleaning the inside (Mt 23:25-26). Proper behavior apart from purity of motive results in being little more than attractive cemetery plots. On the surface all looks beautiful, but underneath are rotting bones and stinking flesh (Mt 23:27-28).

Numerous attempts have been made to systematize the ethical teachings of Jesus. Most usually focus on one aspect of Jesus' teachings to the exclusion or neglect of others. Some of the most influential of these attempts are the Catholic, utopian, Lutheran, liberal, interim ethic and existentialist interpretations.

The *"Catholic" interpretation.* This view sees Jesus as teaching a two-level ethic. The first level involves an ethic that all Christians must follow, such as the Ten Commandments, the various commands to love and the golden rule. The second level is "evangelical advice," which the more dedicated may seek to follow. This involves such commands as selling all one's possessions, denying one's family and denying marriage. Whereas in Roman Catholicism this leads to a distinction between laypeople and clergy, in Protestantism it leads to such distinctions as being justified versus being sanctified, being born again versus being baptized by the Spirit, being a carnal Christian versus being a victorious Christian, having Christ in one's heart versus having him seated on the throne of one's heart and knowing Jesus as Savior versus knowing him as Lord.

The *"utopian" interpretation.* Here the teachings of Jesus are understood as being directed to all Christians with the intention of forming a new society of love and peace on earth. Certain commands are usually emphasized: not judging; shunning litigation; practicing nonresistance; not swearing oaths; refraining from marriage; rejecting such institutions as the police, army, judicial systems and civil authority.

The *"Lutheran" interpretation.* This view sees the teachings of Jesus as an uncompromising demand for ethical perfection that is unattainable. The teachings of Jesus, like the Old Testament commands (according to Paul's teachings), are simply impossible to fulfill. Any serious attempt to keep them can lead only to guilt and despair. But this is their purpose, for in our despair we are driven to seek God's grace. The ethical teachings of Jesus are not meant to lead to a personal righteousness.

The "liberal" interpretation. Jesus' teachings, according to this view, seek to implant within our hearts a new attitude. Jesus was not interested in expounding specific laws or commandments. This would lead only to legalism. Jesus was much more concerned with what his followers should be than with what they should do. One should concentrate therefore on following the teachings of Jesus that focus on the inner condition of the heart rather than on specific external behavior. Correct actions will flow from a heart of love.

The "interim ethic" interpretation. Made famous by Albert Schweitzer, this interpretation sees the teachings of Jesus as involving an interim, emergency ethic. This temporary ethic was for the short period of time that remained before the end of history. As a result of the shortness of the time remaining, there was no time to worry about seeking justice in the courts, being concerned about marriage, resisting evil and so on. Schweitzer went on to add that since the end did not come, Jesus' ethical teachings were wrong. They represent an impractical idealism. Nevertheless, Schweitzer added, the singleness of focus and the heroic dedication of Jesus to such an ethic can still be admired.

The "existentialist" interpretation. According to this view, Jesus' ethic does not consist of a system of rules but of a call to decision. It is an ethic in which the individual is continually encountered with God's demand and call to total and radical decision. Thus Jesus' teachings are meant to lead to a radical obedience that does not need specific commands or guidance.

Evaluating the interpretations. Although these interpretations capture various aspects of Jesus' ethical teachings, each fails to understand them in their entirety.

The Catholic interpretation loses sight of the fact that Jesus did not call people to a two-level discipleship. On the contrary, he said, "If any want to become my followers, let them deny themselves and take up their cross and follow me" (Mk 8:34), and, "Whoever comes to me and does not hate father and mother, wife and children, brothers and sisters, yes, and even life itself, cannot be my disciple" (Lk 14:26). The convenience of the two stages is shipwrecked on such sayings.

The utopian interpretation flounders on the fact that Jesus did not reject the role of civil government in the life of the believer (Mk 12:13-

17). Also, when the various teachings used in support of this view are properly interpreted in light of their literary form (such as hyperbole and metaphor), they no longer support this interpretation.

The Lutheran interpretation correctly understands that Jesus, like Paul, taught that the life of faith begins with and rests on grace. It loses sight of the fact, however, that these ethical teachings, which supposedly are meant to drive us to grace, are directed at those who have already experienced the grace of God and are already followers of Jesus. The Sermon on the Mount, for example, is directed to those who were already disciples (compare Mt 5:1-2).

Similarly, the liberal interpretation seems to ignore that, for Jesus, doing and being go hand in hand. The separation of the sheep from the goats in the final judgment (Mt 25:31-46) is not based on one's *being* but on one's *doing*. "Every good tree bears good fruit, but the bad tree bears bad fruit. . . . Thus you will know them by their fruits" (Mt 7:17, 20).

The interim ethic interpretation fails to do justice to the fact that Jesus based his ethical teachings on creation (Mk 10:6-9), the Old Testament commandments (Mk 7:9-13) and God's character (Lk 6:36) rather than on an imminent future crisis.

Whereas Jesus taught the need for a radical decision, he did not leave his followers on their own. He was concerned with guiding the disciples who made that radical decision as to how a life of radical obedience should be lived. Thus Jesus' ethical teachings cannot be seen as contentless demands for decision as in the "existentialist" interpretation, for he believed that a life of radical obedience requires guidance and direction. As a result, he gave ethical teachings to provide direction for that life.

The kingdom interpretation. To understand Jesus' ethical teachings, we must recognize that his teachings on ethical behavior are intimately connected to the coming of the kingdom of God. Since the God of the kingdom is the God of Abraham, Isaac, Moses and the prophets, we should expect continuity with the ethical teachings God gave to his people in the Old Testament. Those teachings stem from the moral character of God himself. As a result, ethical holiness in the new covenant corresponds with the ethical holiness in the old. Yet with the coming of the kingdom the attainment of that holiness has been enhanced because of the "already." With the coming of the kingdom of God the "childhood" of the old covenant gives way to the maturity of "adulthood" in the new.

Thus certain teachings concerning clean/unclean give way to the freedom (and responsibility) found in the new covenant (Gal 4:1-7). Whereas this was alluded to in germ form by Jesus (Mk 7:14-23), it would become clearer to the church after the resurrection (Rom 14:1-23; Acts 10-11).

In the ministry of Jesus, a unique understanding of God's grace and love is given. Now it is seen as never before what it means to love outcasts, sinners and enemies. The call for disciples to live as God's children is supported by the knowledge that they are indeed his children and can call him *Abba*. The call to forgive is carried out in the realization that they have been forgiven and receive continual forgiveness (Lk 11:4). When called to renounce the world, the flesh and the devil, they realize that Satan has already been defeated and that they are heirs of the kingdom. It is true that the coming of the promised Spirit was still future, but until his coming at Pentecost the ethic of the kingdom was to be lived out in the presence of the Anointed One. Shortly the Spirit would come (Jn 16:5-15), and in his presence the ethic of the kingdom would be lived out with a new heart and a new power (Rom 8:2-5). Thus the ethic of the kingdom, like the kingdom, itself, is realized in the "already."

Conclusion

The ministry of Jesus was marked by the announcement that something new was taking place. The day awaited and longed for had arrived. The promises of the Old Testament were being fulfilled. The kingdom of God had come. This new day brought with it such joy and excitement that fasting was inappropriate. It was rather a time for celebration, as at a wedding (Mark 2:18-19).

A new covenant was inaugurated. Yet this new covenant was not a repudiation of the past covenant but its fulfillment. It involved not a new religion or movement but the fuller realization of the covenant God made long before with the people of Israel. Unlike Marcion and some later church leaders, Jesus did not see the coming of the kingdom as a repudiation of the covenant God made with Israel. Nor, as some would later argue, did he understand the new covenant as identical with the earlier one. The fact that he called it "new" (1 Cor 11:25) reveals this.

The coming of the kingdom brought with it a certain sameness, for the God of the new covenant was the same as the God of the old covenant. The same God was worshiped in both, although a new intimacy was apparent in the use of the title *Abba*. The same ethic that stems from the character of the unchangeable God is found in both, although the deeper intention of that ethic and a new empowering is now present. Paradoxically the ethic Jesus taught was both the same and different, old and new!

References

Barr, James. "Abba Isn't Daddy." *Journal of Theological Studies* 39 (1988): 28-47.

Beasley-Murray, G. R. *Jesus and the Kingdom of God.* Grand Rapids, Mich.: Eerdmans, 1986.

Caragounis, C. C. "Kingdom of God/Heaven." In *Dictionary of Jesus and the Gospels,* edited by Joel B. Green, Scot McKnight and I. Howard Marshall, pp. 417-30. Downers Grove, Ill.: InterVarsity Press, 1992.

Chilton, Bruce, and J. I. H. McDonald. *Jesus and the Ethics of the Kingdom.* Grand Rapids, Mich.: Eerdmans, 1987.

Harvey, A. E. *Strenuous Commands: The Ethic of Jesus.* Philadelphia: Trinity, 1990.

Hurst, L. D. "Ethics of Jesus." In *Dictionary of Jesus and the Gospels,* edited by Joel B. Green, Scot McKnight and I. Howard Marshall, pp. 210-22. Downers Grove, Ill.: InterVarsity Press, 1992.

Jeremias, Joachim. *New Testament Theology.* New York: Scribner's, 1971.

Ladd, George Eldon. *Jesus and the Kingdom.* New York: Harper, 1964.

Schrage, Wolfgang. *The Ethics of the New Testament.* Philadelphia: Fortress, 1988.

Stein, Robert H. *The Method and Message of Jesus' Teachings,* pp. 60-114. Rev. ed. Louisville, Ky.: Westminster/John Knox, 1994.

10
THE PERSON OF JESUS
"Who Then Is This,
That Even the Wind &
the Sea Obey Him?"

HROUGHOUT HIS MINISTRY JESUS ELICITED THE QUESTION "WHO IS
this person, who . . . ?" from those who witnessed his healings (Lk 5:21;
Jn 5:12), his control over nature (Mk 4:41) and his forgiving of sins (Mk
2:7; Lk 7:49). It was raised by his disciples (Mk 4:41), by a questioning
John the Baptist (Lk 7:18-23), by those who challenged his authority (Mk
11:28; Jn 8:25), by Herod, the tetrarch of Galilee (Lk 9:9), by the high
priest at Jesus' trial (Mk 14:61) and by the Roman governor, Pontius
Pilate (Mk 15:2). While teaching his disciples Jesus himself raised this
question: "Who do people say that I am?" (Mk 8:27).

At times Jesus challenged people to reflect on who he was. In the case
of the rich young ruler who frivolously addressed him "Good Teacher,"
Jesus asked, "Why do you call me good? No one is good but God alone"
(Mk 10:18). During his ministry various answers were given to this
question: a teacher sent from God; a prophet; "the" Prophet; Elijah; Jeremiah; John the Baptist raised from the dead; the Christ. Others suggested that he was a demon, a false prophet, a deceiver, a national threat to
the peace of the nation.

Jesus' Understanding of Himself

Jesus revealed his own understanding of who he was in three ways: by his actions, through his speech and by the titles he used or accepted.

The actions of Jesus. There is present in his actions a unique claim of authority. Jesus saw himself as one who had authority over the temple (Mk 11:15-19; compare 11:27-33), over the demons (Mk 1:27, 32-34), over the prince of demons (Mk 3:27), over sickness and disease (Mk 1:29-31, 40-45), over nature (Mk 4:35-41), over the sabbath (Mk 2:23-28) and even over death itself (Mk 5:21-43; Lk 7:11-17; Jn 11:1-44). Such actions naturally raised the question "By what authority are you doing these things? Who gave you this authority to do them?" (Mk 11:28; Jn 2:18). Such behavior carried with it a clear christological claim.

At times Jesus performed certain actions that were the exclusive prerogative of God. When Jesus forgave the sins of a paralytic, the scribes protested: "Why does this fellow speak in this way? It is blasphemy! Who can forgive sins but God alone?" (Mk 2:7). Similarly when he forgave a woman of her sins, some of those present responded, "Who is this who even forgives sins?" (Lk 7:49). Attempts have been made to interpret these actions ("your sins are forgiven" [Mk 2:5]) as examples of "divine passives"—a reverent way of avoiding the name of God by using the passive. The words of Jesus, according to this view, should be interpreted "God has forgiven you of your sins," rather than "I personally have forgiven you of your sins." It is evident that neither Mark nor Luke understood these sayings in this manner.

Nor did Jesus' audience understand his words in this way, for they were greatly upset. They all believed that Jesus was exercising a prerogative belonging to God alone. The accounts furthermore do not give the slightest hint that Jesus sought to explain to his opponents that they misunderstood this action. There is no hint of Jesus' saying, "You have misunderstood me. I was simply using the 'divine passive' and stating that God had forgiven him/her." The Gospel accounts clearly portray Jesus as consciously exercising a divine prerogative and personally forgiving sins.

Another action of Jesus possessing christological significance is his miracle-working activity. The miracles of Jesus bear witness to his uniqueness. The Gospel of John even refers to them as "signs" that revealed who he was (Jn 2:11). Although Jesus rejected the giving of signs to vindicate his ministry, his miracles nevertheless functioned as signs of his uniqueness. The miracles naturally raised questions: Who is this who controls the wind and waves (see Mk 4:35-41)? Who is this who can heal the unhealable and even raise the dead (see Mk 5:1-43)? The response caused by the healing of the man born blind is typical. Never since the world began were such miracles performed (compare Jn 9:32).

To plunder Satan's domain and free the demonized required one stronger than Satan (Mk 3:27). Furthermore Jesus did this apart from incantations, complicated rituals, magic spells or uttering nonsense syllables. (The Aramaic terms found in the Gospels are not magical incantations but have simple and uncomplicated meanings.) In his exorcisms Jesus did not seek to tap or manipulate impersonal or demonic forces. On the contrary, he commanded the demons by his words alone (Mk 9:25). Such authority of course raised the question of who this was who commanded the unclean spirits (Mk 1:27).

It is true that others in the past could work miracles. One thinks here of Moses and Elijah. Jesus even acknowledged that some of his contemporaries could cast out demons (Lk 11:19). Yet the extent of Jesus' miracles was such that opponents and friends alike marveled, "We have never seen anything like this!" (Mk 2:12). The miracles were not only signs of the arrival of the kingdom of God; they were a manifestation of the kingdom (Lk 11:22). Unlike John the Baptist, the ministry of Jesus was typified by miracles.

Thirty-four separate miracles are performed by Jesus in the Gospel accounts. Along with these are fifteen Gospel texts that refer to Jesus' miracle-working activity. In addition, we have other accounts in which Jesus is the recipient of a miraculous act, such as the virginal conception, the events surrounding his baptism and transfiguration, his resurrection and his ascension.

One cannot read the Gospel accounts without the question arising, "Who is this man who is master of nature, disease and even death?" In Jesus' actions people saw a bold claim to a unique authority. Even as the prince dressed as a pauper unconsciously revealed who he was by his behavior, so Jesus, despite his modest dress and occupation, revealed his understanding of who he was by his actions.

The words of Jesus. Another way Jesus disclosed his self-understanding was through his speech. Jesus claimed that he possessed authority over

Israel's greatest treasure, the law of God (Mt 5:31-32, 38-39; Mk 10:2-12). Whereas it was considered damnable to contradict or minimize even the minutest detail of the law (*b. Sanhedrin* 99a), Jesus felt free on certain occasions to revise and even annul various aspects (Mt 5:31-32; Mk 7:1-23). His justification for doing so did not depend on tradition or logic. It was because of who he was that he was able to make such pronouncements. The justification for such actions was simply "But I say to you . . ."

Another aspect of Jesus' speech that has christological significance is found in his use of "*Amēn* [translated 'Truly' (NRSV) or 'Verily' (KJV)] I tell you." This expression was quite new and without parallel. Some have even seen in this single word a "Christology in a nutshell." By his unique use of this term Jesus claimed that his words possessed an absolute certainty. This certainty did not rest on Old Testament scriptural support or on the amassing of rabbinic quotations. It was not based on impeccable logic. No, the certainty of what he was saying was based on the fact that he said it. "Truly I tell you" (Mt 6:5; Mk 10:29-30) should be understood, "You can be certain of what I am saying, *because I say so!*" It is no wonder, therefore, that the crowds were astounded at Jesus' teaching, for "he taught them as one having authority, and not as their scribes" (Mt 7:28-29; compare Mk 1:27).

On a number of occasions Jesus compared himself to the great men of the past. Jesus saw himself as greater than Jonah and Solomon (Mt 12:38-42). When the question was raised, "Are you greater than our father Abraham, who died?" (Jn 8:53), the Gospel writer expects his readers to respond, "Yes, he is. Jesus is unique and greater than all others." He is greater than Jacob (Jn 4:12). Jesus refers to his coming as bringing something greater than the temple itself (Mt 12:6). Such words contain within them a high Christology indeed.

In his teaching Jesus understood himself as the revealer of divine wisdom. He taught using the forms of past wisdom teachers: proverbs, riddles, poetry, paradox, parables and so on. His sayings often resemble earlier words of wisdom. (Compare, for example, Mt 5:42 with Sirach 4:4-6; Mt 24:18 with Job 39:30; Mk 4:25 with 2 Esdras 7:25.) Jesus, however, did not see himself simply as another teacher of wisdom. He was wisdom's final spokesman. He possessed a wisdom greater than Solomon's (Mt 12:42). His unique relationship with God (Mt 11:25-27) made him the ultimate wise man. Thus the rejection of him and his teachings would bring terrible judgment (Mt 23:29-39), for in so doing people were rejecting the personification of wisdom itself.

Above all, it is in those sayings concerning human destiny that Jesus' high view of his calling and person is most evident. Whereas his contemporaries focused their attention on ritual and law, Jesus claimed that the deciding issue that determined one's future centered on a person's response to him. Jesus maintained that a person's future happiness depended on his or her relationship with him. Heaven or hell, bliss or damnation—one's eternal destiny is determined by the acceptance or rejection of him (Mt 10:32-33; 11:6; Mk 8:34-38; 9:37)! In the person of Jesus one is confronted with salvation or judgment.

The "totalitarian" nature of Jesus' demand for allegiance must not be lost sight of or compromised. To require loyalty greater than that due to father or mother, wife or children (Luke 14:26) is to demand the kind of allegiance that only God can make. In light of all this, one cannot avoid the questions "Who is this who thinks that the world revolves around himself? A deranged egomaniac? A false prophet? Or can it be that this is indeed the King of kings and Lord of lords?"

The titles of Jesus. What is implicit in Jesus' actions and words becomes more explicit in the christological titles Jesus used or accepted as self-descriptions. During his ministry such titles were acknowledged by Jesus privately and with great reservation due to popular misconceptions surrounding them.

Some of his contemporaries understood him as the Son of David (Mt 9:27; 15:22; Mk 10:47-48; 11:1-10), and in their genealogies Matthew (1:1, 6) and Luke (3:31) clearly saw him as the promised successor and fulfillment of the Davidic dynasty. Although acknowledging this title, Jesus avoided the designation due to the political dimensions associated with it. What the title connoted to most of Jesus' contemporaries had little in common with his own understanding of his role and mission.

One title he both accepted and used was "prophet" (Mt 21:11, 46; Mk 6:4, 14-15; 8:27-28; Lk 7:39; 24:19). The fact that Jesus was thought by some to be the returning Elijah (Mk 8:28) or Jeremiah (Mt 16:14) indicates that the people perceived him not just as another prophet but as the eschatological prophet. Jesus was not simply another prophet preaching repentance and uttering future prophecies but "the" prophet (Deut 18:15) who brought with him what the earlier prophets foretold. Jesus did not merely announce the arrival of the kingdom of God; he brought it with him. He did not simply predict the destruction of the temple; he brought it about (Mk 15:29). Thus the title "prophet" is both correct and yet inadequate. Unlike the prophets of old, the authority of Jesus' words lay not in "Thus saith the Lord" but in "Truly, I say to you."

Another title used and accepted by Jesus was "Lord" (*mar* in Aramaic). "Lord" could be used as a title of respect, similar to "Sir," or could possess a more noble dimension, such as when used of God (Mt 7:21-23; Lk 6:46; compare 1 Cor 16:22). The titles that play the largest role in Jesus' self-understanding, however, are "Son of God," "Messiah/Christ" and "Son of Man."

1. Son of God. The title "Son of God" occurs frequently in the Bible and intertestamental literature. It is used of angels, kings, the people of Israel, and in the present form of 2 Esdras (7:28; 13:32, 37, 52; 14:9) and Enoch (105:2) as a title for the Messiah. It is used in this latter capacity in the Dead Sea Scrolls as well when such passages as Psalm 2:7 and 2 Samuel 7:14 are discussed. In the New Testament it is used as a description of the Christian believer (Rom 8:14; Gal 3:26; 4:5-6). In the Gospels, Jesus is addressed as the Son of God by demons, Satan, the disciples, a Roman centurion and the Voice from heaven, and it is used as a self-designation.

Probably the most important example of Jesus' use of this title as a self-designation is found in Mark 13:32. Reflecting on the final consummation of all things, Jesus states, "But about that day or hour no one knows, neither the angels in heaven, nor the Son, but only the Father." The historical nature of this saying receives strong support from the fact that Jesus as the Son of God confesses ignorance about the future. This is clearly not the kind of saying that the early church would have created and placed on the lips of the Son of God. One need only note the tendency of the early church in the apocryphal Gospels to heighten the divine dimension of Jesus' life to realize this (see chapter two under "Extrabiblical Sources"). The difficulty this saying creates (how could the Son of God not know this?) guarantees it as being an authentic saying. This saying reveals that Jesus understood himself as possessing a unique relationship with God. He is distinct from other humans ("no one") and even angels. He is the "Son." In several other places Jesus used this title to indicate his uniqueness.

In the parable of the evil tenants, Jesus portrayed himself as different from the Old Testament prophets. They were "slaves." He, on the other hand, was "a beloved son" (Mk 12:6). The authenticity of this parable is supported by the fact that the "son" is killed and his body is thrown out of the vineyard, apparently to rot. There is no reference to the resurrection in the account. This would be most strange if it, or the reference to the Son, were the creation of the early church. It is doubtful that they would have created this parable without referring in some way to the son rising from the dead.

Still another significant passage in which Jesus teaches that he possessed a unique relationship to God as the Son is found in Matthew 11:25-27:

At that time Jesus said, "I thank you, Father, Lord of heaven and earth, because you have hidden these things from the wise and the intelligent and have revealed them to infants; yes, Father, for such was your gracious will. All things have been handed over to me by my Father; and no one knows the Son except the Father, and no one knows the Father except the Son and anyone to whom the Son chooses to reveal him."

Here again Jesus indicated that he possessed a relationship with God unlike any other. As the Son he had no parallel. True, his followers through faith in him can become "sons" of God by adoption (Gal 4:4-7 RSV). But Jesus' sonship is unique. He is the Son of God by nature. The difference in relationship is not simply quantitative; it is qualitative. Jesus understood himself to be the "only Son" (Mk 12:6; Jn 3:16).

2. Christ. Another important title Jesus used as a self-designation is "Messiah" (Hebrew) or "Christ" (Greek). Because of the political and militaristic connotations associated with this title, however, Jesus avoided using it openly. Some scholars have argued that Jesus never used this title as a self-designation. After the disciples believed that Jesus rose from the dead, this title was read back into Jesus' ministry. Yet neither the empty tomb nor the resurrection appearances demonstrated that Jesus was in fact the Messiah. And certainly the crucifixion did not give birth to such a view. The title was associated with Jesus because in his ministry he acknowledged that he was the Anointed One, the Messiah/Christ awaited by the Jewish people, and because he was crucified as the King of the Jews. After his death and resurrection this title (Acts 5:42; 17:3)

became so associated with who he was that it became part of his name—Jesus Christ.

During his ministry, however, Jesus refrained from using the title publicly, for it would have hindered his ministry and brought about an immediate confrontation with Rome. Rome could not tolerate a popular and gifted leader claiming that he was the promised King of Israel, the Son of David, for according to popular thinking the Christ would free the people of Israel from Roman bondage and reestablish the Davidic monarchy. The public use of this title would be understood as a call for revolution and war and could not have been ignored by Rome. Attempts by Jesus to qualify the title and to refute misconceptions associated with it would probably have gone unheeded and been drowned out by a mobilization for the great war of liberation.

Privately Jesus did acknowledge on occasion that he was the promised Messiah. He shared this with a Samaritan woman (Jn 4:25-26). After a time he shared it with his disciples near Caesarea Philippi (Mk 8:27-30), but he warned them not to announce it to others. Attempts have been made to argue from this passage that Jesus at Caesarea Philippi rejected this title as a self-designation or that Mark in his account teaches that Jesus rejected it, but there is no evidence in the texts to support such a view. (See chapter eleven under "The Confession of Peter" for further discussion of this incident.)

Later, when placed under oath during his trial by the high priest and required to answer, Jesus acknowledged that he was the Christ. Matthew and Luke reveal that he did so, however, with reservation. His response to the question whether he was "the Messiah, the Son of God" (Mt 26:63) was an affirmative "You have said so" (v. 64). Immediately, however, he added, "But I tell you, from now on you will see the Son of Man seated at the right hand of Power and coming on the clouds of heaven." Jesus recognized that due to the misconceptions associated with the title "Messiah" he could not simply affirm his messiahship. Yet he could not, on the other hand, deny it. As a result he replied, "Yes . . . but . . ." (See chapter seventeen under "The Trial Before Caiaphas and the Jewish Leadership" for further discussion of this passage.)

Jesus gave a similar response to Pontius Pilate's questioning. When asked "Are you the King of the Jews?" Jesus replied, "You say so" (Mk 15:2). In the Johannine account of the trial Jesus qualified his answer by saying, "My kingdom is not from this world. If my kingdom were from this world, my followers would be fighting to keep me from being handed over to the Jews. But as it is, my kingdom is not from here" (Jn 18:36). During his trial and crucifixion he was mocked for having claimed to be the Messiah (Mk 15:18, 32; Lk 23:35-39). The clearest historical support for Jesus' having used this title as a self-designation is found in the titulus placed on his cross. It was customary for the charge for which a victim was being executed to be displayed. The charge recorded in various forms was "The King of the Jews." It is clear from this that Jesus was condemned to death by Rome on political grounds for claiming to be the Messiah. No other explanation for his crucifixion is convincing.

3. Son of Man. The most important self-designation of Jesus is the title "Son of Man." That is evident because of its frequency (sixty-nine times in the Synoptic Gospels and thirteen times in John), because it is found in all the Gospel layers (Mark, Q, M, L, John) and because with only two exceptions it is found exclusively on Jesus' lips. (Even in the two exceptions, Lk 24:7 and Jn 12:34, those using the title are doing so in response to Jesus' earlier use of the title.) Thus it is clear that this was Jesus' favorite way of describing his person and work. Despite the importance of this title, however, there is much disagreement as to its meaning.

In the Old Testament the expression "son of man" is found in Psalms (Ps 8:4; 80:17; 144:3—see RSV), Ezekiel (ninety-three times) and Daniel 7:13. In the Psalms it refers to a "man" or a "human being," and in Ezekiel it is the term God uses in addressing the prophet. In Daniel, as well as in *Enoch* 37-71 and 2 Esdras 13, the expression is a title applied to the Messiah. (The question whether the references in *Enoch* and 2 Esdras are pre-Christian or reveal a post-Christian understanding of the title is much debated.) At the present time much debate centers on whether the Aramaic expression for Son of Man *(bar enasha)* could have been used as a title. Would Jesus' hearers have interpreted this expression as a circumlocution for "I" (Jesus referring to himself) or as a general reference to a "human being?"

When the Gospel traditions were translated from Aramaic into Greek, the expression *bar enasha* was understood as a title. This translation was done very early in the life of the church because of the presence of Greek-speaking Jewish Christians (compare the Hellenists of Acts 6). It was furthermore done in the bilingual environment of Jerusalem. It is highly unlikely that under such circumstances a nontitular *bar enasha* would have been translated incorrectly into the titular Son of Man that we find in our Gospels. It seems more reasonable to assume that these translators, many of whom were eyewitnesses (Lk 1:2), understood that this Aramaic expression was used by Jesus as a title.

Furthermore, in several places (Mt 10:23; 19:28; 25:31; Mk 8:38; 13:26; 14:62) Jesus used this expression in relation to Daniel 7:13, where it refers to a particular individual. The facts that this was not a clearly known messianic title in Judaism at the time of Jesus and that it was not a title used by the early church to describe the person of Jesus (it occurs only four times in the rest of the New Testament and only once in the sense that Jesus used it—Acts 7:56) argue strongly that its use as a title in the Gospels is due to Jesus' having used this self-description for himself.

One of the reasons Jesus chose this expression as his favorite self-designation was its very ambiguity. As already pointed out, Jesus avoided the open use of such well-known messianic titles as "Son of David" and "Messiah/Christ." The confusion surrounding the title "Son of Man" served Jesus well. It functioned much like a parable. To those on the inside it revealed Jesus' messianic calling; to those on the outside it had a riddlelike quality (Mk 4:10-12). To the latter it was perhaps understood as a circumlocution or as a general reference to Jesus as a human being. Thus it served Jesus' purpose admirably. He could use it openly without fear and yet privately explain its meaning to his disciples (Mk 4:34). "The Son of Man has come . . ." explained well that he had come from God and had an "otherness" about him. It also explained that though the kingdom of God had now been realized in his coming, the consummation of the kingdom still lay in the future. Its ultimate completion still awaited the coming of the Son of Man with the "clouds of heaven" (Dan 7:13; Mk 13:26; 14:62).

Jesus' Understanding of His Mission

At the beginning of his ministry Jesus announced that the kingdom of God had arrived. He had come "to bring good news to the poor . . . to proclaim release to the captives and recovery of sight to the blind, to let the oppressed go free, to proclaim the year of the Lord's favor" (Lk 4:18-19). He came to inaugurate a new covenant. With this new covenant came a new intimacy, the privilege of addressing God as "Father." And with this covenant came the supreme Gift—the Spirit. These are the *results* of Jesus' ministry and work. What is not stated in these pronouncements is the *means* by which Jesus would achieve them. He did not assume that the coming of the kingdom, the new covenant and the Spirit were simply the results of the ongoing course of history. Nor did he believe that they would come about as the result of human achievement. He did not believe that they were the natural results of evolutionary progress in history. The new covenant and all that was associated with it were the result of what he would accomplish by his ministry.

Jesus' thinking and understanding developed in a culture founded on the religion of the Old Testament. Like other Jews he believed that the new covenant would bring with it the forgiveness of sins (compare Jer 31:31 and 34). The sealing of that covenant, furthermore, required the pouring out of sacrificial blood. The yearly reliving of God's covenant with Moses and the people of Israel at Passover had at its very heart the sacrifice and pouring out of the blood of the Passover lamb. At the beginning of Jesus' ministry John the Baptist, as a prophet, understood this dimension of Jesus' work when he referred to him as "the Lamb of God who takes away the sin of the world!" (Jn 1:29; compare v. 36; 1 Cor 5:7; 1 Pet 1:19). It is not surprising, therefore, that Jesus believed that the means by which the kingdom and its benefits would be achieved involved giving himself as a sacrifice to seal the new covenant.

Attempts to portray Jesus as a social reformer or political activist lose sight of this dimension. They focus almost totally on horizontal concerns dealing with one's "neighbor." To be sure, this dimension does exist in Jesus' teachings: "You shall love your neighbor as yourself" (Mk 12:31). Yet this horizontal command is preceded by a vertical one, "You shall love the Lord your God" (Mk 12:30). Matthew's account adds, "This is the greatest and first commandment" (Mt 22:38). For Jesus the concern for one's relationship with God is of primary importance. The prodigal son had above all sinned against "heaven" (Lk 15:18, 21); the unjust judge did not fear God nor respect people (Lk 18:2; note also how the vertical and horizontal go together in Lk 11:42). For Jesus and his contemporaries, forgiveness of sins was essential (Mk 10:17; Jn 3:3), and forgiveness was associated with sacrifice (Heb 9:22).

Whereas Israel longed for the coming of the Messiah to restore its political fortunes and free it from its enemies, Jesus saw Israel's need differently. What Israel needed was the once-and-for-all sacrifice that would solve the deeper and more important need of its relationship with God. How could human forgiveness be achieved? And how could the righteous standing before God resulting from this forgiveness be lived out in daily life? Jesus saw that this was the greatest need facing the people of Israel. As a result, he understood his messianic mission as bringing about the new covenant promised by the prophets through the sacrificial offering of himself. With this would come the answer to Israel's and humanity's greatest need—forgiveness, which allowed sinful people fellowship with a holy God. This also brought with it the gift of God's Spirit, which would enable them to live out the divine ethic.

In the early part of his ministry Jesus did not share this understanding with his disciples. On occasions, however, he made allusions to his future death. He explained fasting as being inappropriate in the present time of joy and celebration. Yet a time would come when he would be taken from the disciples (Mk 2:18-20). At that time fasting would take place. Such fasting and mourning seems to fit only a brief period in the life of the early church, the period between Good Friday and Easter, for the early church did not see itself as living in a time of mourning. As a result it is unlikely that this saying was created by them and placed back on the lips of Jesus to justify the practice of fasting. Jesus alluded elsewhere to his death, when he spoke of fulfilling his baptism in a way that can only be understood as referring to his death (Mk 10:38-39), not perishing somewhere other than Jerusalem (Lk 13:33), and the Son of Man's being three days and nights in the heart of the earth (Mt 12:40). The time reference in the latter passage does not match well the period between Jesus' death and resurrection and thus argues for its authenticity.

It was at Caesarea Philippi that Jesus began to teach his disciples explicitly of his future death (Mt 16:21; Mk 8:31). There is no doubt that the passion predictions of Jesus have been artistically organized by Mark. In Mk 8:31—10:45 we have three passion predictions (8:31; 9:31; 10:33-34) followed in each instance with an error made by the disciples, which is followed in turn by a section of Jesus' teachings on discipleship. Some of the passion predictions may also be more detailed and "filled out" by what subsequently happened. Yet the Gospel accounts clearly teach that Jesus sought to prepare his disciples beforehand for his forthcoming death. He would even allude to his death publicly in the parable of the evil tenants (Mk 12:1-12), and he would struggle with its reality at Gethsemene (Mk 14:32-50).

Jesus did not believe that he needed to provide detailed explanations of how his death would bring forgiveness and seal the new covenant. He would leave to his followers the theological explanation (for example, Rom 3:24-26; 2 Cor 5:21; Tit 2:14; Heb 9:11-28; 1 Pet 1:18-19; 2:24; 3:18; 1 Jn 2:2). His own understanding of his death as sacrificial and sealing a covenant is found primarily in two places: "For the Son of Man came not to be served but to serve, and to give his life a ransom for many" (Mk 10:45); "This is my blood of the covenant, which is poured out for many" (Mk 14:24). In the first reference Jesus taught that his mission would culminate in the offering of his life as a "ransom for many." Here the idea of sacrifice and substitution are both present. With regard to the Last Supper, Jesus referred to his death as achieving human forgiveness (Mt 26:28) and sealing the new covenant. This teaching would provide the nucleus from which the church's later interpretation of the meaning of Jesus' death would develop.

Many critics deny the authenticity of these references to Jesus' death and to their sacrificial nature. These prophetic pronouncements are all understood as *vaticinia ex eventu* (alleged prophecies after the fact, created by the early church and placed on the lips of Jesus). That is not surprising, for if one denies the supernatural and thus the possibility of true prophecy, this is a natural conclusion. Often the dislike of a theology involving sacrifice or a substitutionary atonement also causes a rejection of the authenticity of these passages. Yet Jesus must have wrestled with the possibility of death and martyrdom. After all, he was aware that John the Baptist was put to death due to the animosity of those who opposed his preaching. Since he was experiencing a similar hostility and plotting (Mk 3:6; 11:18; 14:1-2; Jn 11:49-53), he must have reflected over the possibility that what had happened to John might happen to him as well. In fact, it would have been incredible for Jesus not to see the likelihood, if not the eventuality, of his martyrdom.

Furthermore, Jesus lived in a culture that believed that the death of the righteous brought atonement for the sins of the nation:

Be merciful to your people and let our punishment be a satisfaction on their behalf. Make my blood their purification and take my life as a ransom for theirs. (4 Macc 6:29; James H. Charlesworth, ed., *The Old Testament Pseudepigrapha* [Garden City, N.Y.: Doubleday, 1985], 2:552)

Through the blood of these righteous ones and through the propitiation of their death the divine providence rescued Israel. (4 Macc 17:22; Charlesworth, ed., *Old Testament Pseudepigrapha*, 2:563)

As a result, even if Jesus had never received a supernatural revelation concerning his role as the Lamb of God, he could well have foreseen the inevitability of his death and understood it as having redemptive significance. And where was it more likely for this to take place than the headquarters of his most vigorous opposition—Jerusalem?

The Gospels maintain that from the beginning of his ministry Jesus was aware of the cost involved in following God's will. From his later reference to the baptism awaiting him (Mk 10:38-39), it appears that his surrender to the will of God at the time of his baptism was a surrender unto death, perhaps even death on the cross. No developmental understanding of this is found in the Gospel portrayal of Jesus' ministry. When exactly Jesus became aware of all this is locked up in the mystery of the incarnation. Speculation is possible, but the value of such speculation is questionable, for it is essentially an outworking of one's christological presuppositions. A reading of the noncanonical infancy Gospels raises serious questions as to the value of such an exercise. Historically we possess no evidence that would allow us to come to a conclusion on this matter.

Conclusion

The Gospels reveal that Jesus progressively provided his followers with an understanding of both who he was and what he would do. During his ministry this understanding caused great confusion. At times his disciples even refused to accept this teaching because it conflicted with the prevailing understanding of the messianic role. With the resurrection this was remedied, and what was previously unclear and even rejected came to be understood as the power (1 Cor 1:18) and wisdom of God (1 Cor 2:7).

References

Bayer, Hans F. *Jesus' Predictions of Vindication and Resurrection*. Tübingen, Germany: J. C. B. Mohr, 1986.

Blackburn, B. L. "Miracles and Miracle Stories." In *Dictionary of Jesus and the Gospels*, edited by Joel B. Green, Scot McKnight and I. Howard Marshall, pp. 549-60. Downers Grove, Ill.: InterVarsity Press, 1992.

Brown, Raymond E. *The Death of the Messiah*, pp. 1468-91. New York: Doubleday, 1994.

Dunn, James D. G. *Christology in the Making*. Philadelphia: Westminster Press, 1980.

Kim, Seyoon. *The "Son of Man" as the Son of God*. Tübingen, Germany: J. C. B. Mohr, 1983.

Marshall, I. Howard. *The Origins of New Testament Christology*. Rev. ed. Downers Grove, Ill.: InterVarsity Press, 1990.

Meyer, Ben F. *The Aims of Jesus*. London: SCM Press, 1979.

Sanders, E. P. *The Historical Figure of Jesus*, pp. 238-48. New York: Penguin, 1991.

Stein, Robert H. *The Method and Message of Jesus' Teachings*, pp. 115-51. Rev. ed. Louisville, Ky.: Westminster/John Knox, 1994.

Vermes, Geza. *Jesus the Jew*. London: Collins, 1973.

Witherington, Ben, III. *The Christology of Jesus*. Minneapolis: Fortress, 1990.

11
THE EVENTS OF
CAESAREA PHILIPPI
The Turning Point

AT A CERTAIN POINT IN HIS MINISTRY JESUS MADE A JOURNEY THAT took him outside the confines of Galilee, Judah and Samaria into the predominantly Gentile territories of Tyre, Sidon, Caesarea Philippi and the Decapolis (a federation of ten [deca] Greek cities [polis; compare Minneapolis]). The reason Matthew (15:21—18:35) and Mark (7:24—9:50) recorded this journey is clear. They wanted to demonstrate to their Gentile readers that even during his lifetime Jesus was concerned for them. He came to bring the good news not just to the children of Abraham but to Gentiles as well.

Possible Reasons for Jesus' Trip to the Gentiles
When the specific question is asked as to why Jesus took this journey, there is less certainty. Several suggestions have been made: to preach the gospel to the Gentiles; to find privacy and rest; to reflect on the success of his ministry; to escape the hostility of Herod Antipas; to teach his disciples.

To preach the gospel to the Gentiles. The journey was, in fact, a Gentile mission. This suggestion, however, runs into difficulty in light of the context Mark gives this journey: "From there he set out and went away to the region of Tyre. He entered a house and did not want anyone to know he was there" (Mk 7:24). Other sayings indicate that Jesus did not envision a "Gentile mission" during this journey or for that matter during his earthly ministry (Mt 10:5; Mk 7:27-28). A Gentile mission there would indeed be, but only after the death and resurrection of Jesus, his Great Commission (Mt 28:19-20; Acts 1:8) and the persecution of the early church (Acts 8:1-4). It is true that some Gentiles did hear the good news during this journey, but that was not its primary purpose.

To find privacy and rest. This suggestion does receive support from Mark 7:24. At times Jesus did seek privacy (Mk 4:34; 6:31-32), but there appears to be a better suggestion for the journey.

To reflect on the success (or lack of success) of his ministry. At this time Jesus came to the realization that he must go to Jerusalem and die. Others have proposed that Jesus came to the decision to go to Jerusalem to confront the people and their leaders with the need to recognize that the kingdom of God had come and that he was the heir to the Davidic throne. Such speculations find no support from the text but are examples of the "psychologizing" of Jesus popular in the nineteenth century. They run counter to those passages in which Jesus alludes to his death before this journey, and it is special pleading to argue that all these references (for example, Mt 12:38-40; Mk 2:18-20; Jn 2:19-22; 3:14; 8:28; 10:11; 12:7, 23, 32) are nonhistorical and should be dated after Jesus' death.

To escape the hostility of Herod Antipas, ruler of Galilee. The incident in Luke 13:31-35, where some Pharisees warned Jesus that Herod wanted to kill him, is often cited to support this view. Yet if anything, this passage indicates that Jesus had no fear of Herod and that he believed he must head toward Jerusalem rather than to Gentile territory.

To teach his disciples and prepare them for coming events. This is the best suggestion. It was at this time that their understanding of his person and work came to a climax. Jesus elicited from them a confession of his messiahship and began to teach them of the inevitability and necessity of his death. What was learned during this journey became the foundation of their later preaching.

Both Matthew (Mt 16:13) and Mark (Mk 8:27) indicate that this key event, which marked the turning point of Jesus' ministry, occurred at a place called Caesarea Philippi. Many rulers were fond of building cities and dedicating them to the emperor—Caesar(ea). As a result there were numerous Caesarea(s). This Caesarea was called Caesarea Philippi to indicate that it was the Caesarea that Philip the tetrarch had built and not the Caesarea of Herod the Great, a larger and more important city lying on the coast. The latter was simply called Caesarea (compare Acts 8:40; 9:30; 10:1, 24).

Caesarea Philippi was situated at the southwest foot of Mount Hermon, which is the largest mountain in that part of the world, rising to ninety-one hundred feet. There is no obvious or clear theological reason for the mention of Caesarea Philippi in this incident. It appears to be a historical reminiscence associated with this event and serves as a strong witness to its historicity.

The Confession of Peter

As a master teacher, Jesus sought to lead his disciples into a deeper understanding of who he was. To elicit from them a correct response he posed a question: "Who do people say that I am?" (Mk 8:27). The disciples repeated some of the speculations they had overheard from the crowds. In politeness they did not repeat the negative things Jesus' opponents were saying.

One suggestion of the people was that Jesus was John the Baptist. This identification of Jesus with John the Baptist, perhaps raised from the dead (Mk 6:16; Lk 9:7), seems strange in that Jesus and John the Baptist were contemporaries whose ministries overlapped. No clear parallel exists in Judaism for the idea that those who suggested this believed that John the Baptist had after his death become reincarnate in Jesus of Nazareth. Probably it is best to envision that those who believed this thought that the "spirit" of John the Baptist had passed on to Jesus much as the "spirit" of Elijah had come to rest upon Elisha (compare 2 Kings 2:1-15).

Others thought that Jesus might be the fulfillment of the prophecy concerning Elijah, who was to return before the Day of the Lord (compare Mal 4:5). The widespread nature of the belief in the return of Elijah is seen in the references to this by the disciples (Mk 8:28) and Herod Antipas (Mk 6:15). Jesus believed that this prophecy was fulfilled in the ministry of John the Baptist (Mk 9:11-13), and the Baptist, by wearing a skin of camel's hair and a leather belt around his waist, apparently believed that he was fulfilling this role (see chapter six under "The Coming of John the Baptist"). Once again the common belief surrounding the fulfillment of this prophecy should be understood as involving less a view of reincarnation than the fulfilling of a common role and mission so that the kind of ministry manifested by Elijah would once again be seen.

Other suggestions as to who Jesus was involve his being "one of the prophets" (Mk 8:28) or "Jeremiah" (Mt 16:14). The return of the Old Testament prophets Isaiah and Jeremiah is referred to in 2 Esdras 2:18. Again the least likely explanation involves a belief in some sort of reincarnation. More probable is either the belief that the dead Old Testament prophets would reappear supernaturally in history or that God would raise up new prophets such as Isaiah and Jeremiah, their "spiritual" heirs, to carry out the divine mission.

After the disciples recounted some of the rumors as to who he was, Jesus then asked them, "But who do *you* say that I am?" (Mk 8:29). The Greek text contains an emphasis on the plural word *you*. What had *they* observed and learned as a result of their time with Jesus? They had seen his miracles. They had observed his authority and had heard his teachings. What had they learned? Could they see beyond the nationalistic hopes of many of their contemporaries? Peter responded for the disciples, "You are the Messiah [or Christ]." (Luke has "the Messiah of God" [Lk 9:20] and Matthew "the Messiah, the Son of the living God" [Mt 16:16].) Upon receiving this confession Jesus commanded the disciples to tell no one about it. Such an open confession of his messiahship would raise false nationalistic hopes among many and would bring about an immediate confrontation with Rome. Jesus' understanding of his messiahship stood in sharp contrast with that of his contemporaries and, as we shall see, even with that of his disciples.

Some have argued that Jesus or the Evangelist Mark in his account rejected the title "Messiah" as an acceptable description. (It is evident from Mt 16:17 that Matthew did not understand the account in this way.) Jesus' command to silence (Mk 8:30), it is argued, should be understood as a rejection of this title by Mark and should be interpreted "Don't tell anyone such a foolish and false thought." Yet if Mark was seeking to convey this idea, he was singularly inept, for no one ever interpreted his words that way until the latter half of the twentieth century.

The very way Mark begins his Gospel, "The beginning of the good news of Jesus *Christ*," indicates that Mark wanted his readers to understand that Jesus was indeed the Messiah. Clearly he did not reject "Messiah" as a legitimate title to describe Jesus. On the contrary, it is exactly the way he wanted his readers to understand Jesus. Mark wanted all the rest of his Gospel (Mk 1:2—16:8) to be read in light of the fact that Jesus is the Messiah/Christ. Mark 8:30 itself also refutes such a view, for in this verse Jesus does not command the disciples to refrain from telling the people that he is the Messiah but to refrain from telling anyone *about him*, that is, about the fact that he was indeed the Messiah.

It is likewise difficult to believe that on this occasion Jesus rejected this title, for we are confronted by the fact that all the Evangelists understood the confession positively. They truly believed that Jesus was the Messiah. That an indignant rejection of this title by Jesus was later turned into the church's favorite confession ("Jesus is the Christ") and that this confession became part of his name ("Jesus Christ") would be simply incredible. Jesus' denial of this title as a personal description would furthermore make the crucifixion incomprehensible. Jesus was crucified on political charges. Apart from his having acknowledged that he was the Christ, his crucifixion is simply unexplainable (see chapter eighteen under "And They Crucified Him").

Jesus Predicts His Passion

Along with the disciples' confession that he was the Christ, the events surrounding Caesarea Philippi were a watershed in Jesus' ministry for another reason. This is evident in both Matthew and Mark. Mark points out that upon Peter's confession, Jesus *"then . . . began to teach them* that the Son of Man must undergo great suffering, and be rejected by the elders, the chief priests, and the scribes, and be killed, and after three days rise again. He said all this quite openly" (Mk 8:31-32). Matthew makes this turning point in Jesus' ministry even more explicit: *"From that time on, Jesus began to show his disciples* that he must go to Jerusalem and undergo great suffering at the hands of the elders and chief priests and scribes, and be killed, and on the third day be raised" (Mt 16:21).

Although Jesus had alluded to his forthcoming death on different occasions, at this point in his ministry he sought to prepare the disciples for this event. Henceforth Jesus concentrated his teaching on the disciples in order to prepare them for his future passion. From here on the references to his death became clearer and more frequent (Mk 8:31; 9:9, 31; 10:32-34, 38-39, 45; 12:1-12; 14:3-9, 34; Lk 13:33).

There is no denying that the arrangement and wording of the passion predictions in Mark (and thus in Matthew and Luke) betray the editorial artistry of the Evangelist. Mark consciously arranged this material so that we have three passion predictions (Mk 8:31; 9:31; 10:32-34), succeeded by three errors on the part of the disciples (Mk 8:32-33; 9:33-34; 10:35-41), followed by three sets of teachings concerning discipleship (Mk 8:34—9:1; 9:35-50; 10:42-45). Yet each of the Synoptic Gospels points out that Jesus on several occasions taught the disciples that he would go to Jerusalem, experience rejection by the Jewish leadership, be killed and rise from the dead three days later. Whereas some of these predictions may be worded in light of the subsequent events (compare Mk 10:33-34), other predictions appear to have been little altered by those events (compare Mk 9:31; 10:38-39). For example, the "after three days" of Mark 8:31 does not fit the time frame of the events as neatly as the more traditional "on the third day" found in Matthew 16:21; 17:23; 20:19; Luke 9:22; 18:33; 24:7, 46; Acts 10:40; 1 Corinthians 15:4.

The necessity of preparing the disciples for the future passion was understandable. One need only observe the response of Peter to this teaching to see why. Despite the verbal correctness of his earlier confession that Jesus was the Christ, Peter's understanding of what this confession implied was seriously flawed. In his thinking, as in the thinking of most of his contemporaries, there was no place for the suffering, rejection and death of which Jesus spoke. Jesus had altered in part the disciples' nationalistic preconceptions about the person and work of the Messiah, but there was no room for a messianic passion in their understanding. Consequently Peter began to criticize and even rebuke Jesus for teaching this. No wonder that Jesus had commanded the disciples not to tell anyone that he was the Christ. If the disciples were still confused and harbored misconceptions concerning the work of the Messiah, how much more confused must the crowds have been.

Peter's rejection of Jesus' teaching should be noted. Its realistic nature and the subsequent rebuke by Jesus lend credibility to the incident. In light of the fact that the other disciples were privy to Peter's rebuke,

Jesus replied, "Get behind me, Satan! For you are setting your mind not on divine things but on human things" (Mk 8:33). The theology suggested by Peter's rebuke stemmed not from God but from this world and the prince of this world. A crossless messiahship has its origin not in divine wisdom but in the flawed reasoning of this world. Thus Jesus rebuked Peter as representing Satan and advocating his views. (There is no need to assume that somehow Satan had "entered" into the body of Peter and was personally speaking through the apostle.)

It is most difficult to imagine that this incident is anything other than the recalling of a historical experience. Who in the church would have created a story in which Peter, one of the greatest heroes of the church, was called Satan? The glorification of the apostles found in the apocryphal Gospels makes obvious how unlikely this would have been. The harshness of Jesus' rebuke is a guarantee of the historicity of the incident. Attempts to interpret Mark as involved in a vendetta against Peter and the other disciples are misguided (cf. Mk 16:7).

The importance of Jesus' preparing the disciples for his death is also seen in that despite this teaching, the passion caught them unawares and brought total confusion. For those well acquainted with the story of Jesus' resurrection, this confusion may seen strange. Some critics even claim that the later consternation and confusion of the disciples refute the claim that Jesus had predicted his passion to them. Yet such confusion can be understood because of how foreign and strange such predictions were in light of their preconceived messianic expectations. A "suffering Messiah" was not a theological doctrine for them but a contradiction of terms. Whether the disciples thought that Jesus would one day come around to their way of thinking about the messianic role is impossible to say. We cannot reconstruct how the disciples dealt with Jesus' teaching concerning his passion, but psychologically their later confusion is understandable.

Peter and the "Rock Saying"

In Matthew's account of the events surrounding Peter's confession is an addition that has exerted an enormous influence in the history of the Christian church. Upon Peter's confession Jesus replies,

Blessed are you, Simon son of Jonah! For flesh and blood has not revealed this to you, but my Father in heaven. And I tell you, you are Peter, and on this rock I will build my church, and the gates of Hades will not prevail against it. I will give you the˙ keys of the kingdom of heaven, and whatever you bind on earth will be bound in heaven, and whatever you loose on earth will be loosed in heaven. (Mt 16:17-19)

From the beginning of the third century this passage has played a critical role in the history of the Christian church in discussions of church government. In Roman Catholicism it has been the major textual support for the institution of the papacy. According to this view, Jesus established the apostle Peter as his vicar upon earth until he returned. This leadership role was then passed on, upon his death, to apostolic successors called "popes." This view can be seen throughout the art of the church, for in the paintings and sculpture depicting Peter and the apostles, one can always recognize Peter. He is the one with the ring of keys in his belt. The Orthodox and Protestant exegesis of this passage has denied this interpretation.

In the past one could usually tell if a commentator on the Gospel of Matthew was Roman Catholic or Protestant simply by observing how he or she interpreted this passage of Scripture. If the rock was interpreted as referring to Peter, the commentator was Roman Catholic. If the rock was interpreted as alluding to Peter's confession that Jesus was the Christ, he or she was Protestant. It is unfortunate when the interpretation of a text is predetermined from the start by one's religious affiliation. One's religious background predisposes how one interprets a text such as this. Such awareness should serve as a first step in trying to be more objective.

The basic issue involved in interpreting this text involves the term *rock*. A play on words between the term *rock* and the name *Peter* appears to be present. The two terms come from the same Greek root: *petra* (rock) and *petros* (Peter). Those who deny the Roman Catholic interpretation argue that the difference between these two words indicates that they should not be understood as a pun. Rather, Jesus' words should be interpreted, "You are Peter and on this confession, that is, the 'rock' that I am in fact the Christ, I shall build my church." In support of this interpretation are various New Testament passages that indicate that Jesus is "the church's one foundation": for example, 1 Corinthians 3:11; Ephesians 2:20; 1 Peter 2:4-8; Revelation 1:18; 3:7.

On the other hand, the difference in Greek between *rock* and *Peter* is due to the fact that *rock* is a feminine word (first declension requiring the *-a* ending), whereas *Peter* is a masculine term (second declension requiring the *-os* ending). Thus the difference between these two words was not due to a conscious decision on the part of the Evangelist but was necessitated by the Greek language. Furthermore, if one translates the terms *rock* and *Peter* back into Aramaic, the language of Jesus and the disciples, there is no difference whatsoever in the terms. They are both translated by *Kepha*. Thus in Aramaic a pun is present in the passage. Jesus says, "You are *Kepha* and upon this *Kepha* . . ."

The easiest way of understanding this pun is to assume that Jesus is referring to Peter as a "rock" due to the future role he would play in the church. Peter is the one who would serve as the early leader of the church; it would be through him that the gospel would be proclaimed in Jerusalem, Judea (Acts 2:1—4:31) and Samaria (Acts 8:14-25), and it would be through Peter that the first Gentiles would hear the gospel and believe (Acts 10:1—11:18). There is a real sense, therefore, that it would be through the ministry of Peter, the leader of the apostles, that the church would be established and grow.

One cannot deny, however, that the ultimate foundation of the church is none other than Jesus Christ himself. There is no other foundation that the church is built upon (1 Cor 3:11). Furthermore, Peter's behavior was far from infallible both during Jesus' ministry and after (Gal 2:11-21). A church that would withstand the gates of hell had to be built on a firmer foundation than Peter. Yet there is no need to deny the leadership role of Peter within the early church. Protestants and Orthodox can join with Roman Catholics in joy over the gift of this man to the church. However, there is no hint anywhere in this text or in the rest of the New Testament that this leadership role was passed on in perpetuity to a successor of any sort.

On the contrary, whereas the one apostle who was a traitor was replaced (Acts 1:21-26), other apostles were not replaced upon their deaths (Acts 12:2). With respect to the "keys" given to Peter, it should also be noted that in Matthew 18:18 this same authority to "bind and loose" is given to all the disciples, and in Revelation 1:18 Jesus is pictured as the one who ultimately holds the keys of Death and Hades. Whatever this "binding and loosing" may mean, it is evident that it was not the sole possession of the apostle Peter.

The authenticity of this passage has been questioned for several reasons. (Some of the reasons for this are that the term *church* is not found in any other Gospel passage except Mt 18:17 and that the degree of authority given to Peter here is not found elsewhere in the New Testament.) On the other hand, its authenticity receives support from the Semitic nature of the saying. The importance given to this passage in the history of the church is nonetheless out of proportion with the role it plays in the New Testament. It is unwise to build a heavy theological system or structure on a single passage of the Bible. Just as it is foolish to build a large theological practice on a single, confusing reference to baptism for the dead in 1 Corinthians 15:29, so it is unwise to build a large ecclesiastical framework on this single reference to Peter as the rock.

Conclusion

The events of Caesarea Philippi were clearly the watershed and turning point of Jesus' ministry. It is at this point that the disciples came to acknowledge, despite their own misconceptions, that Jesus was indeed the Christ. Upon receiving this confession Jesus began to prepare the disciples for his forthcoming passion. This new teaching would cause even more confusion during Jesus' ministry, but after the resurrection the disciples would be able to see clearly that the cross was not a tragedy or mistake but part of the divine mystery. The resurrection would not create a new understanding of the person and work of Jesus, the Christ. Rather, it would confirm what he had taught all along: Jesus of Nazareth was indeed the Christ, the Son of God, the Savior of the world.

References

Bayer, Hans F. *Jesus' Predictions of Vindication and Resurrection.* Tübingen, Germany: J. C. B. Mohr, 1986.

Brown, Raymond E., Karl P. Donfried and John Reumann, eds. *Peter in the New Testament.* Minneapolis: Augsburg, 1973.

Caragounis, Chrys C. *Peter and the Rock.* Berlin: Walter de Gruyter, 1990.

Cullmann, Oscar. *Peter: Disciple, Apostle, Martyr.* Philadelphia: Westminster Press, 1962.

Hooker, Morna D. *The Gospel According to Saint Mark,* pp. 199-207. Peabody, Mass.: Hendrickson, 1991.

Lane, William L. *The Gospel According to Mark*, pp. 287-304. Grand Rapids, Mich.: Eerdmans, 1974.

Marcus, Joel. "The Gates of Hades and the Keys of the Kingdom." *Catholic Biblical Quarterly* 50 (1988): 443-55.

Wilkins, Michael J. *The Concept of Disciple in Matthew's Gospel*. Leiden: E. J. Brill, 1988.

12
THE TRANSFIGURATION
A Glimpse of the Future

THE TRANSFIGURATION ACCOUNT IS ATTACHED TO THE EVENTS OF Caesarea Philippi by one of the few chronological connections found in the Gospels. According to Mark 9:2 and Matthew 17:1 the transfiguration took place "six days later" than the confession of Peter at Caesarea Philippi. In Luke 9:28 the chronological tie is "about eight days after." (Luke may be reckoning the time period inclusively whereas Mark and Matthew thought exclusively.) Apart from the events between Palm Sunday and Easter, we find no other temporal designation this specific.

Since it would have been impossible in the oral period to recount a story "Six days later . . ." without raising the question "Six days later than what?" the transfiguration was probably connected to the events of Caesarea Philippi before Mark wrote his Gospel. (It is doubtful that Mark created the temporal designation, because we do not find such designations elsewhere in his Gospel outside the passion narrative. It may also be that Luke's reference to "about eight days later" witnesses to a separate tradition of this chronological tie.) As we shall see shortly, any understanding of what happened at the transfiguration must keep in mind the events of Caesarea Philippi.

The Place
In all three accounts we read that this event took place on a "mountain" (Mt 17:1; Mk 9:2; Lk 9:28). Matthew and Mark add that it took place on a "high" mountain. Much debate has occurred as to which "mountain" the Evangelists meant.

The traditional sight of the transfiguration is Mount Tabor, which is located about ten miles southwest of the Sea of Galilee. It is essentially a round hill lying in the Plain of Esdraelon rising some thirteen hundred feet above the plain and reaching a height of more than eighteen hundred feet above sea level. Standing in splendid isolation above the plain, its appearance is striking. It is referred to as a mountain in Judges 4:6, 12, 14 (compare also Jer 46:18 and Ps 89:12). Yet it is very difficult to conceive of its being described as a "high" mountain. If a Roman garrison occupied the top of Mount Tabor during Jesus' day, as some suggest, that would further argue against this being the actual site (compare Josephus *War* 2.20.6 [2.573]; 4.1.8 [4.54-61]).

A second suggestion is that the transfiguration took place on Mount Carmel on the Mediterranean Sea, by present-day Haifa. It also is called a mountain, although its height of 1,742 feet is even lower than that of Mount Tabor. Thus it also is far from being a "high" mountain. It furthermore suffers by being out of the way with respect to the events and places surrounding the transfiguration: Bethsaida (Mk 8:22), Caesarea Philippi (Mk 8:27), Galilee (Mk 9:30), Capernaum (Mk 9:33). If these place designations are to be taken seriously, Mount Carmel is too far removed from Jesus' activities in these locations to be accepted as the correct site.

The best suggestion is Mount Hermon, which towers above the area and reaches a height of more than ninety-one hundred feet. Caesarea Philippi lies on the slopes of this mountain, whose snow-covered peaks can be seen from far away. Mount Hermon is indeed a "high" mountain in the fullest sense. The fact that the previous event of Peter's confession at Caesarea Philippi is located on this large, broad mountain argues in favor of its being the best possibility.

In our quest to find "the" mountain, we must not lose sight of the fact that the Evangelists were not concerned with designating the exact location of the event. In their accounts, and probably in the oral tradition before them, the description of the place is simply "a high mountain." This should caution us that although such geographical questions are legitimate and interesting, the heart of the story does not lie in its geographical location. Of course, if one designates this account as a myth because of its miraculous nature, the question of where it took place is nonsensical. Yet even for those who accept the historicity of this account, it is not the "where" that is of primary importance. It is "what" took place that matters.

The Transfiguration

On this occasion Jesus took with him three disciples—Peter, James and John. These three formed an inner core within the Twelve. They were present with Jesus at the raising of Jairus's daughter from the dead (Mk 5:37), at Gethsemane (Mk 14:33) and, with Andrew, at Jesus' apocalyptic discourse (Mk 13:3). No reason is given for Jesus' selection of them on these occasions, but they do not appear to have served as a leadership hierarchy among the Twelve.

On the mountain Jesus was *transfigured* before the disciples. This English term translates the Greek *metemorphōthē* (Mk 9:2). Jesus experienced a supernatural transformation. Naturalistic explanations, such as the sun breaking through the clouds and shining brightly upon Jesus' white garments, will not do. Jesus' garments became dazzling white (Mk 9:3), but the appearance of his face also changed (Lk 9:29). The Evangelists did not understand it as some outside force shining on Jesus. Rather, they portray this brilliance as radiating outward from inside Jesus. Jesus was transfigured, and his face shone as the sun (Mt 17:3).

Luke adds that Moses and Elijah appeared "in glory" with him. The Evangelists understood this as a temporary glorification of Jesus, and the sight was such that the disciples were "terrified" (Mk 9:6). Thus whereas Moses in his encounter with God on Mount Sinai radiated God's glory (Ex 34:29, 30, 35), Jesus on this occasion radiated a foretaste of his own future glory.

Some have attempted to explain the transfiguration as a visionary experience of the three disciples. Support for this comes from Matthew 17:9, where Jesus orders them not to tell anyone about the "vision" until after the resurrection. This term, however, can also refer to historical events. In Exodus 3:3 and Deuteronomy 28:34, 67, for example, the historical "sights" referred to use the same term in the Greek translation of the Old Testament as here in Matthew 17:9. (Compare also "displays" in Deut 4:34, a translation of the same Greek term.) More important, the whole tenor of the account prohibits one from interpreting it as a vision. The words of Peter stand in the way of seeing the transfiguration as a vision or myth, as does the temporal designation.

No doubt the similarities between the present account and various Old Testament motifs and incidents (Moses on the mountain, Moses' face shining, the presence of a cloud, perhaps the "six days") have been heightened in the telling, but that does not mean that the account has been created out of nothing by someone who dreamed it up. On the contrary, it is much easier to understand it as a real incident in the life of Jesus that was worded in light of these Old Testament accounts.

Another explanation of this account is that it was originally a resurrection story that was read back into the life of Jesus. Support for this has been seen in the reference to a cloud (compare Acts 1:9), a high mountain (Mt 28:16), the reference to Jesus' glory (compare 1 Pet 1:11, 21), the idea that the disciples' unbelief during Jesus' lifetime is unexplainable if they had witnessed a transfiguration, the similarity of Jesus' clothing to that of the angels at the empty tomb and so on. There are numerous reasons, however, why the transfiguration is best understood as an account that occurred during the ministry of Jesus.

The first is that all the Gospel writers understood it this way. This is also true of the account in 2 Peter 1:16-18. Second, the use of the title "Rabbi" (Mk 9:5) would be strange indeed in a resurrection account. It is true that Matthew and Luke have "Lord" and "Master," but clearly Mark's use of "Rabbi" indicates that he did not inherit it as a resurrection story. It is also difficult to understand the presence of Peter, James and John if this were originally a resurrection story. Whereas these three appear together as a group during the ministry of Jesus, they do not appear as a trio in any of the resurrection accounts. Finally, Peter's impulsive words to build three dwellings—one for Jesus, one for Elijah and one for Moses—would be strange after the resurrection. Could such a foolish equation of Elijah and Moses with Jesus have been made then? But during the ministry of Jesus such an error is conceivable.

What actually took place during Jesus' transfiguration? One of the

earliest explanations is found in the New Testament itself:
> For we did not follow cleverly devised myths wheñ we made known
> to you the power and coming of our Lord Jesus Christ, but we had
> been eyewitnesses of his majesty. For he received honor and glory
> from God the Father when that voice was conveyed to him by the
> Majestic Glory, saying, "This is my Son, my Beloved, with whom I am
> well pleased." We ourselves heard this voice come from heaven, while
> we were with him on the holy mountain. (2 Pet 1:16-18)

In this passage the transfiguration is seen as foreshadowing the glory
Jesus will possess at the parousia (his second coming). This is probably
the best way of interpreting the difficult passages which introduce the
account in each of the Gospels. Mark understood the transfiguration as
fulfilling Jesus' statement "Truly I tell you, there are some standing here
who will not taste death until they see that the kingdom of God has come
with power" (Mk 9:1).

It should also be remembered that this verse immediately follows Mark
8:38, which refers to the future coming of the Son of Man in glory.
Matthew 16:28 ties the transfiguration even more closely to the parousia
by saying that they would not taste death "before they [saw] the Son of
Man coming in his kingdom." It would appear, therefore, that both
2 Peter and the Gospel writers understood the transfiguration as a
glimpse of the future splendor of the Son of Man at his glorious return.

Still another possible interpretation is that the transfiguration was a
manifestation of the preexistent glory of the Son of God. Some have
suggested that John 1:14 (compare also Jn 12:27-33) may be an allusion
to it. According to this understanding, the emptying, or "kenosis," of the
Son of God (Phil 2:7) temporarily disappeared on this occasion, the veil
of his humanity was pierced, and the glory of the preincarnate Word
broke through. In light of the clear association of the transfiguration
with the parousia in 2 Peter and Matthew 16:28, however, it seems best
to interpret the transfiguration primarily as a glimpse of the future glory
of Jesus, the beloved Son.

The Appearance of Moses and Elijah

All three Gospel accounts state that Elijah and Moses (Mk 9:4) appeared
to Jesus at the transfiguration. Matthew 17:3 and Luke 9:30 reverse the
order of names in order to give a more correct chronological scheme—

Moses and Elijah. The significance of their presence is debated. Are they present because they represent the fulfillment of the Scriptures, namely, the Law (Moses) and the Prophets (Elijah)? This may be Luke's understanding (compare Lk 16:29, 31; 24:27). But if so, would not Isaiah or Jeremiah better represent the Prophets? Note, however, the tie between Moses and Elijah in Malachi 4:4-5. It should also be remembered that Elijah is the first major prophet referred to in the "Former Prophets" (the books of Joshua through 2 Kings).

Or are Moses and Elijah present because according to tradition both ascended into heaven? (Despite Deut 34:5, Jewish tradition refers to Moses' having ascended into heaven [Josephus *Ant.* 4.8.48 (4.326)].) But if so, would not the pairing of Elijah with Enoch be better? Are they present because they are the only two Old Testament saints who witnessed a theophany on a mountain (Ex 24; 1 Kings 19)? Are they here in order to refute the view that Jesus might in fact be Elijah or one of the prophets (Mk 8:28; compare Deut 18:15)? Or are they present because these two Old Testament figures were expected to appear before the coming of the messianic age? Possibly this future eschatological role of the two best explains their appearance on the scene.

The transfiguration of Jesus and the appearance of Moses and Elijah caused Peter to suggest the building of three "tabernacles." The error of trying to enshrine and perpetuate that which is only temporal by building tabernacles is compounded by the more serious christological error of equating Moses and Elijah with Jesus. The confession at Caesarea Philippi, properly understood, should have protected Peter from this error, but as the subsequent rebuke reveals (Mk 8:31-33), Peter and the disciples lacked a proper understanding of the implications of that confession. Mark points out that Peter made the present suggestion because he did not know what else to say (Mk 9:6; compare Lk 9:33).

The Voice from Heaven

Another major event that took place at the transfiguration was the speaking of a Voice from heaven. The Voice must be understood with respect to Peter's previous erroneous suggestions here and at Caesarea Philippi. In contrast to the Voice at Jesus' baptism, which was addressed to Jesus (compare Mk 1:11; Lk 3:22), here the Voice is addressed to Peter, James and John.

The first part, "This is my Son, the Beloved," must be understood as a rebuke of the suggestion that tabernacles be built. It has been suggested that Peter's error here is that he wanted to make permanent a fleeting experience. Soon there would be no one else with them on the mountain, "only Jesus" (Mk 9:8). More important, however, is the error of seeking to build tabernacles *equally* for Jesus, Elijah and Moses. The latter greats of the Old Testament were servants, not "sons." Jesus is the only Son. (Compare this distinction in the parable of the wicked tenants in Mk 12:2-7.) Moses and Elijah were prophets through whom God spoke, but Jesus is the "Son, whom he appointed heir of all things" (Heb 1:2). The Jesus of the transfiguration was far greater than they.

Peter and the disciples had not grasped the implications of the confession uttered at Caesarea Philippi. Jesus' sonship involved not just a quantitative distinction—that Jesus was a greater prophet than Elijah and Moses. There existed a qualitative distinction as well. It was Jesus alone who was transfigured, not Elijah and Moses. Even Luke, who mentions that Moses and Elijah appeared "in glory" (Lk 9:31), understood that there was a significant difference between their appearance and that of the Son, who possessed his own glory. (Compare Lk 9:32 "his glory"; compare also 9:26.)

The second part of the divine message, "Listen to him," points back to Caesarea Philippi. The present account does not refer to Jesus' teachings, so we must look elsewhere to understand what words of Jesus they are to listen to. Because of this, as well as the temporal tie to the preceding account, we must look back to what happened at Caesarea Philippi. There, after his confession, when Jesus began to teach about his forthcoming passion (Mk 8:31), Peter rebuked him concerning this. He was unable to accept Jesus' teaching concerning the messianic role and to modify his own messianic perceptions, which were no doubt more political in nature. Peter could not accept Jesus' understanding that his divine call and mission involved suffering and death. At that time Jesus pointed out that Peter's rejection of Jesus' messianic role was Satanic. For Jesus this issue had been settled at the temptation.

At the transfiguration the Voice from heaven revisited Peter's rejection of Jesus' passion prediction. The command "Listen to him" was a rebuke of Peter and the disciples. They had to understand and accept Jesus' teachings concerning the messianic role. Now, along with Jesus' claim that the rejection of a suffering Messiah was Satanic, came the divine Voice. The original readers of the transfiguration accounts, of course, knew that Jesus' messianic mission involved his arrest-trial-crucifixion-resurrection-ascension. Such a comprehensive understanding, however, was not available for Peter, James and John at the transfiguration. What they could know and needed to accept was that the transfiguration was a divine verification of the confession and passion prediction made at Caesarea Philippi. It was God's seal of approval, the heavenly ratification, of Jesus' teaching concerning his messianic calling. Jesus was indeed the Christ, the Son of God. (The tie between these two titles is explicitly made in Mt 16:16, but each of the Evangelists understood these titles as appropriate and complementary descriptions of Jesus [compare Mk 1:1; 14:61; Lk 4:41; 22:67-71.]) Precisely because he was the Christ, Jesus had to suffer and die and rise on the third day.

The Voice affirmed that the disciples had to accept Jesus' understanding of his mission as involving suffering and death. Whatever previous understandings they possessed concerning the messianic role must give way to Jesus' own teaching. The disciples dare not force Jesus' mission into their own mode of thinking. On the contrary, they must "listen to him." They must not try to make Jesus into a messiah that met with their approval. Their contemporaries might claim that a suffering and dying Messiah was a stumbling block for faith and plain foolishness (1 Cor 1:23). The one, however, who was willing to listen to the divine Voice would know that in Jesus' suffering and death God's power and wisdom were in fact revealed (1 Cor 1:24).

The Voice from heaven still speaks this way to the followers of Jesus. What is deemed wise in this world may ultimately be foolishness before God; what may be deemed foolishness in this world (such as Jesus' sacrificial death to reconcile God and humanity) may ultimately be wisdom before God.

From Here to Jerusalem

Each Synoptic Gospel points out that after the transfiguration Jesus headed toward Jerusalem. Matthew refers to Jesus' coming to Galilee (Mt 17:22), and in particular Capernaum (Mt 17:24), leaving Galilee for Judea on the other side of the Jordan (Mt 19:1), going up to Jerusalem (Mt 20:17), passing through Jericho (Mt 20:29) and finally entering Jerusalem

(Mt 21:10). Mark, like Matthew, has Jesus passing through Galilee (Mk 9:30), entering Capernaum (Mk 9:33), going to Judea across the Jordan (Mk 10:1), going up to Jerusalem (Mk 10:32), passing through Jericho (Mk 10:46) and then entering Jerusalem (Mk 11:11). Luke points out that after the events of Caesarea Philippi and the transfiguration (Lk 9:18-36), Jesus resolutely set his face toward Jerusalem (Lk 9:51). What follows is the largest block of Q material in his Gospel (Lk 9:51-18:14), but even within this material we read of Jesus going through Samaria (Lk 9:52), gradually making his way to Jerusalem (Lk 13:22), traveling to Jerusalem along the border between Samaria and Galilee (Lk 17:11), coming to Jericho (Lk 19:1), nearing Jerusalem (Lk 19:11) and finally entering it (Lk 19:41-45).

Since the arrangement of much of the Gospel material is frequently due to nonchronological motives, it is impossible to postulate how soon after the events surrounding Caesarea Philippi and the transfiguration Jesus came to Jerusalem. Both Matthew and Luke place large collections of materials between these events (Mt 18:1-35, the fourth major collection of Jesus' sayings in his Gospel; Lk 9:51—18:14, the largest Q section in his Gospel). The placement of these materials is due to literary concerns. Thus we cannot argue that this journey must have taken a considerable amount of time for Jesus to have taught all this material. The nonchronological nature of Luke's placement of Jesus' teachings found in Luke 9:51—18:14 is also seen in that much of this material is found in Matthew before his accounts of the events surrounding Caesarea Philippi and the transfiguration.

If we take the Synoptic Gospels seriously, the focus of Jesus' ministry underwent a major turning point at this time. The period of teaching in Galilee had come to an end. There would still be teaching on the way to Jerusalem and in Jerusalem, but that was secondary to his fulfilling of the divine purpose. "The Son of Man must undergo great suffering, and be rejected, . . . and be killed, and after three days rise again" (Mk 8:31). As a result, Jesus sought to prepare his disciples for the passion. This theme would be repeated to them on numerous occasions (compare Mk 9:31-32; 10:33-34, 45; 12:6-11; 14:6-9, 18-21, 22-25). Even if we allow that some of this may be due to the editorial work of the Evangelists, it would appear that Jesus sought to prepare the disciples for his forthcoming passion. Yet even more important still was Jesus' need to fulfill his calling.

His face was therefore set for Jerusalem, because he "came not to be served but to serve, and to give his life a ransom for many" (Mk 10:45).

Conclusion

The transfiguration of Jesus is intimately tied to the events of Caesarea Philippi. That is true not only temporally but also theologically. What had occurred at Caesarea Philippi was affirmed, and its implications were further spelled out. What Peter had confessed was now verified by the divine Voice. Jesus was not Elijah, Moses, a prophet or John the Baptist. The Voice affirmed what Peter had said. Jesus was the Messiah/Christ, the beloved Son of God. This implied that he had no equals. People could not treat him on the same terms as Moses and Elijah—he was much greater.

What this meant concerning his mission had to be learned from Jesus himself. Peter earlier had sought to impose his own messianic conceptions on Jesus. The result was a Satanic understanding of the messianic role. At the transfiguration the Voice told Peter and the others that they must "listen to Jesus." He alone was the one who could and must interpret the messianic role that God intended. And this role led to Jerusalem and a cross.

References

Boobyer, G. H. *St. Mark and the Transfiguration Story.* Edinburgh: T & T Clark, 1942.

Caird, G. B. "The Transfiguration." *Expository Times* 67 (1955): 291-94.

Hooker, Morna D. " 'What Doest Thou Here, Elijah?' A Look at St. Mark's Account of the Transfiguration." In *The Glory of Christ in the New Testament*, edited by L. D. Hurst and N. T. Wright, pp. 59-70. Oxford: Clarendon, 1987.

Liefeld, Walter L. "Transfiguration." In *Dictionary of Jesus and the Gospels*, edited by Joel B. Green, Scot McKnight and I. Howard Marshall, pp. 834-41. Downers Grove, Ill.: InterVarsity Press, 1992.

McGuckin, John Anthony. *The Transfiguration of Christ in Scripture and Tradition.* Lewiston, N.Y.: Edwin Mellen, 1987.

Murphy-O'Connor, Jerome. "What Really Happened at the Transfiguration?" *Bible Review* 3, no. 3 (1987): 8-21.

Ramsey, Arthur Michael. *The Glory of God and the Transfiguration of Christ.* London: Longmans, Green, 1949.

Stein, Robert H. "Is the Transfiguration (Mark 9:2-8) a Misplaced Resurrection-Account?" *Journal of Biblical Literature* 95 (1976): 79-96.

13
THE TRIUMPHAL
ENTRY
Israel's King
Enters Jerusalem

AFTER THE EVENTS ASSOCIATED WITH CAESAREA PHILIPPI AND THE transfiguration, Jesus led his disciples toward Jerusalem. For Jesus the crowning event of his mission was much nearer than a superficial reading of the Gospels might suggest. As already pointed out (see chapter twelve under "From Here to Jerusalem"), the Evangelists placed at this point in their Gospels various collections of traditions. This gives the impression that a longer period of time transpired before Jesus' arrival in Jerusalem. That is especially true of Luke, who placed his larger collection of the Q material (Lk 9:51—18:14) at this point. With the triumphal entry, the Evangelists now began focusing their attention on the events of passion week. Six of Mark's sixteen chapters (11—16) are devoted to this.

The accounts in Mark and Matthew suggest that the route Jesus took to Jerusalem was along the eastern side of the Jordan River (Mk 10:1; Mt 19:1) via Jericho (Mk 10:46; Mt 20:29; compare Lk 18:35). Luke suggests that part of this journey went through Samaria as well (Lk 9:52; compare also Lk 17:11). From Jericho (ten miles northwest of the Dead Sea and

825 feet below sea level) they traveled up the steep desert road called "The Ascent of Blood" some fourteen miles to Jerusalem (2,500 feet above sea level). During this period Jesus continued to minister to the needs of the people and his disciples. For the latter, this involved continued teaching concerning his coming passion (Mk 9:31; 10:32-34, 45). For the former, it involved continued teaching and healing.

The Event As Understood by Jesus
For the Gospel writers, Jesus' entry into Jerusalem was of great importance. That is evident because it is one of the few incidents from the life of Jesus recorded in all four Gospels. The Synoptic Gospels give the impression that the events associated with Jesus' triumphal entry took place immediately upon Jesus' arrival at Jerusalem. John, however, suggests that Jesus came to Bethany first (compare Jn 10:40; 11:1, 6-7, 17) and then stayed in a nearby area before his entry into Jerusalem (Jn 11:54—12:19). John furthermore indicates that some of the enthusiasm that greeted Jesus at the triumphal entry was elicited by the recent miracle of raising Lazarus from the dead (Jn 12:9). If, as will be suggested, the use of a colt to ride into Jerusalem was prearranged by Jesus, this lends additional support to the view that Jesus did not enter Jerusalem on the same day he left Jericho.

Jesus' entrance into Jerusalem is associated with several geographical designations: Bethphage, Bethany and the Mount of Olives. The Mount of Olives consists of a ridge of summits, the tallest of which is about 3,000 feet above sea level. It lies directly east of Jerusalem and is separated from it by the Kidron Valley. The exact locations of Bethphage and Bethany are uncertain. Some suggest that Bethphage was located on the eastern side of the Mount of Olives about a half-mile below the summit and that Bethany was still farther east, about two miles from Jerusalem.

On the day Jesus entered Jerusalem, he sent two disciples ahead to an unnamed village to find a colt on which no one had ever ridden. They were to untie it and bring it to Jesus. If those present asked what they were doing, they were simply to reply, "The Lord needs it and will send it back here immediately" (Mk 11:3). Upon arriving in the village they found the colt, just as Jesus said. As they untied it, they were asked what they were doing, again just as Jesus said. They replied as Jesus directed and were permitted to take the colt.

A great deal of discussion has taken place over exactly how to understand this incident. Is this to be understood primarily as an example of Jesus' supernatural foreknowledge of events? Several other events in the life of Jesus indicate that he possessed such a foreknowledge, as for example in his passion predictions. Do we have another example of such foreknowledge here? Or is this to be understood as a prearranged event? In other words, did Jesus arrange beforehand for the colt to be left at a designated place so that he could ride it into Jerusalem?

The strongest argument in favor of the latter is the fact that supernaturally knowing that an unridden colt was tied up in the neighboring village does not explain what happened when the disciples untied it. Why would those who were present have allowed the disciples to untie and take the colt? Foreknowledge of the colt's presence does not explain it. If Jesus had prearranged this, however, it is understandable. When asked why they were untying the colt, the two disciples simply said, "The Lord needs it," and this satisfied the questioners. Their response was something like "Oh, okay." This suggests that here, as in the case of finding a prepared upper room for the Last Supper, Jesus had prearranged what was about to take place. Attempts have been made to explain the answer of the two disciples as implying that the "Lord" referred to in their reply was the human owner of the colt and that his owner, a follower of Jesus, wanted them to bring the colt to him. Such an explanation, however, does violence to the authorial intention of all the Synoptic texts. For the Gospel writers, it is clear that "Lord" here can only refer to the "Lord Jesus," not the human owner of the colt.

The suggestion that Jesus had prearranged for an unridden donkey to be prepared for his use carries significant christological implications. The attempt to explain what took place as being due to weariness on the part of Jesus completely misunderstands the event. From Bethany to Jerusalem is about two miles. It is difficult to believe that the Jesus who walked throughout Galilee to Tyre, to Caesarea Philippi, down to Jericho and up to Jerusalem had all of a sudden become tired. The Gospel writers want us to understand that Jesus consciously sought to enter Jerusalem not on foot, as other pilgrims did, but in this specific manner.

Attempts to see the triumphal entry as a later messianic myth created by the early church as they sought to fulfill Old Testament messianic prophecies are unsatisfactory. The reason for this is that the earliest account (Mark's) lacks any explicit reference to the quotation in Zechariah 9:9, which is supposed to have provided the basis for this so-called mythical account. This would require that the source that supposedly gave birth to the myth, the Old Testament quotation from Zechariah, was very early omitted from the story. (Luke also omits it.) Later, in Matthew 21:5 and John 12:14-15, the Old Testament quotation supposedly resurfaced.

It seems simpler to see in this event a conscious and symbolic act of Jesus revealing that he understood himself to be the Christ, Israel's long-awaited king. Yet in contrast to the messianic king of the *Psalms of Solomon* (17:21-46), he came unrecognized in lowliness and meekness. Even his own disciples did not fully understand the significance of what had happened (Jn 12:16).

It was an unridden donkey that was brought to Jesus. Because of its never having been ridden, it was fit for the sacred task it was about to perform (compare 1 Sam 6:7). Upon its arrival the disciples placed their cloaks on it. Whether they did so in order to make a kind of "saddle" for Jesus or because they purposely were treating him as a royal messianic figure is difficult to say. The latter is not impossible in light of the exuberance of the moment. The spreading of garments and branches on the road (Mk 11:8; compare 2 Kings 9:13) suggests this. The Gospel accounts are probably best interpreted as understanding this as a messianic act, whether consciously or unconsciously done by the disciples. (Matthew's account speaks of the disciples bringing two animals to Jesus, a colt and the foal of a donkey, and his sitting on "them" [Mt 21:7]. It is unlikely that Matthew wanted his readers to believe that Jesus sat on both animals at once, so the "them" is best interpreted as referring to the garments mentioned in the preceding part of the verse.)

As they descended the Mount of Olives toward Jerusalem, people brought palms with them. (It is from the reference to palms in Jn 12:13 that the name "Palm Sunday" comes.) These were carried by the crowds. There has been some debate as to whether palm trees were native to Jerusalem, due to its cold winter climate. Yet on other occasions palms seem to have been available in Jerusalem (1 Macc 13:51). It is quite possible that at least on the warmer, eastern slopes of the Mount of Olives palm trees grew. Their presence gave a royal and messianic quality to the event, for they were a sign of Jewish nationalism, especially Maccabean nationalism, and they appear on the coins minted during the Bar Kokhba revolt in A.D. 132-35.

As they proceeded, Jesus was greeted with shouts from Psalm 118, a psalm used to greet pilgrims during such festivals as the Feast of Tabernacles and the Passover: "Hosanna! Blessed is the one who comes in the name of the Lord! Blessed is the coming kingdom of our ancestor David! Hosanna in the highest heaven!" (Mk 11:9-10). The term *Hosanna* is literally a prayer for help—"Save us [please]!" Yet as time went on, it became a greeting much like our present use of the expression "Praise the Lord" (compare *m. Pesaḥim* 5:7; 10:5-7). Luke understood it as a greeting of praise. Consequently he omitted it and introduced the words of this pilgrim psalm with "the whole multitude of the disciples began to praise God joyfully with a loud voice" (Lk 19:37).

The fact that this is a pilgrim psalm and was shouted to pilgrims in general explains how Jesus could receive this kind of a welcome into Jerusalem and not arouse Roman reaction or suspicion. No doubt the welcome given to Jesus was more enthusiastic than that given other pilgrims (Lk 19:39-40). After all, he was a well-known teacher and was viewed by many as a prophet (Mt 21:11). For some of his followers who made up the crowd, Jesus was not a mere pilgrim coming to Jerusalem, but "the" Pilgrim, their Teacher, their Master and Lord. There may even have been some who entertained ideas that he might indeed be "the coming one." (Compare how this expression has messianic overtones in Mt 11:3 and 23:39.)

For Jesus this entry was indeed messianic in nature. Intentionally he arranged for an unridden colt to be prepared for him. Its virginal nature indicates that the colt would serve a special use. It was fit for Israel's King. Intentionally he entered the holy city in fulfillment of Zechariah 9:9, for he was Israel's Messiah. As he entered Jerusalem, he was greeted, as noted above, with a traditional pilgrim psalm. Even those who greeted him enthusiastically in this manner did not truly understand what was taking place, for Jesus was not just a pilgrim or even a special pilgrim. He was rather "the one who came in the name of the Lord." What was implicit in the original scene the Gospel writers later tended to make explicit. Matthew 21:5 and John 12:15 do so by quoting Zechariah 9:9, whereas Luke 19:38 and John 12:13 do so by adding "the king" and "the King of Israel."

The Event As Understood by the Crowd

For the crowds what happened at the triumphal entry was understood differently. For them the event was more like a natural and traditional welcome of a famous pilgrim into Jerusalem. The traditional greeting of Psalm 118 was shouted to Jesus and those coming with him. Among the enthusiastic crowds coming with Jesus were his own disciples and followers, along with numerous other Galilean pilgrims. Their positive attitude and devotion toward Jesus added to the fervor and spirit of the occasion. The placing of cloaks and branches on the road before him was certainly a greater act of welcome than a normal pilgrim received.

In a sense, then, those who claim that the triumphal entry was nothing more than an enthusiastic welcome of a famous pilgrim that was later interpreted as a messianic event in fulfillment of the Old Testament are partially correct. In the minds of most of Jesus' audience that day, this event was essentially a pilgrim's welcome of Jesus of Nazareth. Yet for some of Jesus' followers there was something "more" about this event. What this "more" involved, however, was unclear. Even though the crowd in John's Gospel says, "Hosanna! Blessed is the one who comes in the name of the Lord—the King of Israel!" (Jn 12:13), the Evangelist goes on to say, "His disciples did not understand these things at first; but when Jesus was glorified, then they remembered that these things had been written of him and had been done to him" (v. 16). The other Gospel writers also reveal this ambiguity concerning what took place.

What Jesus intended was indeed messianic and fulfilled Zechariah 9:9 (Mt 21:4-5). But only in Luke 19:38 and John 12:13 is a clear messianic title shouted out during the event, and John, as we have mentioned, points out that the disciples themselves did not fully understand everything that was involved in this event. Thus if some of the crowd that day (no doubt a minority) saw this event as messianic, most did not. In their minds, what was taking place was a fervent and enthusiastic pilgrim's welcome of the prophet Jesus of Nazareth into Jerusalem.

Conclusion

For Jesus the triumphal entry was a carefully orchestrated messianic act. It was a parabolic act that could be perceived by those with eyes to see but that was concealed for others. His messianic entry was shrouded in the same type of secrecy that characterized his parabolic teaching concerning the kingdom of God and his use of the title "Son of Man." In conscious fulfillment of the Old Testament prophecy found in Zechariah 9:9, he arranged for an unridden donkey to be ready for him. Having fetched it, he rode into Jerusalem. He did not walk into the city as other pilgrims did; he rode. Yet he mounted no warrior stallion, for he was meek and humble. He rode into Jerusalem not to mount a kingly throne but to fulfill his Father's mission. In majesty he rode on—to die!

The crowds knew little, if any, of this. The festive occasion and the coming of a famous celebrity worked together to inspire an enthusiastic pilgrim's welcome. No doubt his own followers and the crowds from Galilee added greatly to this enthusiasm. The greeting of this pilgrim psalm was more fitting than realized, however. He who "comes in the name of the Lord" was indeed coming to "save" (hosanna). Yet here, as at Caesarea Philippi, the confession or greeting of the people was not understood. Jesus was greeted as "the prophet Jesus from Nazareth in Galilee" (Mt 21:11), not as Messiah and King. The people's understanding and messianic hopes were radically different; they could not understand this event. No doubt this lay within the divine will. The consequences of an open messianic welcome for Jesus would have brought about an immediate confrontation with Rome. Rome could not tolerate any Messiah or King of Israel. There was no room for both Caesar and God's Messiah.

At the trial, when witnesses were sought to condemn Jesus and justify Roman political action, no mention was made of the triumphal entry. Clearly in the minds of Rome and the Jewish leadership this event was not understood as a messianic claim or challenge. This clearly refutes those who would interpret Jesus' entry into Jerusalem as a political act possessing a revolutionary and Zealotlike purpose. We also should not understand the triumphal entry as a later mythical legend created under the influence of the church's study of Zechariah 9:9. Apparently Zechariah 9:9 was not interpreted messianically in Judaism until the fourth century of our era.

The triumphal entry was a real event that Jesus had purposely arranged and carried out in fulfillment of his divine mission. Within a short time the enthusiasm greeting Jesus on this day would turn to a more hostile "Crucify him!" (Mk 15:13-14). Yet this was his day. It was fitting to receive this enthusiastic welcome. In fact, if the crowds and disciples had not so responded, if they had remained silent, "the stones would [have] shout[ed] out" (Lk 19:40).

References

Catchpole, D. R. "The 'Triumphal' Entry." In *Jesus and the Politics of His Day,* edited by E. Bammel and C. F. D. Moule, pp. 319-34. Cambridge: Cambridge University Press, 1984.

Gundry, Robert H. *Mark: A Commentary on His Apology for the Cross,* pp. 623-34. Grand Rapids, Mich.: Eerdmans, 1993.

Guthrie, Donald. *Jesus the Messiah,* pp. 267-70. Grand Rapids, Mich.: Zondervan, 1972.

Harrison, Everett F. *A Short Life of Christ,* pp. 165-75. Grand Rapids, Mich.: Eerdmans, 1968.

Losie, Lynn A. "Triumphal Entry." In *Dictionary of Jesus and the Gospels,* edited by Joel B. Green, Scot McKnight and I. Howard Marshall, pp. 854-59. Downers Grove, Ill.: InterVarsity Press, 1992.

Sanders, E. P. *Jesus and Judaism,* pp. 306-8. Philadelphia: Fortress, 1985.

14
THE CLEANSING
OF THE TEMPLE
God's House—
a Den of Thieves

I N THE SYNOPTIC GOSPELS THE CLEANSING OF THE TEMPLE IS INTIMATELY associated with the triumphal entry. In Mark it takes place "on the following day" (Mk 11:12). In Matthew and Luke it takes place immediately following the triumphal entry. (Compare "Then Jesus entered the temple and drove out . . ." [Mt 21:12] and "Then he entered the temple and began to drive out . . ." [Lk 19:45].) It may be that Mark intentionally placed the cleansing of the temple in its present position to help the reader understand how to interpret this event. On several occasions Mark "sandwiched" two separate events in his Gospel (compare, for example, Mk 3:22-30 between vv. 19-21 and 31-35; 5:25-34 between vv. 21-24 and 35-43; 6:14-29 between vv. 6-13 and 30ff.; 14:3-9 between vv. 1-2 and 10-11). As we shall see, Mark "sandwiched" the cleansing of the temple (Mk 11:15-19) between the cursing of the fig tree (vv. 12-14 and 20-25) so that his readers would understand that the "cleansing" was not simply an act of purification or reformation but one of judgment.

The Problem of John's Account

A greater problem arises when one compares the account of the cleansing in the Synoptic Gospels with the same account in John. The importance of this incident in the life of Jesus is witnessed to by the fact that it is one of the few events recorded in all four Gospels. The location of this story in John 2, however, immediately raises a problem: the cleansing of the temple appears at the beginning of Jesus' ministry, whereas in the Synoptic Gospels it appears during the last week.

It has been pointed out on several occasions that the canonical Gospels were not written primarily with chronological considerations in mind. Mark (and Matthew and Luke, who used Mark) organized his Gospel geographically. Jesus' ministry in Galilee and the traditions associated with his ministry there occur at the beginning of the Gospel, and his ministry in Jerusalem occurs at the end. Since Jesus' mission in Jerusalem begins at Mark 11:1, the cleansing of the temple can only be located somewhere after that verse. For John, who has Jesus traveling back and forth from Galilee to Jerusalem, the cleansing of the temple could be inserted in any of several places.

It has been popular in harmonizing the Gospel accounts to speak of two separate cleansings of the temple. One supposedly occurred early in Jesus' ministry (so John) and the other at the end (so the Synoptic Gospels). This explanation is certainly possible. Two factors, however, argue against it. One is the close similarity between the accounts (selling sacrificial animals and overturning the tables of the money changers). Another is that, in John as well as in the Synoptic Gospels, there is closely associated with this event the question of Jesus' authority (compare Mk 11:27-33 and Jn 2:18-22). A significant difference, however, between the accounts is that John alone refers to Jesus' "making a whip" (Jn 2:15) to drive out those buying and selling in the temple.

If, as most scholars believe, there was one cleansing of the temple, it more likely occurred at the end of Jesus' ministry. Possibly John placed this incident in the life of Jesus at the beginning of his Gospel so that it could serve as a typical example of the hostility Jesus faced from the religious leadership. Thus its location in John may be due primarily to literary considerations. By placing the account at this point in his Gospel, John provided his readers with a helpful preview of what took place in his ministry. As a result, it is evident from the very beginning that the death of Jesus was inevitable because of the hostility of official Judaism toward him.

The Cleansing of the Temple

The temple of Jerusalem in Jesus' day was a magnificent structure. Bordered on the east and west by the Kidron and Tyropean valleys, on the south by the old city of David, and to the north by the fortress of Antonia, the temple occupied an area of more than 170,000 square yards. The area did not form a perfect square but was trapezoidal in shape, with the north and west sides being longer than the south and east.

The temple area was the largest such site in the ancient world. The platform was surrounded by massive walls that supported the large amount of material used to level the area as well as the great weight of the temple and its other structures. The walls descended more than fifty feet below the level of the street and rested on bedrock. They also towered more than eighty feet above street level. Many of the stones used in the wall were enormous. Some of the stones visible today are forty feet long and weigh more than a hundred tons. Josephus mentions even larger stones used in the construction of the temple, some as large as forty-five by five by six cubits (*War* 5.5.6 [5.224]). Elsewhere he describes them as twenty-five by eight by twelve cubits (*Ant.* 15.11.3 [15.392]). (A cubit was about eighteen inches.) Even the lesser dimension would mean that these stones were enormous in size.

The temple of Jesus' day was the result of continual work and alteration. After the Solomonic temple was destroyed by the Babylonians in 587 B.C., it was rebuilt by the returning exiles led by Zerubbabel in 538 B.C. This temple was continually modified, but the most influential and monumental work occurred under the rule of Herod the Great. In 20 B.C. he began a massive rebuilding of the entire platform, walls and temple. Some ten thousand workmen, a thousand wagons and a thousand priests were involved in the rebuilding (Josephus *Ant.* 15.11.2 [15.390]). These priests were specially trained in various construction techniques so that they could perform the necessary work in the sacred areas of the temple, which were off limits to the general public. Work continued on the temple after Herod's death until shortly before its destruction in A.D. 70.

The temple was mostly covered with gold. What was not covered consisted of bright white stone. The roof contained gold spikes to prevent the birds from defiling it. In bright sunlight the temple reflected the sun so brilliantly that one could not look directly at it. The magnificence of the temple was such that it could be compared favorably with any of the seven wonders of the ancient world.

Numerous gates gave access to the temple area. From the south were Huldah Gates 1 and 2; on the north side was the North Gate; from the west were what is now called Warren's Gate, Barclay's Gate, Wilson's Arch and the West Gate; the Golden Gate gave access from the east. Each gate led people into a large area called the Court of the Gentiles. This made up most of the temple area. Around the walls of the temple were covered walkways or porticoes. In the middle of the temple area was a stone fence or balustrade that led into the temple proper. This fence marked the end of the Court of the Gentiles and separated it from the inner court of the temple. The stone balustrade was about four and a half feet high. All the gates leading through the balustrade into the inner court of the temple had inscriptions written in Greek and Latin warning non-Jews that they were prohibited upon pain of death from entering.

Upon passing through the balustrade one encountered a tier of fourteen steps that led to another wall. This wall was more than thirty-five feet high. Nine gates led through it into another courtyard area. The eastern third of this courtyard area was called the Women's Court. The larger western part of the courtyard was called the Court of Israel (the men's court). Even as Gentiles were not allowed into the inner court of the temple, so women were not allowed into the Court of Israel. From the Court of Israel one then entered the Court of the Priests, which contained the altar of burnt offering and the temple proper. The latter, proceeding from east to west, contained the porch leading into the temple, the holy place and the holy of holies.

As Jesus entered the temple area, probably through the Golden Gate facing the Mount of Olives, he saw in the Court of the Gentiles the selling of sacrificial animals and the exchanging of money. Each year around the time of the Passover, every adult Jewish male had to pay a temple tax of a half-shekel (compare Mt 17:24-27). This was based on Exodus 30:13-15:

> This is what each one who is registered shall give: half a shekel according to the shekel of the sanctuary (the shekel is twenty gerahs), half a shekel as an offering to the LORD. Each one who is registered,

from twenty years old and upward, shall give the LORD's offering. The rich shall not give more, and the poor shall not give less, than the half shekel.

Since much of the coinage of ancient times possessed idolatrous images and terminology, the only coin that was acceptable for the temple tax was the Tyrian silver half-shekel (technically the silver didrachma of Tyre). To facilitate the paying of the tax, on the fifteenth day of the month preceding the Passover (the month of Adar), money-changing tables were set up in the provinces surrounding Jerusalem, and on the twenty-fifth they were set up in the Court of the Gentiles in the temple (*m. Šeqalim* 1:3). Needless to say, the changing of money was not done on a "nonprofit" basis (*m. Šeqalim* 1:6). A premium of 4-8 percent was charged.

Jesus also saw the selling of sacrificial animals within the same court. Viewed from one perspective, this, along with the exchanging of money, was a service for pilgrims coming to Jerusalem, albeit for a charge (*m. Bekorot* 4.5-6). The bringing of the appropriate sacrificial animal would be a tedious process, and even if a person brought his own sacrifice, this would have to be checked by the priests to ensure that it did not possess any blemish. And what would the owner then do if the animal brought to be sacrificed was unacceptable? Thus the selling of sacrificial animals and the exchanging of money could be seen as an attempt by the priest-hood to make the temple more "user friendly." From a different perspective, however, it could be seen as the transformation of the temple from a place of worship to a kind of priestly bazaar. Far from assisting the temple in functioning as a house of prayer for all people, the smell of the animals, their refuse, their cries and so on detracted attention from the God-ordained purpose of the temple.

There is also evidence that for the priestly leadership such "commercial" activities were quite profitable. The Talmud records an incident where an outrageous price was being charged for sacrificial pigeons:

> Once in Jerusalem a pair of doves cost a golden *denar*. Rabban Simeon b. Gamaliel said: By this Temple! I will not suffer the night to pass by before they cost but a [silver] *denar*. He went into the court and taught: If a woman suffered five miscarriages that were not in doubt or five issues that were not in doubt, she need bring but one offering, and she may then eat of the animal-offerings; and she is not bound to offer the other offerings. And the same day the price of a pair of doves stood

at a quarter-*denar* each. (*m. Keritot* 1.7)
This incident indicates that at times the cost of purchasing sacrifices in the temple was excessive. One golden denar was worth some twenty-five silver denars. The incident also reveals the antagonism of at least some Pharisees toward the Sadducean priesthood and toward their practice of selling sacrifices. Consequently Rabbi Simeon b. Gamaliel pronounced a ruling in which he reinterpreted the law involving sacrifices so that fewer sacrifices would be needed. The result was a drastic drop in the "stock" market. The incident also suggests that Jesus' action in cleansing the temple could well have found support from Pharisees who were present.

What Jesus saw in the temple distressed him. Far from fulfilling its intended usage and being "a house of prayer for all the nations," the selling of sacrificial animals and exchanging of money had made the temple "a den of robbers" (Mk 11:17). In so describing the temple Jesus quoted from Isaiah and Jeremiah:

> And the foreigners who join themselves to the LORD, to minister to him, to love the name of the LORD, and to be his servants, all who keep the sabbath, and do not profane it, and hold fast my covenant—these I will bring to my holy mountain, and make them joyful in my house of prayer; their burnt offerings and their sacrifices will be accepted on my altar; for my house shall be called a house of prayer for all peoples. (Is 56:6-7)

> Has this house, which is called by my name, become a den of robbers in your sight? (Jer 7:11)

(Matthew and Luke omit this double quotation. That may be because they wrote their Gospels after the destruction of the temple and thus saw no possible fulfillment of these passages.)

Some have suggested that the term *robbers* in Mark 11:17 refers to revolutionary or nationalistic rebels and that Jesus was complaining that a Zealotlike mentality was dominating the temple. Yet this is precisely the term found in Jeremiah 7:11 and thus should not be pressed. Within the present context there is nothing that deals with political revolution. What is in the forefront is the profiteering going on in the temple. Thus the term *robbers* is best understood as referring to the thievery involved in the selling of sacrifices and exchanging of coins.

In righteous indignation Jesus cleansed the temple. He interrupted the business of changing money by overturning the tables of the money changers. He chased away those in the business of selling sacrifices. He even chased away those who were seeking to buy sacrifices (note "those who were selling and those who were buying" [Mk 11:15]), for they too contributed to this shame. In the Johannine account the intensity of Jesus' action is described by his making a whip out of rope and using it as a kind of scourge to chase away the guilty (Jn 2:15).

Certainly the picture of Jesus given in the Gospel accounts is far from the weak, effeminate Christ found in so much Christian art. In this scene Jesus is portrayed as God's righteous servant. Armed with right, empowered with zeal for God, confident of the correctness of his actions, he was irresistible. No one could stand against his prophetic action, for his moral power, virtue and holy action melted away the will of any who might seek to resist. If temple and Roman officials witnessed this activity in one part of the temple, they did not see it as a major threat to the order of the temple or as an attempt to rally people to rebel. Perhaps some Jews, like Rabbi Simeon b. Gamaliel, might even have agreed with Jesus' action.

It would be wrong, however, to exaggerate the extent of Jesus' action in cleansing the temple. The Gospel writers focus their attention on this event because of its theological importance. Yet only a small part of the massive temple area was affected. The incident was probably on a smaller scale than a simple reading of the Gospels might suggest.

The Meaning of This Event
The issue of exactly what took place at the cleansing of the temple and whether it was in fact a "cleansing" is greatly debated. How the Evangelists interpreted this event is easier to understand.

The understanding of the Evangelists. The Evangelists' understanding of this incident can best be seen by the way Mark has "sandwiched" this event in the middle of his account of Jesus' cursing of the fig tree:

> On the following day, when they came from Bethany, he was hungry. Seeing in the distance a fig tree in leaf, he went to see whether perhaps he would find anything on it. When he came to it, he found nothing but leaves, for it was not the season for figs. He said to it, "May no one ever eat fruit from you again." And his disciples heard it. (Mk 11:12-14)

After then recounting the story of the cleansing (Mk 11:15-19), Mark completes the story of the cursing of the fig tree (vv. 20-24). By sandwiching the cleansing of the temple between the cursing accounts, Mark indicates to his readers that they should interpret the cleansing of the temple in light of what happened to the fig tree. The cursing of the fig tree was not an example of proper horticultural practice. No, it was an acted-out parable. Even as a fig tree (a well-known Old Testament symbol for Israel) that did not bear fruit was judged, so also the temple, which represented official Judaism, was judged because it did not bear fruit.

To assist his readers in understanding the judgment aspect, Mark added the comment "for it was not the season for figs" (Mk 11:13). This comment has caused great confusion for interpreters. Why should a fig tree be cursed for not having fruit when it was not the time for fruit? This difficulty is alleviated when we understand it as a comment to the readers, calling them not to misunderstand what took place at the temple. By this comment Mark is saying, "What took place had nothing to do with the issue of a fig tree bearing fruit. It was a parabolic act of Jesus. You should understand this event in light of the cursing of the fig tree. It should be interpreted as follows: The Son of God came to the temple and, instead of finding fruit and faithful worship, he found nothing but empty form, mere leaves of thievery; thus he judged official Israel and the temple." Mark reinforced this theme of judgment by the context in which he placed it, which includes the parable of the wicked tenants in Mark 12:1-11 and the eschatological discourse involving the destruction of Jerusalem and its temple (Mk 13).

The understanding of Jesus. Numerous explanations exist as to exactly what Jesus was doing when he cleansed the temple. Some of the more important ones are as follows:

□ Jesus intended this act to be purely religious and reformatory, seeking to cleanse the temple of its impurities by removing the commercial pollution and thievery practiced in the selling of sacrifices and exchanging of coins.

□ Jesus intended to protect Gentile access to the temple and to show that the time had arrived for Jewish-Gentile barriers to be broken down so that the full inclusion of Gentiles into the worship of Israel could take place.

□ Jesus sought to end the entire sacrificial system in favor of a more spiritual form of worship.

□ Jesus prophesied by this action the forthcoming destruction of the temple and its future restoration.

☐ Jesus wanted to make a political statement and overthrow the Jewish religious leadership as well as the Roman government, in effect calling for a revolution.

Some of these suggestions have little merit. The third was popular within nineteenth-century theological liberalism but finds no support in the Gospels. On the contrary, Jesus told a cleansed leper to go to the priest and offer the required sacrifice (Mk 1:40-45). He told ten lepers on another occasion to do the same (Lk 17:11-19). He assumed the continuing offering of sacrifices by his followers (Mt 5:23-24). He told his disciples to pay the temple tax (Mt 17:24-27). There is no evidence that Jesus was opposed to the sacrificial system. For him the temple was a holy place (Mk 11:16), and the essence of the temple's worship was the offering of sacrifices to God.

Similarly, nothing in the cleansing accounts suggests that Jesus was attempting to bring about a political revolution. The cleansing of he temple was not an act of rebellion. If it were, one would have expected the Roman soldiers stationed in the Fortress of Antonia and the temple police to have stepped in. Most probably it was seen by them as an intrareligious Jewish squabble in which they should not intervene. Furthermore, one would expect that if Jesus' intention had been to incite a rebellion this would have been raised at his trial. Yet despite all the attempts to find evidence against him during his trial, nothing was ever said concerning his cleansing of the temple. Whereas some scholars argue that the cleansing of the temple was perhaps the crucial event that led to Jesus' death, the complete lack of any mention of it in the trial narrative refutes it. Surely, if it were the major reason for Jesus' trial, one would expect to read about it in the Gospel accounts. The event itself must have seemed so innocuous and nonpolitical to both the Jewish and Roman leadership that it was not even considered worthy of mention.

The second explanation of the cleansing as an attempt to make Judaism more open and friendly to Gentiles lacks any supporting evidence in the account and the other Gospel traditions. A time was coming when Jesus would tell his followers to go into the Gentile world and preach the gospel there, but he told this to his followers only—not to official Judaism. Such an explanation appears to be a modern politically correct drive for inclusivism, even as the explanation that Jesus was seeking to do away with the sacrificial system represents the value system of nine-teenth-century liberalism.

To understand Jesus' motivation for cleansing the temple, we must observe that in all four Gospel accounts it is intimately associated with casting out those selling sacrificial animals and exchanging money. Jesus was not opposed to these activities in themselves. On the contrary, by his actions and teachings Jesus supported the sacrificial system. Jesus did not seek to cleanse the temple of sacrifices. Rather, he cleansed it of abuse. The temple was not to be a "marketplace" (Jn 2:16). Along with this commercializing of God's house, Jesus was aware that dishonesty was involved in these activities. The temple had not only become a mar-ketplace but a dishonest "den of robbers" (Mk 11:17). Jesus' comment is best understood as his assessment of the financial dealings involved in the selling of sacrifices and the exchanging of coins.

There is a sense, then, that Jesus did indeed intend to purify his Fa-ther's house. Mark includes an interesting comment that affirms this: "He would not allow anyone to carry anything through the temple" (Mk 11:16). Jesus taught that it was wrong to use the temple as a shortcut for going from one part of the city to another. The house of God was sacred and was to be used for its intended and holy purpose of worship. He did not, therefore, see a straight line through the temple court as the shortest distance between two points but as disrespect for God's house. (For an interesting parallel in the Mishna, see *m. Berakot* 9.5.)

On the other hand, it appears that Jesus' action involved more than a mere desire to purify and cleanse the temple. It was also a parabolic act signifying that judgment was coming upon the temple and the nation. In John the cleansing of the temple is closely associated with Jesus' predic-tion of the destruction of the temple: "The Jews then said to him, 'What sign can you show us for doing this [cleansing of the temple]?' Jesus answered them, 'Destroy this temple, and in three days I will raise it up' " (Jn 2:18-19). This same saying is found at the trial of Jesus (Mk 14:57-59), at his crucifixion (Mk 15:29-30) and in Acts 6:13-15, where witnesses refer to these words of Jesus. Other sayings of Jesus also refer to this forthcoming judgment of the temple (Mk 12:1-12; 13:1-23; Lk 19:41-44).

Like the Old Testament prophets, Jesus saw in the priestly supervision of the temple a corruption of God's intended purpose (compare Jer 8:10; 14:18; 23:11, 33-34; 32:31-32; 34:18-19; Lam 4:13; Ezek 22:26; Zeph 3:4;

Zech 14:21; compare also *Testament of Levi* 14:1-8; Josephus *Ant.* 20.8.8 [20.181]; *Targum of Jeremiah* 7:1-11). And like the Old Testament prophets Jesus prophesied of its destruction (compare Jer 4:5—5:31; 7:14; 25:1-38; 26:1-24; Ezek 4:1—7:27; Mic 3:9-12). Like the Old Testament prophets he also illustrated this judgment by a symbolic act, both in cleansing the temple and by the cursing of the fig tree (compare Jer 19:10; 27:2-7; Ezek 4:9-17). Jesus' prediction, however, goes beyond that of the Old Testament prophets. Jesus did not simply predict the destruction of the temple and Jerusalem. As in the cursing of the fig tree, so here also Jesus brought about that cursing/judgment. He himself would see that it happened. He had passed judgment on the situation and would bring it about. Unlike the Old Testament prophets, however, Jesus predicted the destruction of the temple without hinting that a new temple would be built to take its place. Through his ministry such a temple would be unnecessary (Jn 4:21-23).

Conclusion

The cleansing of the temple is best understood as a symbolic act of Jesus in which he sought to purify the temple and at the same time proclaim divine judgment on it. It was a purifying act in that he rebuked the commercialization of God's house. The temple was not meant to be a stock market or bank exchange. It was not meant to be a profit-making enterprise for the high priests. Jesus' action, consequently, must be understood, in part at least, as a cleansing. His reference to the temple as a "den of robbers" (Mk 11:17) and his prohibition of using the temple as a shortcut (Mk 11:16) demonstrate that.

Yet the cleansing involved more. It was a prophetic act as well. Unlike the Old Testament prophets, however, Jesus did not merely predict the future destruction of the temple. His actions were not simply a prognostication of what would soon happen to the temple. He would bring about its destruction. He would cause it to take place.

The christological implications of Jesus' cleansing of the temple were apparent not only to the Evangelists but also to those who witnessed this event. Consequently they asked, "By what authority are you doing these things? Who gave you this authority to do them?" (Mk 11:28). "What sign can you show us for doing this?" (Jn 2:18).

Jesus' sense of authority over the temple stemmed from his unique relationship to the God of the temple. Earlier he had told his parents, "Did you not know that I must be in my Father's house?" (Lk 2:49). The cleansing of the temple reveals that the Son of Man has divine authority on earth. He claimed authority to forgive sins (Mk 2:10), and he demonstrated this by healing (Mk 2:11-12). He claimed authority over Satan's realm and the demonic (Mk 3:27), and he demonstrated this by casting out demons. He claimed authority over life and death (Jn 11:25-26), and he demonstrated this by raising the dead (Mk 5:21-43; Lk 7:11-15; Jn 11:43-44). Here by this action Jesus claimed authority to purify the temple and to pronounce judgment on it, and he would demonstrate this by the events of A.D. 70.

References

Barrett, Charles Kingsley. "The House of Prayer and the Den of Thieves." In *Jesus und Paulus*, edited by E. Earle Ellis, pp. 13-20. Göttingen, Germany: Vandenhoeck & Rupprecht, 1978.

Chilton, Bruce. *The Temple of Jesus: His Sacrificial Program Within a Cultural History of Sacrifice*. University Park: Pennsylvania State University Press, 1992.

Eppstein, Victor. "The Historicity of the Gospel Account of the Cleansing of the Temple." *Zeitschrift für die neutestamentliche Wissenschaft* 55 (1964): 42-58.

Evans, Craig A. "Jesus' Action in the Temple: Cleansing or Portent of Destruction?" *Catholic Biblical Quarterly* 51 (1989): 237-70.

Gaston, Lloyd. *No Stone on Another: Studies in the Significance of the Fall of Jerusalem in the Synoptic Gospels*. Leiden: E. J. Brill, 1970.

Herzog, W. R., II. "Temple Cleansing." In *Dictionary of Jesus and the Gospels*, edited by Joel B. Green, Scot McKnight and I. Howard Marshall, pp. 817-21. Downers Grove, Ill.: InterVarsity Press, 1992.

Horsley, Richard A. *Jesus and the Spiral of Violence: Popular Jewish Resistance in Roman Palestine*. San Francisco: Harper & Row, 1987.

Sanders, E. P. *Jesus and Judaism*, pp. 61-76. Philadelphia: Fortress, 1985.

15
THE LAST SUPPER
Jesus Looks
to the Future

IN THE DISCUSSION OF THE EVENTS SURROUNDING PALM SUNDAY AND Easter, we frequently find a detailed order of what took place during "holy week." A popular chronology for this period is as follows.

Palm Sunday   Jesus' entry into Jerusalem (Mk 11:1-11)

Monday   The cleansing of the temple (Mk 11:12-19)

Tuesday   Jesus teaches in the temple and answers questions
                (Mk 11:20—13:37); and Judas's plan to betray Jesus
                (Mk 14:1-11)

Wednesday   Jesus rests

Thursday   The Last Supper, Gethsemane, Judas's betrayal, Je-
                sus' arrest (Mk 14:12-52)

Friday   The trial, crucifixion and burial

Saturday   Jesus in the tomb

Easter Sunday   The resurrection

Although such a chronology is tidy and neat, when one looks more closely at it several problems arise. One of these problems was discussed in the last chapter: whereas in Mark the cleansing of the temple takes place on the day after Jesus' entry into Jerusalem, in Matthew and Luke it seems to take place on the same day. Another problem concerns whether Mark and the other Gospels intend to give a chronological description of this week in Jesus' life. It is likely that here, as elsewhere in the Gospels, the order is influenced more by topical than by chronological considerations. For example, the material in Mark 12:13-40 is similar in nature. It consists of controversy stories involving the Pharisees (vv. 13-17), Sadducees (vv. 18-27) and a scribe (vv. 28-34), followed by a counterquestion from Jesus (vv. 35-40). The same can be said concerning the unified nature of the eschatological material in Mark 13:3-37. Also, there are no explicit temporal designations between Mark 11:20 and 14:1. It is probably incorrect to assume that the material found between these two references all took place on the same day. Still another problem we encounter with respect to such a chronology is whether we are dealing with the Jewish reckoning of time (a day begins and ends at 6:00 p.m.) or a modern-day reckoning of time.

Basically the biblical writers want us to know several facts: Jesus' entry into Jerusalem took place shortly before his death and resurrection (the idea that this took place on a Sunday comes from Jn 12:1, 12); the Last Supper occurred just before the crucifixion (1 Cor 11:23); the crucifixion took place on Friday (Mk 15:42); and the resurrection was on a Sunday (Mk 16:1).

The Historical Setting
On the eve of the Passover Jesus sent two of his disciples (Peter and John, according to Lk 22:8) into Jerusalem to prepare the Passover meal. Jesus told them to look for a man carrying a jar of water and to follow him. They were then to ask the owner of the house this man entered if the

room was prepared for the "Teacher" and his disciples to eat the Passover. There they were to prepare for the celebration. •

Since carrying water was considered "women's work," a man doing this would be an unusual sight. The view that Jesus prearranged this meeting receives support from the simple mention of the "Teacher" to the owner and from the fact that a room was already prepared and awaiting their coming. Thus as in the fetching of the colt (see chapter thirteen, under "The Event As Understood by Jesus"), the arrangement for Jesus to eat the Passover with his disciples in this "upper room" (Mk 14:15 RSV) appears preplanned.

Peter and John were to prepare for the meal. Whether this involved the sacrificing and roasting of the Passover lamb as well as the collecting and preparation of the other parts of the meal is uncertain. The owner may already have done this. If so, the two disciples were to make certain that all was ready and to take care of anything that still needed to be done.

No reason is given for the secrecy in all this. Some have suggested that Jesus wanted to keep Judas from knowing beforehand where he would be during this time. In this way Jesus made certain that the betrayal would not take place until after he had shared the Last Supper with his disciples. (Note that the reference to Judas's seeking an opportunity to betray Jesus is recorded immediately before the instructions for the preparation of the Last Supper [Mk 14:11-12].) Others suggest that Jesus' great fame and popularity among the people required such secrecy. Only in this manner could he be alone with the disciples (compare Mk 3:20; 6:30-31). Both theories have merit, but we must acknowledge that we cannot be certain as to the exact reason for this secrecy.

John 13—17 records several additional incidents that took place during this meal. The setting and many of the activities referred to in these five chapters are quite similar to the accounts in the Synoptic Gospels: the material in John 13—17 takes place on the night of Jesus' betrayal (Jn 13:2; 18:1-12); there is a meal involved (Jn 13:1-4); the meal was associated in some way with the Passover (Jn 13:1); Peter's threefold denial is foretold (Jn 13:36-38); Jesus tells of his departure (Jn 14:1-4, 28; 16:16-24); and after the meal Jesus and the disciples leave for a garden across the Kidron Valley, namely, Gethsemane (Jn 18:1). These similarities suggest that John 13—17 took place during the night of the Last Supper. On the other hand, John includes a great deal of material not found in the Synoptic accounts: Jesus' washing the disciples' feet (Jn 13:3-20); his teachings on love (Jn 13:34-35; 15:12-17), the coming of the Spirit (Jn 14:15-17, 26; 15:26; 16:4-15) and other subjects (Jn 14:8-14, 18-24; 15:18—16:3); and Jesus' prayer for his disciples (Jn 17:1-26).

In all four Gospel accounts Jesus foretells his betrayal by one of his disciples. Why Jesus told the disciples this is uncertain. It is easier to understand why the Gospel writers recorded it. For them it was not just to provide another christological example of Jesus' uniqueness. It portrays Jesus as a prophet who foreknew the future and what was about to happen. More important for the Evangelists, however, was their desire to show that the cross was not a tragedy or accident. It was rather part and parcel of the divine plan and will from the beginning. They wanted to show their readers that the cross was the reason for Jesus' coming. The crucifixion was not some tragic mistake or human derailment of what God intended. On the contrary, as Jesus taught at the Last Supper, the betrayal that led to the cross lay completely within the sovereign plan of God. Jesus went to the cross willingly, knowing that it was God's plan. His hour had now come.

The Date of the Last Supper

All four Gospels agree that the crucifixion of Jesus took place on Friday (Mt 27:62; Mk 15:42; Lk 23:54; Jn 19:31, 42). This means, by the Jewish reckoning of time, sometime between 6:00 p.m. Thursday and 6:00 p.m. Friday. Two main questions arise with respect to the dating of the Last Supper. The first involves Mark 14:12, and the second concerns whether the Last Supper came at a Passover celebration or whether it was a meal that preceded the Passover.

The problem of Mark 14:12. In telling the story of the Last Supper, Mark states that Jesus told his disciples to prepare the Passover "on the first day of Unleavened Bread, when the Passover lamb is sacrificed" (Mk 14:12). The problem is that the Passover lamb was actually sacrificed on the afternoon of the fourteenth of Nisan, whereas the Passover, which was the first day of the Feast of Unleavened Bread, technically began on the fifteenth.

This apparent discrepancy is best explained by seeing here a difference between the popular understanding of when the Passover began and the technical description of its beginning. In the minds of most people the Passover celebration began on the fourteenth of Nisan, when they searched their homes for leaven and slaughtered the Passover lamb. Compare our modern-day celebration of Christmas. For many Christmas begins on Christmas Eve, when presents are exchanged, the Christmas story is read or the church service is held (or even sooner, when decorations are hung or displayed). Technically, of course, Christmas begins at 12:00 a.m. on December 25. In a similar way, the Passover began for most Jews on "Passover Eve," the fourteenth of Nisan. (Compare Josephus *Ant.* 14.2.1 [14.21]; 17.9.3 [17.213]; 18.2.2 [18.29] and *War* 2.1.3 [2.10]; 5.3.1 [5.98-99] for references to the Passover beginning on the fourteenth of Nisan.)

The Last Supper and the Passover. The most serious problem involved in the dating of the Last Supper involves its relationship to the Passover celebration. According to the Synoptic Gospels, the Last Supper took place in association with a Passover meal: "Where do you want us to go and make the preparations for you to eat the Passover?" (Mk 14:12; compare also vv. 14, 16). At the end of the meal Luke records Jesus as saying, "I have eagerly desired to eat this Passover with you before I suffer" (Lk 22:15). On the other hand, in John it appears that the trial and crucifixion took place before the Passover: "Then they took Jesus from Caiaphas to Pilate's headquarters. It was early in the morning. They themselves did not enter the headquarters, so as to avoid ritual defilement and to be able to eat the Passover" (Jn 18:28; compare also 13:1, 29; 19:31). Here the Passover is portrayed as still being in the future.

Was the Last Supper associated with a Passover meal (as in the Synoptic Gospels), or did it precede the Passover (as in John)? Numerous attempts have been made to answer this question. Some choose one view over the other.

One suggestion is that the Synoptic Gospels are correct and that the Last Supper was in fact part of a Passover celebration. Those who hold this view suggest that the term *Passover* in John 18:28 does not refer to the actual Passover itself but to other meals and celebrations associated with the Feast of Unleavened Bread (compare 2 Chron 30:22). The problem is that it is very difficult to interpret the Greek term *pascha* ("Passover") in John 18:28 as meaning anything other than the Passover meal.

An alternative suggestion is that John is correct. The Last Supper was not part of a Passover meal but was eaten a day or so before it. According to this view, Jesus celebrated the Passover early because he knew that he would be dead at the time of the Passover. Yet it is very unlikely that the private celebration of the Passover according to one's own choice of time was permitted in Judaism.

Some have therefore suggested that Jesus celebrated a different kind of festive meal. Support for this is seen in the fact that no mention is made at the Last Supper of the Passover lamb and that the word for "bread" (*artos*) is not the normal word used for unleavened bread (*azyma*). This line of reasoning is not convincing, however. One would expect that only those aspects important for the celebration of the Last Supper would be retained in recounting the tradition. Those which were not, such as the Passover lamb, would be omitted. As for the term *artos* and its Hebrew equivalent, they are the terms used in the Old Testament, the LXX, the Mishna and the Targums to describe the shewbread, which consisted of unleavened bread. Philo, a first-century Jewish scholar, furthermore explicitly refers to the unleavened bread of the Passover as *artos* (see *De Specialibus Legibus* 2.158). The main difficulty with this alternative suggestion is that the writers of the Synoptic Gospels clearly wanted their statements to be understood as indicating that the Last Supper was part of a Passover celebration (see, for example, Mk 14:12, 14, 16; Lk 22:15).

Perhaps both John and the Synoptic Gospels are correct. Numerous suggestions have sought this middle ground:

☐ In the year of Jesus' crucifixion the Passover fell on the sabbath, so the Pharisees celebrated the Passover a day earlier (as did Jesus, according to the Synoptic Gospels), whereas the Sadducees celebrated it on the normal day, which was a day later (so the priests in Jn 18:28).

☐ That year a question arose as to when the month of Nisan actually began, and since the Pharisees believed it started one day earlier than the Sadducees, they (and Jesus) celebrated it a day earlier than the Sadducees (and the priests).

☐ So many lambs were required for the Passover celebration that it took two days to slaughter them, and as a result the Galileans (and Jesus) celebrated the Passover a day earlier than the Judeans (and priests).

☐ Two different calendars were in use during that time, one solar (Qumran) and the other lunar (the rest of Judaism), and the difference between John and the Synoptic Gospels is due to their use of two different calendars.

There are others, but each one has difficulties associated with it, and at this time it must be admitted that no satisfactory solution has been offered.

The Last Supper as a Passover Meal

The question of how to reconcile the Gospel accounts of the Last Supper remains unresolved. It would appear for several reasons, however, that the meal Jesus ate with his disciples on the night of his betrayal was indeed the Passover.

First, Jesus and the disciples did not return to Bethany that night, as they had on previous days. They remained instead within the walled city of Jerusalem to eat this meal. That is best explained by the fact that the Passover had to be eaten within Jerusalem proper.

Second, Jesus and the disciples ate this meal reclining. The expression "had taken their places and were eating" in Mark 14:18 actually means "while they were reclining and eating." Normally people sat at meals. It was only at festive meals, such as the Passover, that they would recline with pillows under their arms facing a low table. (That explains why the woman of Lk 7:36-50 was able to wash Jesus' feet and anoint them. At festive meals the participants reclined facing the table with their feet radiating outward like spokes. Compare also Jn 12:1-8.)

Third, people usually ate two meals during a normal day. The first meal was at 10:00-11:00 a.m., and the second was in the late afternoon. The meal associated with the Last Supper was eaten in the evening (Mk 14:17; 1 Cor 11:23). According to Exodus 12:8 the Passover had to be eaten at night.

Fourth, the Last Supper ended with a hymn (Mt 26:30; Mk 14:26). It was customary to end the Passover by singing the last part of the Hallel Psalms (Ps 113—118).

Fifth, during the Passover meal it was customary to interpret the symbolic significance of the various elements in the meal (Ex 12:26-27). This was done with respect to the Last Supper.

Finally, the night of the Passover had to be spent within Jerusalem. At the time of the Passover the normal population of Jerusalem (about 25,000-30,000) swelled in size to 125,000 or more. It was impossible for all the pilgrims to find lodging within the walled city. As a result Jerusalem was redefined to include all the hills facing the city. Thus whereas the Passover had to be eaten within the walled city, the night could be spent in "greater Jerusalem." The Garden of Gethsemane lay on the western slopes of the Mount of Olives facing Jerusalem. On the night of the Last Supper, Jesus and the disciples did not return to Bethany but stayed at Gethsemane, which was part of "greater Jerusalem." This fits well the Last Supper's being associated with a Passover meal.

In light of these and other reasons it seems best to conclude that the Last Supper took place at the end of a Passover celebration. If so, this provides us with a most useful context for understanding it. The Passover meal, which required the presence of ten people, consisted essentially of six elements, all of which had symbolic significance.

1. The Passover lamb could be cooked only by being roasted over a fire. All of it had to be eaten that night. Nothing could be saved. What remained had to be burned. The lamb reminded the participants of the time of the exodus, when in the evening the angel of death visited all the firstborn in Egypt. Only those homes protected by the blood of the Passover lamb escaped.

2. The unleavened bread reminded them that their salvation from Egypt was so quick and swift that they did not have time to bake bread.

3. The bowl of salt water reminded them of the sorrow and tears of their captivity, as well as the crossing of the Red Sea.

4. The bitter herbs reminded them of the bitterness of their bondage in Egypt.

5. The *charosheth*, a kind of fruit puree, reminded them of the clay that was used to make bricks during their bondage in Egypt.

6. Last, four cups of red wine were mixed with water. These four cups reminded them of the promises God made in Exodus 6:6-7. It may have been the third of these cups that Jesus used in the Last Supper (Lk 22:20; 1 Cor 10:16; 11:25). The fourth and final cup was followed by a benediction and the singing of a psalm.

At the end of the Passover meal, it was customary for someone (usually the youngest son) to ask the question "Why is this night different from other nights?" The host would then explain the significance of the meal and retell the story of the exodus, using the symbolism of the various elements in so doing. The story was told from the viewpoint of the participants. "*We* were once slaves in Egypt. . . . God raised up *for us* a deliverer, Moses. . . . Plagues. . . . Passover. . . . Deliverance . . ." As the host of the meal, Jesus would have been the one to tell the story. In light of this historical context, certain parallels between the Passover and the Last Supper become quite clear:

The Passover	The Lord's Supper
God remembered his covenant with Abraham	A new covenant is enacted
Slavery in Egypt	(Slavery to sin?)
Deliverance from Egypt	Forgiveness of sins (Mt 26:28)
Blood of Passover lamb	Blood of Christ, our Passover (1 Cor 5:7), the Lamb of God (Jn 1:29, 36)
Interpretation of elements of Passover	Interpretation of elements of Lord's Supper
Call for continual celebration	Call for continual celebration

In light of this context the teachings of the Last Supper take on an even deeper significance.

The Interpretation of the Lord's Supper

A number of different terms have been associated with the Lord's Supper. Some arise from biblical descriptions: the "breaking of bread" (Acts 2:42, compare 2:46; 20:7, 11), the "Eucharist," (from the Greek term for "giving thanks" in Mt 26:27; Mk 14:23; Lk 22:17, 19; 1 Cor 11:24), the "table of the Lord" (1 Cor 10:21), "communion" (1 Cor 10:16 KJV), the "Lord's supper" (1 Cor 11:20). The following, on the other hand, do not: the "mass" (from the Latin ending of the rite, *Ite, missa est*—"Go, you are dismissed") and the "Last Supper." The New Testament contains a number of references and allusions to the Lord's Supper (Mk 6:42; 8:6;

Lk 24:30; Acts 2:42, 46; 20:7, 11; 27:35; Jn 6:25-59; 1 Cor 10:1-22; 11:20-22). The most important, however, are Matthew 26:26-29; Mark 14:22-25; Luke 22:14-20; and 1 Corinthians 11:23-26.

The last four accounts fall into two distinct groups representing two different traditions concerning the Lord's Supper:

Matthew and Mark	Luke and 1 Corinthians
"blessing" bread	"giving thanks" for bread
"Take"	[lacking]
"this is my body"	"This is my body" + "which is given for you"
[lacking]	"Do this in remembrance of me"
"giving thanks"	[lacking]
"this"	"This cup"
"Drink from it, all of you"	[lacking]
"my blood of the covenant"	"new covenant in my blood"
"which is poured out for many"	Luke has "that is poured out for you," but this is lacking in 1 Corinthians

The account in Luke is quite unusual because it alone has a reference to the drinking of a cup and to the coming of the kingdom of God before the bread (Lk 22:17-18). There is also a serious textual problem associated with Luke's version of the Last Supper. A few significant Greek manuscripts (mainly Codex Beza, or D) and several Old Latin manuscripts omit Luke 22:19b-20, " 'Do this is remembrance of me.' And he did the same with the cup after supper, saying, 'This cup that is poured out for you is the new covenant in my blood.' " Most probably, however, these manuscripts represent the work of a scribe who was confused by the cup-bread-cup sequence in Luke and omitted the second reference to the cup.

The meaning of the Last Supper centers on four "sayings": (1) "This is my body"; (2) "Do this in remembrance of me"; (3) "This is my blood of the covenant, which is poured out for many"; and (4) "I will never again drink of the fruit of the vine until that day when I drink it new in the kingdom of God."

"This is my body." All four accounts contain this first saying, although Luke and 1 Corinthians add "which is given for you." It is uncertain whether this last phrase goes back to Jesus himself or simply makes explicit what was already implicit in Jesus' teaching. Over the centuries there has been great debate over the meaning of the word *is*. Should it be understood literally to mean that the bread (and cup) are truly the body (and blood) of Christ? This is essentially the view held over the years in Roman Catholic and Lutheran churches. The former (transubstantiation) holds that during the supper, when the priest speaks the appointed words, the bread and wine become transformed into the body and blood of Christ, even though they may look and test out to be bread and wine. The latter (consubstantiation) maintains that the bread and wine remain bread and wine but that in, around and through the elements there is present the actual body and blood of Christ.

Or should this saying instead be understood metaphorically? This latter view emphasizes the word *remembrance* rather than *is:* "This is my body that is for you. Do this in remembrance of me" (1 Cor 11:24). One representation of this view interprets what is taking place as essentially a memorial in which believers remember the life and deeds of Jesus. This view is represented by Zwingli, Congregationalists, Baptists and Methodists. Another version of this view, that of Calvin and the Reformed church, is that Jesus is spiritually present in the eating of the bread and wine by faith.

In light of Jesus' frequent use of metaphor and various other figures of speech, there is no need to insist on a literal interpretation of his words here. Elsewhere Jesus spoke of himself as a vine, a door, the good shepherd and so on without intending that these metaphors should be understood literally. The fact that the elements in the Lord's Supper are still called "bread" and "the cup" after they are partaken of (1 Cor 11:26-28) also suggests this. If the disciples were asked during their participation in this meal, "Where is the body of Jesus?" it is extremely unlikely that they would have pointed to the bread. They would have pointed to Jesus, their host. As we shall see with respect to the third saying, it is even more unlikely that the disciples would have thought that the wine in the cup was the actual blood of Jesus (see below under "This is my blood of the covenant, which is poured out for many").

Jesus in this first saying taught that he came to give his "body," that is, himself as a person (compare Rom 12:1; Phil 1:20; 1 Cor 9:27), on our behalf. The full understanding of what this meant was not available to the disciples at the time. Later, however, as the church came to understand more fully that Jesus had come from the Father (Jn 1:1-14; Phil 2:6-8), they realized that the bread spoke of the Word, who became flesh and bore our sins in his body (1 Pet 2:24). The bread in the Lord's Supper points to the incarnation of the Son of God and his giving himself for the redemption of the world.

"Do this in remembrance of me." Because this saying is not found in Mark's and Matthew's accounts, some scholars have questioned its authenticity. Yet it is contained in the earliest account of the Lord's Supper (1 Cor 11:23-26). In this account, which was written in the mid-fifties, Paul refers to his having "received" and "handed on" the tradition of the Lord's Supper to the Corinthians during his earlier mission to them. The words *received* and *handed on* are technical terms that describe the receiving and passing on of oral tradition. Although Paul claims that ultimately this tradition came from the "Lord," that is, from Jesus' words at the Last Supper, he received it via the oral tradition of the church (compare Lk 1:2; 1 Cor 15:3). Whether Paul received this tradition from the church in Antioch in the mid-forties or from the church in Damascus (Acts 9:19-25; 11:22-26; Gal 1:17) or Jerusalem (Acts 9:26-30; Gal 1:18) in the mid-thirties is impossible to say. What needs to be recognized is that this saying is part of the earliest form of the Lord's Supper that we possess.

In the context of the continual celebration of the Passover, Jesus taught that the Lord's Supper should be similarly remembered. Just as the "old" covenant had its symbolic ritual in the Passover, so Jesus in instituting a "new" covenant also saw the importance of a symbolic repetition of its main teachings and truths. The fact that the early church from the beginning was in the habit of celebrating the Lord's Supper on a regular basis (Acts 2:46) is best explained by Jesus' having said something like "Do this in remembrance of me." Even as Israel celebrated the Passover in order to "remember the day of [their] departure from the land of Egypt" (Deut 16:3), so the church should celebrate the Lord's Supper in order to "remember" the new covenant.

The question has been raised as to what Jesus wanted his followers to remember. One suggestion is that Jesus wanted his disciples to petition God to remember him and deliver him. The emphasis of all four accounts, however, is not for the disciples to intercede with God on behalf of Jesus. In the present context such an interpretation is not possible. A more popular way of understanding this saying is to see it as instituting a continual memorial in which believers are to reflect back on the death of Jesus. Still another suggestion is to interpret the verb *remember* as meaning "to proclaim." This fits well with 1 Corinthians 11:26, where Paul states, "For as often as you eat this bread and drink the cup, you proclaim the Lord's death until he comes." This suggestion understands the Lord's Supper as being primarily an evangelistic proclamation of the gospel. The best way of understanding this saying, however, is to see it as directed to and meant for the church. The command is best seen as ordering the continual celebration and recounting of Jesus' vicarious death and his forthcoming return. Just as the Passover was intended to celebrate-recount-recapitulate the exodus, so the "remembrance" of the Lord's Supper is intended to celebrate-recount-recapitulate the death of Christ, our Passover, and his future coming.

"This is my blood of the covenant, which is poured out for many." During the Passover, after the third cup was drunk there followed the traditional blessing: "Blessed be thou, Lord our God, King of the world, who has created the fruit of the vine." After giving thanks for the cup (Matthew, Mark), Jesus said, "This is my blood of the covenant, which is poured out for many." All four accounts associate the cup with "blood" and a "covenant." This brings to mind the words in Exodus 24:8, where Moses after ratifying the covenant with sacrifices stated, "See the blood of the covenant that the LORD has made with you in accordance with all these words." This "blood of the covenant" was also understood as atoning for the sins of the people. (See the *Targums of Pseudo-Jonathan* and *Onqelos* on this passage.) It is Matthew who most clearly sees this tie when he adds the comment "for the forgiveness of sins" (Mt 26:28). Here he makes explicit what is implicit in the expression "blood of the covenant" (com-

pare Heb 9:20-22; 10:26-29).

The reference to a covenant brings to mind the promise of Jeremiah 31:31, where the prophet speaks of a time when God would "make a new covenant with the house of Israel and the house of Judah." In the Lord's Supper, Jesus taught that this new covenant would be inaugurated and sealed through his blood, that is, through his sacrificial death. In Luke's and Paul's version of the Lord's Supper explicit mention is made of the cup as a "new" covenant (Lk 22:20; 1 Cor 11:25). Mark's and Matthew's versions lack this term, so it is uncertain if Jesus explicitly used this adjective. Nevertheless, even if Jesus did not use this term, it is implicit in his teaching.

The reference to forgiveness of sins associated with the new covenant spoken of by Jeremiah (Jer 31:34) is also associated with the covenant Jesus instituted. This is seen in the reference to the "forgiveness of sins" in Matthew 26:28 and the reference to the "blood of the covenant, which is poured out for many" (Mt 26:28; Mk 14:24). The latter expression comes from Isaiah 53:12, where the suffering servant bears "the sin of many."

In the Last Supper Jesus revealed that he understood his death as involving "blood poured out" for his followers. His death involved the voluntary giving of his life in sacrifice. Jesus' words should be interpreted in light of such passages as Mark 10:45 ("give his life a ransom for many"), 1 Corinthians 15:3 ("Christ died for our sins in accordance with the scriptures") and 1 Peter 2:24 ("He himself bore our sins in his body on the cross. . . . By his wounds you have been healed"). Jesus saw this sacrifice as bringing about a new covenant, which was not, however, a repudiation of the old covenant but rather its fulfillment. In the context of God's dealings with his people, Jesus was inaugurating a new period in the history of salvation.

As with the bread, so with the cup it is difficult to interpret the word *is* literally. The reference to the cup being the "blood of the covenant" is best understood metaphorically. We must remember the context of the Last Supper. It involved Jews who were well acquainted with the Old Testament prohibition against drinking blood (for example, Lev 3:17; 7:26-27; 17:14). If the disciples literally believed that they were being told to drink blood, one would have expected them to protest strongly. One need only recall Peter's protest in Acts 10:9-16 when he was commanded to eat nonkosher meat to see how difficult it would have been for the disciples to drink real blood. Yet they exhibited no qualms in drinking the cup Jesus gave them. The early church also encountered no problems from its Jewish members in this respect. If Peter had believed that he was truly drinking blood, his reaction later to the divine command to "kill and eat" nonkosher meat would likely have been less resistant. It is difficult to imagine Peter saying, "By no means, Lord; for I have never eaten anything that is profane or unclean [although I drink blood regularly]" (Acts 10:14). Furthermore, even after the drinking of the cup, its contents are still referred to in the Lord's Supper as the "fruit of the vine" (Mk 14:25). So it is best to understand Jesus' teaching here as meaning "This cup, that is, the wine in the cup, symbolizes my life given in sacrifice, which seals the new covenant God is now establishing."

"I will never again drink of the fruit of the vine until that day when I drink it new in the kingdom of God." All four accounts of the Lord's Supper make reference to the future. Even as the Passover was an anticipation and longing for that day when God's people would participate in the messianic banquet (Is 25:6-9; 55:1-2; 65:13), so the Lord's Supper looks not only back at Jesus' death but forward to his coming. Even Luke's version contains such a reference, although it occurs before the first three sayings. In 1 Corinthians the reference to the future comes not from Jesus but from Paul: "For as often as you eat this bread and drink the cup, you proclaim the Lord's death until he comes" (1 Cor 11:26).

In the Synoptic Gospels this anticipation of the future takes the form of sharing in the messianic banquet when Jesus returns. This theme appears frequently in Jesus' teaching (Mt 5:6; 8:11; Mk 7:24-30; Lk 12:35-38). The feedings of the five thousand (Mk 6:30-44) and the four thousand (Mk 8:1-10) were probably meant by the Gospel writers to be understood as foretastes of the Lord's Supper and the messianic banquet. (Compare "blessed and broke" and "giving thanks he broke" in Mk 6:41 and 8:6 with "blessing it he broke it" in Mk 14:22.) In some Jewish circles it was believed that Israel's future redemption would come on the night of the Passover (*Mekilta Exodus* 12:42). The Passover celebration, therefore, was highly anticipatory. Similarly Jesus at the Last Supper pointed his followers to the time when history would come to its conclusion by his return (1 Cor 11:26) and all those who followed him would joyously share the messianic banquet with him (Mt 26:29; Mk 14:25; Lk 22:16).

Jesus did not see his death as a tragic human error or a quirk of fate. The conviction that this was the will of God would be reinforced by his experience at Gethsemane. Now as he saw his hour coming, he taught his disciples not only the necessity of his death but also its significance. By his death God would inaugurate the new covenant promised in the Old Testament. He spoke of his sacrificial death in Old Testament terms as the pouring out of his blood to make redemption and forgiveness available "for many." Yet he pointed his disciples not only to the soon-to-be crucifixion but past this event to the future consummation of all things. The bread and the cup, therefore, pointed not just to the immediate future but also to the more distant future when he would share the messianic banquet with his disciples in the realized kingdom.

Conclusion

Aware that his hour had come, Jesus used the context of a Passover celebration to institute a new "rite." In this rite-ordinance-sacrament he spoke of his purpose and mission in life, which involved a two-dimensional focus. Like his teachings on the kingdom of God, it consisted of a soon-to-be "now" and a future "not yet."

The "now," which would come in just hours, involved his giving himself in sacrifice to seal the new covenant God had promised. Bread and wine were invested with eternal symbolic significance. They represented the body he would give and the "blood," or sacrificial purpose, for which he would give that body. From that day until the end of history the Lord's Supper would remind the church that the cross was not an accident or misfortune but the crowning event of human redemption. Many may view it as a stumbling block, foolishness or an unfortunate act of human barbarism. For the followers of Jesus, however, it has been and will always be the object of faith and hope, and the cross will always be the single most distinctive symbol of Christian faith. The bread and the cup continually point to the "old rugged cross" and the redemption achieved there by Jesus.

The second dimension of the Lord's Supper points to the more distant future. Jesus looked to the cross with both horror and confidence. The horror of crucifixion is clearly understandable. Jesus' confidence is seen in his last saying. He goes to the cross knowing he will be victorious. He will rise from the dead; he will ascend to the Father; he will return again in glory. Any celebration of the Lord's Supper that focuses only on the horror of the cross is decidedly unbiblical. The Lord's Supper also speaks of a glorious reunion of Jesus with his followers. Even such a sad hymn as " 'Man of Sorrows,' What a Name," which dolefully sings of Jesus' death, ends "When he comes, our glorious King, / All his ransomed home to bring, / Then anew this song we'll sing, / 'Hallelujah, what a Savior!' " The church must never lose sight of or minimize this dimension of the Lord's Supper.

References

Barclay, William. *The Lord's Supper*. Nashville: Abingdon, 1967.

Barth, Markus. *Rediscovering the Lord's Supper*. Atlanta: John Knox, 1988.

Green, Joel B. *The Death of Jesus*, pp. 234-44. Tübingen, Germany: J. C. B. Mohr, 1988.

Jeremias, Joachim. *The Eucharistic Words of Jesus*. London: SCM Press, 1966.

Klappert, Bertold. "Lord's Supper." In *New International Dictionary of New Testament Theology*, edited by Colin Brown, 2:520-38. Grand Rapids, Mich.: Zondervan, 1976.

Leon-Dufour, Xavier. *Sharing the Eucharistic Bread*. New York: Paulist, 1987.

Marshall, I. Howard. *Last Supper and Lord's Supper*. Grand Rapids, Mich.: Eerdmans, 1980.

Reumann, John. *The Supper of the Lord*. Philadelphia: Fortress, 1985.

Stein, Robert H. "Last Supper." In *Dictionary of Jesus and the Gospels*, edited by Joel B. Green, Scot McKnight and I. Howard Marshall, pp. 444-50. Downers Grove, Ill.: InterVarsity Press, 1992.

Wainwright, Geoffrey. *Eucharist and Eschatology*. New York: Oxford University Press, 1981.

16
GETHSEMANE, BETRAYAL & ARREST

God's Will, Human Treachery & Governmental Evil

AFTER EATING THE PASSOVER AND INSTITUTING THE LORD'S SUPPER in Jerusalem proper, Jesus and the disciples proceeded to the Garden of Gethsemane (Mt 26:36; Mk 14:32). Leaving the city through one of its eastern gates, they descended into the Kidron Valley and climbed up the western side of the Mount of Olives. Located on the lower slopes facing the city, Gethsemane lay within what was considered "greater Jerusalem." There Jesus planned to spend the evening rather than return to Bethany. In so doing he fulfilled the Jewish requirements concerning the celebration of the Passover. Yet he would not spend the entire night in Gethsemane because his "hour" had come.

Gethsemane

When they arrived, Jesus took with him Peter, James and John and separated himself from the rest to pray. On at least two previous occasions these three alone accompanied Jesus. They were at the healing of Jairus's daughter (Mk 5:37) and at the transfiguration (Mk 9:2). Here he urged them to share his agony and to "keep awake" (Mk 14:34). Jesus appealed to the three disciples to pray for him as well as for themselves, for their time of trial was also approaching (Mk 14:38). In his time of struggle and agony Jesus sought the comfort and understanding of his faithful friends (compare 2 Tim 4:9). Proceeding ahead of these three disciples but within their hearing (Lk 22:41 says "about a stone's throw"), Jesus agonized in prayer. Probably our knowledge of the content of Jesus' prayer comes from the three disciples. As was normal, Jesus no doubt prayed aloud. What he prayed was overheard by the disciples during their wakeful periods.

The biblical accounts emphasize Jesus' great torment at this time. He was "distressed and agitated" and "deeply grieved, even to death" (Mk 14:33-34). The saying in Luke 22:44 that Jesus' "sweat became like great drops of blood falling down on the ground" has questionable textual support. Note also that the word "like" refers to a comparison, not an actual reality. Jesus' torment is further revealed in that "he threw himself on the ground" (Mk 14:35; literally, "he fell on his face"). It is hard to imagine that the Gethsemane tradition is fictional in origin. Who would have created such an account in the early church? Possible allusions to this experience of Jesus are found in Hebrews 5:7 and John 12:27.

Jesus' prayer to God was "Abba, Father, for you all things are possible; remove this cup from me; yet, not what I want, but what you want" (Mk 14:36). After a time (the "one hour" in Mk 14:37 should not be pressed for exactness) Jesus came to the disciples and found them sleeping. Warning them to "watch" (RSV) and pray because of their own need to be prepared for temptation, he left them and prayed again. Matthew and Mark mention that he prayed the same thing.

It has been suggested that the disciples were told to "watch" for Judas's coming. This, however, ignores the tie between watching and praying (Mk 14:38; compare Lk 21:36; Eph 6:18; Col 4:2) and that they were to watch *with Jesus* as he prayed (Mt 26:38, 40). Upon returning to the disciples, Jesus found them sleeping again. He returned a third time to pray and, according to Matthew 26:44, prayed the same prayer (compare 2 Cor 12:8). Upon returning he found Peter, James and John still sleeping.

The picture of Jesus in Gethsemane is not that of a stoic facing death with a fearless lack of concern. What was it that Jesus feared? Several suggestions have been made.

One is that he feared physical death. According to this view Jesus knew better than anyone else that physical death was a curse. At Gethsemane he saw that rather than being part of human life as originally designed, death was a violation of what God truly intended. If this, however, was what Jesus feared, it is strange that his followers could so often experience and even embrace physical death for his sake without complaint or murmur. The fear of death grips humanity, but Jesus' agony in Gethsemane was due to something more than physical death. There is no hint in the Gospels that what Jesus feared was physical pain or death.

Another explanation is that what Jesus feared was premature death. Some have suggested that Jesus feared that he would be put to death before he was able to fulfill his mission. Yet Jesus had faith in his Father that not even the smallest sparrow could fall without his knowledge. He had confidence that until his "hour had come" God would protect him from the snares of the enemy (Ps 124:7; 141:9-10).

A third suggestion is that Jesus feared the guilt that his death would bring upon Judas, Pontius Pilate and the leaders of the nation. Jesus knew, however, that his mission was one that divided the sheep from the goats, the wheat from the tares. At no time in his career did he shrink from his mission because people would become guilty for rejecting him. There was nothing he could do to change the fact that some love darkness rather than light.

The explanation of what Jesus feared must be understood in light of the unique death he would die. It was not physical death that caused him grief. It was the thought of "giv[ing] his life a ransom for many" (Mk 10:45), of being made sin even though he knew no sin (2 Cor 5:21), of "[bearing] our sins in his body on the cross" (1 Pet 2:24), of "suffer[ing] for sins once for all, the righteous for the unrighteous" (1 Pet 3:18), of "becoming a curse for us—for it is written, 'Cursed is everyone who hangs on a tree' " (Gal 3:13). Jesus, knowing that his "hour" had come, feared the consequences of drinking the "cup" God had ordained for him (Mk 10:38). As elsewhere, this cup symbolizes the experiencing of divine wrath (Ps 11:6; 75:8; Is 51:17, 22; Jer 49:12; Rev 14:10; 16:19; 17:4). For Jesus, however, this cup was not due to his own sin but because he would bear the sins of others.

Jesus feared the agony of experiencing the wrath of a righteous God against sin. Whereas believers go through the experience of death with a real sense of God's presence, Jesus was about to experience abandonment by God. Believers who walk through the valley of the shadow have

God's assurance and promise: "I will never leave you or forsake you" (Heb 13:5). Jesus knew, however, that he "would become accursed" during the very hour he needed God most. Nowhere do the horror and tragedy of sin become more evident than in Jesus' anguished cry from the cross, "My God, my God, why have you forsaken me?" (Mk 15:34).

As he faced this in the garden, Jesus poured out his heart to God and sought for another way to fulfill his mission. Jesus was no masochist. His faith was not some form of play-acting. Like the psalmist before him, he could pray honestly to God. He could express his feelings forthrightly. The Gospel writers are to be commended for their honesty in recording this tradition. They do not place on Jesus' lips some superficial and silly prayer such as "I thank you, Father, for the opportunity facing me this weekend. I have heard that crucifixion is a broadening experience." On the contrary, knowing the evil he was about to experience, Jesus could pray to his Father with complete honesty: "Abba, Father, for you all things are possible; remove this cup from me." Jesus' faith and trust in the Father, however, is clearly seen when he adds, "Yet, not what I want, but what you want" (Mk 14:36).

Jesus' faith and commitment to the will of God serve as a pattern for his followers. Like the psalmist and, above all, like Jesus, believers can pour out their true feelings to their Father. Yet as they pray for healing and deliverance, they are to end their prayer in faith with "Yet, not what I want, but what you want" (compare 2 Cor 12:7-9).

An interesting question arises as to the nature of Jesus' prayer in Gethsemane. Did he believe that there might in fact be another way for him to fulfill his mission? Was he actually pleading that God would remove this cup from him and work out human redemption in some other way? Or was his prayer rather an expression of his great anguish over what he knew must take place? In light of the numerous predictions Jesus gave concerning his death, it seems unlikely that he really believed that what had been decreed in the Scriptures (his forthcoming passion) could be altered or changed. The Scripture must be fulfilled. This could only mean that his passion must take place. Thus it is best to understand Jesus' cry, "Abba, Father, for you all things are possible; remove this cup from me," not so much as a petition to God but as an agonizing expression of pain.

One tragedy must not be overlooked. Throughout his ministry Jesus provided for the needs, guidance and teaching of his disciples. At Gethsemane we see, perhaps for the first time, an occasion when Jesus needed his disciples. How encouraging it would have been as he faced the cross to know that his followers had shared his agony at Gethsemane. How meaningful it would have been for Jesus as he went through his suffering to have remembered that Peter, James and John had shared his sorrow and had fervently prayed on his behalf. But they failed him, for "he came and found them sleeping" (Mk 14:37, 40; compare 13:36). Earlier the disciples failed to understand his teachings concerning his death (Mk 8:32; 9:32; 10:32). Now, when he sought their assistance during this crucial hour, they failed him again. The disciples were already beginning to forsake him (Mk 14:27-31).

The Betrayal
Understanding the betrayal of Jesus centers on two questions: *"Why* did Judas betray Jesus?" and *"What* did Judas betray?"

The why. A great deal of speculation has transpired concerning *why* Judas betrayed Jesus. One interesting explanation is that it was due to his being Jesus' most loving and dedicated disciple. According to this view, Judas was the only disciple dedicated enough to assist Jesus in completing his ministry. Although he hated doing it, he nevertheless dedicated himself to the horrible task of betraying Jesus. He was the only one willing to help Jesus die by crucifixion in order to fulfill God's plan. Such an explanation, however, is shipwrecked on the words of Jesus in Mark 14:21: "The Son of Man goes as it is written of him, but woe to that one by whom the Son of Man is betrayed! It would have been better for that one not to have been born." Other verses in the New Testament speak in negative terms of Judas's "betraying" Jesus (for example, Mt 26:16, 21, 23; Mk 14:10, 11, 18; Lk 22:4, 6, 48; Jn 6:64, 71; 12:4; 13:2, 11, 21; 21:20). There is good reason Christians tend not to name their children Judas.

Another suggestion is that Judas betrayed Jesus in order to obtain money (Mt 26:15). John even mentions that Judas was a petty thief (Jn 12:6). Yet thirty pieces of silver was not a great sum of money; it was the price of a slave (compare Ex 21:32 and Zech 11:13). Others have sought to explain Judas's betrayal as due to the disillusionment caused by Jesus' continued teaching concerning his death. (Notice that Mk 14:10-11 comes after 14:3-9.)

Lacking any clear explanation in the biblical materials, we must admit that we simply do not know why Judas betrayed Jesus. All attempts to "psychoanalyze" Judas's motive are simply speculative. The biblical writers were not interested in explaining the human factors that led him to do this. Their main interest was to emphasize that from the beginning this lay within the divine plan.

The what. The second question concerning *what* Judas betrayed is easier to answer. One suggestion, that Judas betrayed the "messianic secret," can be eliminated at the outset. According to this view Judas betrayed to the leadership of the nation that Jesus was secretly teaching his disciples that he was the Messiah. In so doing, Judas provided grounds for the Sanhedrin to seek Jesus' arrest and death. This view, however, is refuted by the fact that Judas was not present at the trial when the Sanhedrin sought evidence to condemn Jesus. If Judas had been paid to betray Jesus by revealing that he claimed to be the Jewish Messiah, then he would have been present at the trial as a witness of this.

What Judas betrayed seems clear enough from the Gospel accounts: "It was two days before the Passover and the festival of Unleavened Bread. The chief priests and the scribes were looking for a way to arrest Jesus by stealth and kill him; for they said, 'Not during the festival, or there may be a riot among the people' " (Mk 14:1-2). What Judas betrayed was how Jesus' opponents could seize him privately, apart from the crowds. Since the Jewish leaders were not willing to risk a riot by arresting Jesus in public, they sought a way they could arrest him in secret. Judas provided the opportunity.

Leaving the Last Supper early (Jn 13:27-30), he supplied the needed information: Jesus would spend the night in Gethsemane. There in darkness, without the knowledge of the crowds, they could arrest Jesus. In all this, however, God was in control. There is a sense that the "hour" of Jesus' opponents had now come (Lk 22:53), but in an even greater sense this was *God's* hour. Jesus states, "The hour has come" (God has brought about the hour); "the Son of Man is betrayed into the hands of sinners" (God is giving his Son over to sinners through Judas's betrayal) (Mk 14:41; compare Jn 12:27). The verbs in this verse are examples of "divine passives"—the use of the passive voice to avoid using God's name out of reverence. God was in control of all that was taking place. The Scriptures were being fulfilled.

The Arrest

Aware that Judas was approaching with an armed band, Jesus went out to meet them. It is no weak Jesus we see here. His enemies did not need to search the garden for him. On the contrary, Jesus took the initiative and went out to meet them. It is not a defeated victim that we read of in the biblical accounts but a conquering Christ who goes out to meet his opponents and defeat them by his cross. It was his "hour," and he was in charge. His opponents were unaware that they were simply fulfilling the preordained plan of the Father and his Son.

The description of those who came to meet Jesus indicates that there were a considerable number of them. Mark mentions that along with Judas was "a crowd with swords and clubs, from the chief priests, the scribes, and the elders" (Mk 14:43). Luke refers to "chief priests, the officers of the temple police, and the elders" (Lk 22:52), and John adds "a detachment of soldiers together with police from the chief priests and the Pharisees" (Jn 18:3). The makeup of this group is large even apart from John's mention of a "detachment." This term (speira) normally refers to a cohort, which was a tenth part of a Roman legion, or about six hundred men. At times it could refer to a maniple, or two hundred men. That this was a "detachment" of Roman soldiers is seen from the fact that the term is always used in the New Testament to refer to Roman troops and that they had over them an "officer," or chiliarchos. This term refers to a "tribune," who was in charge of a speira. Even if the "detachment" refers to a maniple, the armed group that came to seize Jesus was formidable. They were prepared to handle quickly and efficiently any resistance that might arise. (The Roman province of Judah housed five Roman cohorts. One was posted at the Fortress of Antonia in Jerusalem. The other four were stationed in Caesarea. By contrast, Syria contained four legions, which were more professionally trained.)

To cause as little disturbance as possible, Judas agreed to single out Jesus with a kiss. This was tactically necessary because in the dark it would not be clear which of the persons was Jesus. Remember that this was a time before electric lights. The trees on the Mount of Olives would be blocking out the light from the stars and moon and further hinder visibility. The last thing that Jesus' opponents wanted was to have to proceed from one group of pilgrims to another seeking Jesus. Thus Judas needed to point out for them exactly who Jesus was.

As for the kiss, this was the usual way for a disciple to greet his teacher. The term used in Mark 14:45 to describe Judas's kissing Jesus is not the normal term to describe the act of kissing. It is a more intensive form and suggests that he may have overdone it. Whether this indicates that Judas prolonged his kiss to make sure that everyone saw clearly whom they should arrest is difficult to say.

The response of Jesus to Judas's action is full of pathos and sorrow: "Judas, is it with a kiss that you are betraying the Son of Man?" (Lk 22:48). In no society and at no time in history have "traitors" ever been admired. Within the biblical culture the horror of betrayal was even more despised and shocking. To "break bread" with someone, to share his food and hospitality, resulted in a unique bond. It meant acceptance (Acts 11:1-18) and even the responsibility to defend and protect (Gen 19). To betray someone who shared his bread with you was about as despicable an act as can be imagined. To have accompanied Jesus, to have shared his lodging, to have broken bread with him, to have shared his cup, to have eaten the Passover meal with him, and then to betray him—this was indeed an unspeakable act. And history will forever remember Judas Iscariot for it.

Jesus' response to the crowd coming to arrest him is full of irony, even sarcasm: "Have you come out with swords and clubs to arrest me as though I were a bandit? Day after day I was with you in the temple teaching, and you did not arrest me. But let the scriptures be fulfilled" (Mk 14:48-49). Jesus knew that his opponents lacked the courage to do what they were doing in the presence of the people. So he rebuked them.

The reaction of the disciples in all this was confusion and fear. Their lack of understanding concerning Jesus' sacrificial death and the rapid development of events, even though they had been foretold of them, caused great consternation. The appearance of so many armed enemies caused fear. All this brought about the natural reaction to flee. Perhaps the only exception was Peter. In his confusion he sought to do what seemed natural. He fought. Lashing out with a sword, he struck the ear of the high priest's slave. (Jn 18:10 states that the slave's name was Malchus, and Lk 22:51 refers to Jesus' healing him.) But instead of being encouraged by Jesus, Peter was rebuked, for those who live by the sword die by the sword. As a result, in addition to feeling confused and fearful, Peter felt rejected for doing the only thing he could think of. Therefore, it is not surprising that he too fled.

Associated with the arrest is an interesting story of a young man present at the scene. He is described as wearing only a linen cloth. The reference to the cloth's being "linen" suggests that he came from a well-to-do family. When seized, the young man fled away naked, leaving behind the garment (Mk 14:51-52). The enigmatic nature of this story has caused many to suggest that this was not a real event but a myth that seeks to teach a spiritual truth. But all attempts to find out what this spiritual truth is supposed to be are unconvincing. Consequently it is hard to conceive of why a story like this would have been created. The earliest commentators understood this passage as autobiographical in nature. They believed that Mark, the author, included this passage because he was the young man.

Conclusion

In the events immediately surrounding Gethsemane we see the divine plan unfolding. The human tragedy seen throughout these events should not blind us to the fact that God was fully in control. At Gethsemane, Judas betrayed Jesus, just as Jesus said he would. Jesus was delivered over to the chief priests, as he said he would be. The disciples deserted him, again just as he said they would. Shortly thereafter Peter would deny him, as Jesus had announced. Soon he would be handed over to the Gentile rulers and be put to death, and after three days he would rise from the dead. This he had also predicted.

In the portrayal of Jesus' anguish and surrender to the will of God, we must not fail to see that Jesus was fully in control. What he had foretold was all taking place, and he was in charge. His hour had now come. His purpose and mission in life were about to be fulfilled. All this reveals that he was a true prophet. Yet he was far more, for unlike the prophets he alone could drink the cup that would bring human redemption.

The depth and horror of human sin are seen clearly in these events. They can be seen in Judas's ugly and revolting betrayal of Jesus and in the disciples' weakness in not being able to watch and pray. It is seen in their cowardly flight. In the next chapter we will see it being manifested in human and governmental injustice and brutality. But above all, we see the terrible nature of sin in Jesus' anguish. At Gethsemane the horror of what he was to experience overwhelmed him. His anguish and the horror of the cross reveal that human sin and depravity are not simply "flaws" in our makeup. On the contrary, they are so serious that they deserve the wrath of God. Gethsemane warns us never to minimize sin or its consequences.

References

Barbour, R. S. "Gethsemane in the Tradition of the Passion." *New Testament Studies* 16 (1969): 231-51.

Brown, Raymond E. *The Death of the Messiah*, pp. 110-310. New York: Doubleday, 1994.

Green, Joel B. "Gethsemane." In *Dictionary of Jesus and the Gospels*, edited by Joel B. Green, Scot McKnight and I. Howard Marshall, pp. 265-68. Downers Grove, Ill.: InterVarsity Press, 1992.

_____ . "Jesus on the Mount of Olives (Luke 22:39-46): Tradition and Theology." *Journal for the Study of the New Testament* 26 (1986): 29-48.

Holleran, J. Warren. *The Synoptic Gethsemane: A Critical Study*. Rome: Universita Gregoriana Editrice, 1973.

Lohse, Eduard. *History of the Suffering and Death of Jesus Christ*, pp. 55-68. Philadelphia: Fortress, 1967.

Stanley, David M. *Jesus in Gethsemane: The Early Church Reflects on the Suffering of Jesus*. New York: Paulist, 1980.

Taylor, Vincent. *The Passion Narrative of St. Luke: A Critical and Historical Investigation*. Cambridge: Cambridge University Press, 1972.

Williams, David John. "Judas Iscariot." In *Dictionary of Jesus and the Gospels*, edited by Joel B. Green, Scot McKnight and I. Howard Marshall, pp. 406-8. Downers Grove, Ill.: InterVarsity Press, 1992.

17
THE TRIAL
The Condemning
of the Innocent

T HE EVENTS SURROUNDING THE TRIAL OF JESUS ARE MUCH DEBATED, for a great deal is at stake. At issue is not simply what actually took place. For some, the trial of Jesus is an excuse for practicing a vicious anti-Semitism. As a result, there is pressure in some circles to see no Jewish involvement in the trial at all. According to this view, a trial never took place before the Sanhedrin. The only trial was before Pontius Pilate.

In both instances "history" has become a means for supporting a particular viewpoint. No writer can investigate the materials and discuss the trial of Jesus without being influenced by some agenda. I am no exception. My particular "agenda" is to seek, if possible, to bring the biblical data into a harmonious portrayal of what took place. This assumes that the Gospel writers are reliable witnesses of the events they record.

In investigating the Gospel accounts we are blessed with a number of traditions. Most probably we have three separate traditions concerning the trial. One is found in the parallel accounts in Mark and Matthew. The others are found in the accounts in Luke and John. This "blessing," however, brings with it serious problems, for it is not easy to harmonize the material from these various traditions. The term *harmonize* may cause misgivings to some readers, but it is a perfectly good term. In the past various "harmonizations" of conflicting accounts have been ridiculous and absurd. Consequently the whole process of harmonizing has become suspect. Yet one should at least attempt to see if diverse materials and traditions in the Gospels may in fact be compatible. We should not pass a negative judgment on attempts at harmonizing. Rather, judgment should be passed only on whether such attempts make sense.

The Events Surrounding the Trial

It must be acknowledged that the Gospel accounts of Jesus' trial appear contradictory in places. John, in contrast to the Synoptic Gospels, refers to Jesus' appearing before Annas (Jn 18:13). Luke alone refers to Pilate's sending Jesus to Herod Antipas (Lk 23:7). Matthew and Mark refer to two "trials," one in the evening and one in the morning, whereas Luke refers to only one. In Luke we read of Peter's denial *before* the meeting of the Sanhedrin. In the other Gospels it takes place *during or after* the meeting. The scourging occurs earlier in John than in Matthew and Mark, and although Luke alludes to it (Lk 23:16, 22), he does not mention it.

There are, of course, major agreements: Jesus appeared before Caiaphas and the Jewish leadership and was found "guilty"; he was condemned by Pontius Pilate, the Roman governor; a man named Barabbas was chosen for release instead of Jesus; Jesus was mocked; and many more. The following is a possible arrangement of how the various events fit together.

Jesus taken to Annas. According to John 18:13, after his arrest Jesus was "first" taken to the residence of Annas, the high priest. The use of the term *first* implies the existence of a subsequent hearing. Annas was high priest from A.D. 6 to 15. Caiaphas, the present ruling high priest (A.D. 18-36), was his son-in-law. Although Annas was no longer the officiating high priest when Jesus was arrested, he was still called a high priest (Lk 3:2; Jn 18:19), for the title and many of the responsibilities of the high priesthood were retained until death (*m. Horayot* 3:4). (Compare how the title "president" traditionally has been retained in addressing former living presidents of the United States.) The main purpose of this prelim-

inary inquiry may have been to allow time for Caiaphas to gather the
Sanhedrin together. What took place was not a formal trial but a rough
interrogation seeking evidence that might condemn Jesus. After an un-
successful attempt to find evidence against Jesus, Annas sent him to
Caiaphas (Mk 14:53; Jn 18:24).

The trial before Caiaphas and the Jewish leaders. Those present at the home
of Caiaphas to "try" Jesus are described as consisting of "all the chief
priests, the elders, and the scribes" (Mk 14:53) and "the whole council"
(*synedrion*, v. 55). The latter term refers to the Sanhedrin, the ruling body
of the Jews, which according to *m. Sanhedrin* 1:6 consisted of seventy
elders and the ruling high priest. It is uncertain, however, whether the
description of the Sanhedrin in this passage can be read back into the
time of Jesus. Some scholars have suggested that there actually existed
two Sanhedrins in Jesus' day. One was the Great Sanhedrin, or Beth Din,
which dealt primarily with religious issues and interpretations of the law.
The other was the political Sanhedrin. According to this understanding,
it was the latter, not the Beth Din, that was involved in Jesus' trial. Such
a reconstruction, however, finds no support in the sources, for they
never speak explicitly of two Sanhedrins.

The impression one receives from Matthew and Mark is that Jesus was
involved in a formal trial. Evidence was sought, for the council was "looking for testimony against Jesus to put him to death" (Mk 14:55). Numerous witnesses were called, but their testimony was contradictory and did
not agree. The only agreement of the witnesses was that Jesus had said
something about "destroying the temple and rebuilding it in three days,"
but even here, due to the riddlelike nature of the statement, their testimony did not agree. At this stage in the trial the testimony against Jesus
was clearly insufficient to condemn him. When asked about these accusations, Jesus remained silent.

In order to find evidence to condemn him, Caiaphas took a different
tack. He directed his questions at Jesus. Yet Jesus refused to answer. At
a certain point, however, Jesus broke his silence and responded to the
questions of the high priest. Why the change? It is Matthew who explains why. Caiaphas placed Jesus under an oath: "I put you under oath
before the living God, tell us if you are the Messiah, the Son of God" (Mt
26:63). Unlike judicial systems that protect the accused from having to
testify against himself, Jewish law knew no such right. According to

Leviticus 5:1, "When any of you sin in that you have heard a public adjuration to testify and—though able to testify as one who has seen or learned of the matter—does not speak up, you are subject to punishment" (compare Prov 29:24; 1 Kings 22:16; *m. Šebu'ot* 4:13). Jesus, as a Jew, accepted the legitimacy of this biblical oath. As a result, he now responded.

Jesus' response to the question whether he was the Messiah is reported differently in the various Gospels. Mark 14:62 records Jesus' reply as a straightforward "I am." Both Matthew and Luke, however, record his reply differently: "You have said so" (Mt 26:64) and "You say that I am" (Lk 22:70). Each of the three Gospel writers states that Jesus then added, "And 'you will see the Son of Man seated at the right hand of the Power,' and 'coming with the clouds of heaven' " (Mk 14:62). Matthew and Luke reveal that Jesus' reply to the high priest was a reticent affirmation. Attempts to interpret these words as a denial or rejection of the messianic title are refuted in his following statement. The high priest and the rest all understood the response as an affirmation. Matthew certainly wanted his readers to understand it this way. Earlier in his Gospel, Jesus spoke of one of the disciples betraying him. When Judas asked, "Surely not I, Rabbi?" (Mt 26:25), Jesus replied, "You have said so." The reply here is identical with Jesus' reply to the chief priest, and it must be understood as "Yes."

It is evident that these three Gospel writers agree that Jesus affirmed before the high priest that he was the Messiah. Mark apparently was less interested in sharing with his readers Jesus' hesitancy concerning this question. His account is nevertheless correct. Jesus did respond positively to the question of the high priest. He was the Messiah. Matthew and Luke are likewise correct in their rendering of Jesus' answer. They, however, were more concerned with indicating that Jesus affirmed his messiahship with reservation. Probably he did so because what the high priest and Sanhedrin believed concerning the messianic role was radically different from how Jesus understood it. Thus, whereas he could not and did not want to deny that he was the Messiah, he was aware that his affirmation could be misunderstood. They saw the Messiah as a royal figure, and this had all sorts of political implications associated with it. In effect Jesus' reply appears to have been "You have framed the question of whether I am the Messiah, and I won't deny that I am, but I prefer to refer to myself as the Son of Man."

After Jesus' answer Caiaphas "tore his clothes" and claimed that Jesus' words were blasphemy. The high priest's tearing of his clothes should not be thought of as an act of uncontrolled rage and fury. It does not mean that he "lost his cool." On the contrary, the tearing of the high priest's clothes was a formal judicial act indicating that the accused was guilty. It was an act minutely regulated according to tradition (*m. Sanhedrin* 7:5). All present concurred with his verdict. Jesus was judged guilty and worthy of death (Mk 14:64). He was then subjected to mocking and ridicule.

It is unclear exactly what Jesus said that caused the Sanhedrin to find him guilty of blasphemy. This has been the subject of much discussion. It is questionable whether simply claiming to be the Messiah was considered blasphemy, for in the Jewish revolt of A.D. 132-35 Bar Kokhba claimed to be the Messiah and no charge of blasphemy was leveled against him. Perhaps what was considered blasphemy was Jesus' claim of sitting at the right hand of God, for this assumed that he possessed a unique relationship with God.

Some have suggested that Jesus' blasphemy consisted of his claim to be the Son of Man (Dan 7:13-14) and his having combined this with the claim to be David's Lord and that he would sit at God's right hand (Ps 110:1). Another suggestion is that Jesus' response "I am" (Mk 14:62) was blasphemous because this was the way God described himself in Exodus 3:14. Yet if Jesus' actual response was closer to what Matthew and Luke have recorded than Mark, this suggestion must be rejected. Other previous claims of Jesus, such as the right to forgive sins and the ability to rise from the dead, no doubt also played a role in this verdict. According to *m. Sanhedrin* 7:5 blasphemy was technically defined as requiring the pronouncement of the sacred name YHWH. It would appear, however, that in Jesus' day blasphemy was understood more broadly. In the hostile environment of the trial Jesus' previous claims and his response to the high priest were sufficient in their minds to condemn him.

During this questioning we read that Peter denied Jesus three times. This had been foretold, but it is nevertheless shocking as we read about it. Along with its attestation in all four Gospels, the difficulty of explaining how and why such a tradition could have arisen during Peter's lifetime assures its historicity. (Also supporting the historicity of this account is the common reference in all the Gospels to Peter's warming himself at a fire in the courtyard.)

The question arises as to exactly when this event took place. In Matthew and Mark the account is placed after the questioning of the high priest and Jesus' acknowledgment that he was the Christ. In Luke it occurs before. The reason for this lies less in a confusion of time and more because of Luke's desire to place the traditions of the trial in a more logical order (Lk 1:3). Rather than switching back and forth from the story of Peter's denial (Mk 14:53-54, 66-72) and the trial (Mk 14:55-65), Luke decided to tell the story of Peter's denial all together. So after telling how Peter entered the courtyard of the high priest following Jesus' arrest, Luke simply continued the story. Matthew and Mark, on the other hand, switch from the courtyard scene to the trial and then switch back to the courtyard in order to complete the story of Peter's denial. The sandwiching of one event (the trial) within another (Peter's denial) is a characteristic of Mark's storytelling. The more logical procedure of staying with and telling the whole story in one setting is characteristic of Luke's "orderly account." What we have, therefore, is not contradictory accounts but an example of different authors using differing literary techniques to report the same traditions.

The denial portrays Peter in a very bad light. He is a coward and a liar. No serious attempt is made to provide an excuse for him. If the Gospel writers had wanted to defend Peter, they could have highlighted the fact that only he and another disciple (Jn 18:15) followed Jesus when he was arrested. Whereas the other disciples simply fled, Peter was brave enough to follow Jesus even into the courtyard of the high priest. Emphasis could have been made on the darkness, the confusion, the helplessness and so on. But nothing like this is done in the Gospels. Peter is simply described as having been intimidated by the situation and denying Jesus. He even began to curse and swear an oath (Mk 14:71).

The Gospel writers conclude this story by stating that "the cock crowed" and that upon hearing this Peter broke down and wept. Luke adds that at this precise moment Jesus turned and looked at Peter, although he does not tell us how that was possible (Lk 22:61). For Peter, there would be forgiveness and restoration (Mk 16:7). He would go on to lead the church during its infant years, and tradition tells us that when given the opportunity once again, he made the great confession with his own life as a martyr in Rome.

Matthew and Mark state that another meeting of the Sanhedrin took place early in the morning, during which they "held a consultation" (Mk 15:1). This did not involve another trial, for that would have been unnecessary, since Jesus had already been found guilty. (Luke may have combined the two meetings of the Sanhedrin into one in order to simplify the story for his readers.) The purpose of this meeting was for the Sanhedrin to draw up charges to present to Pontius Pilate, who was governor of Judah. Since the Roman governor would ultimately decide Jesus' fate, the Jewish leadership had to formulate the charges so that Pontius Pilate would be convinced of the need to execute Jesus.

The Sanhedrin had condemned Jesus on religious grounds. He was in their opinion guilty of blasphemy and should be executed. Rome, however, was not interested in Jewish religious questions as to what constituted blasphemy. If Pilate was going to execute Jesus, it would be because he was convinced that Jesus was dangerous and that he threatened the political stability and well-being of the empire. Thus the Sanhedrin met to formulate the political charges they would bring before Pilate: "We found this man perverting our nation, forbidding us to pay taxes to the emperor, and saying that he himself is the Messiah, a king" (Lk 23:2). It would be on these political charges that Jesus' fate would be decided. (We find a similar parallel in the case of Paul. Note how the religious charges against Paul in Acts 21:27—23:10 were changed to political ones in 24:5-6 when he was brought before the Roman governor.)

The trial before Pontius Pilate. All the Gospels agree that Jesus was brought from the home of Caiaphas to the praetorium, where Pilate was headquartered. At this point Matthew provides a short aside and tells the story of Judas's death. When Judas saw what he had done he "repented." This term is not the usual one we find in the New Testament to describe repentance. It refers more to experiencing remorse. Such remorse may lead to repentance, but it is not the same. Judas tried to undo what he had done by returning the money to the chief priests, but upon finding that this was of no avail he hanged himself (Mt 27:3-10).

According to John 18:31 the reason the Sanhedrin brought Jesus to Pilate was that it no longer had the right to carry out capital punishment. This statement finds support in the Talmud: "Forty years before the destruction of the Temple the Sanhedrin went into exile and took its seat in the Trade Halls. . . . They did not adjudicate in capital cases" (*b. Šabbat* 15a). Upon hearing the charges (Lk 23:2) Pilate began his preliminary questioning of the prisoner. What most concerned him was the charge that Jesus was claiming to be the Messiah, the long-awaited King of the Jews. When asked if he was King of the Jews, Jesus gave the same response he gave to the high priest: "You say so." According to John, Jesus qualified his kingship as being of another world (Jn 18:36-38). Whether Pilate understood this or not is unclear. But as a result of his questioning he was convinced that Jesus was not guilty of any crime worthy of death.

The result of this initial questioning led Pilate to believe that Jesus was innocent of the charges brought against him. How or why he came to this conclusion is not stated. We can only speculate as to whether he was convinced that Jesus was politically harmless or that he was impressed with his innocence. Mark attributes to Pilate the typical response Jesus elicits so often in his Gospel: he was "amazed" (Mk 15:5). Having come to the conclusion that Jesus was innocent, Pilate sought at this time to release him. Only the persistence of the Jewish leaders kept him from doing so. They insisted that Jesus was a threat to the peace and security of the land (Lk 23:5). For some reason Pilate was uneasy about condemning Jesus to death. According to Luke, Pilate's first attempt to rid himself of this problem was to send him to Herod Antipas.

Jesus before Herod Antipas. When Pilate discovered that Jesus was from Galilee, he sent him to Herod Antipas, who was tetrarch of Galilee from 4 B.C. to A.D. 39. It is unclear how Luke obtained information concerning this incident in the trial. Perhaps it was through Joanna, the wife of Herod's steward and a follower of Jesus (Lk 8:3), or through Manaen, a member of the court of Herod, who was also a follower of Jesus (Acts 13:1). Herod appears earlier in the Gospel accounts, for he was the one who executed John the Baptist. Now he would meet the even more famous Jesus of Nazareth.

Herod's knowledge of and interest in Jesus centered on his miracle-working ability. Luke points out that Herod was excited about meeting Jesus because he hoped to see him perform some sort of miraculous sign. This reveals a great deal about Herod. He was not interested in hearing the prophet Jesus but in seeing a magician. To be sure, Jesus worked miracles, but even more than this he proclaimed the divine message. He was not an entertainer who sought to titillate audiences with magical wonders.

When questioned by Herod, Jesus remained silent. The religious leaders who had accompanied Jesus to the residence of Herod continued to accuse him. Luke no doubt expected his readers to assume that their accusations were the same as those brought before Pilate. Perhaps in frustration due to Jesus' silence, Herod mocked him. Finally having dressed him in an elegant robe in mockery of his alleged kingship (Lk 23:11), he sent him back to Pilate. (Although the Greek in Lk 23:11 can be interpreted to mean that Herod himself donned this robe, in light of Mk 15:17-20 it is best to interpret the verse as indicating that Herod had the robe put on Jesus.) Herod would not take on himself the responsibility of Jesus' execution. Again, we can only speculate why. Could it be that he had already been burned once in putting John the Baptist to death (Mk 6:14-29)? Certainly executing Jesus would not endear him to his subjects in Galilee.

It is difficult to know why Pilate sent Jesus to Herod. Was he hoping to "pass the buck," believing that Jesus was innocent and not wanting to execute him? Was it because he was seeking to become reconciled to Herod by bestowing on him the honor of handling this famous case? Was it that he sought Herod's wisdom in making a decision concerning Jesus (compare Acts 25:13—26:32)? Luke's reason for recording this incident is clear: Herod provides a second ruler's verdict that Jesus was innocent (Lk 23:15). It is uncertain, however, exactly why Pilate sent him to Herod. Luke goes on to mention that through this Pilate and Herod became friends; it is ironic that by his death Jesus even brought about the reconciliation of such people as Pilate and Herod.

The trial before Pontius Pilate resumed. Upon the resumption of the trial, Pilate continued to seek Jesus' release. Matthew states that some of Pilate's hesitancy was due to his wife's dream concerning Jesus. Aided by the opinion of Herod, Pilate sought to appease Jesus' opponents by offering to flog him before releasing him (Lk 23:16). This was rejected. Still another attempt by Pilate to release Jesus involved the custom of releasing a prisoner at Passover (Mk 15:6). There is no evidence for such a custom outside the Gospels. All the Gospels, however, refer to it. The closest analogy that we have of such a custom is found in Egypt, where a prefect in Egypt says to an accused person, "You deserve to be scourged for the crimes you have committed, but I grant you to the crowd." The Gospel accounts seem to suggest that this custom may have been unique: "But you have a custom that I release someone for you at the Passover" (Jn 18:39). (Compare also Mt 27:15—"Now at the festival the governor was accustomed to release a prisoner for the crowd, anyone whom they wanted.")

Since Passover was a festival in which Jews remembered their deliverance from bondage, it was a most fitting time for such a custom to take place. No doubt Pilate was confident that the crowd would choose the popular Jesus of Nazareth over the other notorious candidate—Barabbas, a revolutionary bandit who had committed murder. To Pilate's surprise, however, the crowds, stirred up by the high priest and his followers, cried out for the release of Barabbas. When asked what he should then do with Jesus, the crowd cried, "Crucify him!"

Seated on the judgment seat (Mt 27:19; Jn 19:13), Pilate continued to seek the release of Jesus. His hesitancy was finally overcome, however, when the Jewish leaders cried out, "If you release this man, you are no friend of the emperor" (Jn 19:12). The expression "friend of the emperor" was a threat to Pilate. If he did not proceed with Jesus' crucifixion, he knew that the Jewish leaders would report to Rome that he had released a dangerous leader who called himself a king. Pilate's hesitancy came to an end. Washing his hands publicly in the sight of all, he stated, "I am innocent of this man's blood" (Mt 27:24). Then he handed Jesus over to his soldiers to be crucified.

The portrayal of Pilate in the Gospels is a tragic one. One can almost feel sorry for him. He held an unfortunate position in an unfortunate place at an unfortunate time. He tried as best he could to release Jesus and only gave in due to overwhelming pressure. But before one becomes too sympathetic toward this man one must remember what he did. He sentenced to a horrible death someone he knew to be innocent. He was unwilling to do what he knew was right. He sent the most innocent person who ever walked on the face of the earth to death while believing in his innocence. Such a person deserves no sympathy or pity, but scorn. And history will always think of him in the following terms ". . . Jesus Christ . . . suffered under Pontius Pilate, crucified . . ." (Compare Tacitus *Annals* 15.44.)

The Historicity of the Trial
Numerous objections have been raised against both the order of the

events given above and their historicity. It has been argued by some that the entire portrayal of the trial of Jesus before the Sanhedrin is fictitious. They contend that, due to the lack of success in the Jewish mission, the early church attempted to transfer the blame for Jesus' death from the Roman government, with which they had to live, to the Jewish leadership. They assert that Jesus' trial had nothing to do with the Jewish leaders but was purely a Roman trial from beginning to end. It was a decision by the church based on first-century "political correctness," which transferred the guilt and responsibility of Jesus' death from Rome to the Jews. They believe that in light of the terrible anti-Semitism that has resulted from this over the centuries, there is a need to correct the misunderstanding created by the New Testament. The anti-Semitism that led to the Holocaust provides a powerful motivation for seeing the trial as being purely a Roman one. After all "anti-Romanism" is not much of a danger for us to worry about today; anti-Semitism is.

The main historical support for questioning the historicity of the trial accounts found in the Gospels comes from two areas. The first involves various discrepancies between the Gospel accounts of the trial and the rules for such a trial found in the Talmud and, in particular, the tractate *Sanhedrin*. The second comes from the claim that since Judaism possessed the right to exercise capital punishment, the Jewish leaders would have had no need to bring Jesus before Pilate. They could have put him to death directly. Therefore the fact that Jesus was sentenced to death by Pontius Pilate and crucified by the Romans indicates that there was no Jewish involvement in the trial.

The Jewish rules for a trial as found in "b. Sanhedrin." Within the tractate *Sanhedrin* we read of various regulations that supposedly governed the activities of the Sanhedrin. There exist in the Gospel accounts of Jesus' trial more than two dozen violations of the Jewish code of law governing Sanhedrin procedures found in this tractate. Five are most significant:

1. A verdict of condemnation could not be reached on the same day as the trial.

2. No cases dealing with capital punishment were to be heard at night.

3. A death penalty could not be passed except at a special meeting place in the temple.

4. A trial could not be held on the eve of the sabbath or the eve of a festival day.

5. An attempt had to be made to find witnesses for the defense.

The above stand in stark contradiction to what we find in the Gospel accounts of Jesus' trial. As a result, some scholars reject the historicity of the Gospel accounts. These accounts of the trial are instead seen as attempts to shift the blame of the crucifixion from the Romans to the Jews. They are carefully crafted propaganda pamphlets written for Gentiles and Christians. Their attempt to shift the blame has furthermore resulted in a great deal of unjust anti-Semitism. But leaving aside for the moment the issue of anti-Semitism, several reasons exist for questioning the historicity of the accounts in the tractate *Sanhedrin*.

For one, the writing of the Mishna was completed about A.D. 200 and the Talmuds were completed approximately A.D. 400 (the Jerusalem Talmud) and 500 (the Babylonian Talmud). In the past it was common to accept at face value what the Mishna and Talmud said concerning the practices of previous centuries. It is now clear, however, that it is very difficult to establish the authenticity of situations described in the Talmud that predate A.D. 70. Often what they describe are idealized portrayals of institutions and practices that in reality were quite different. In this respect the question can also be raised whether a Sadducean-dominated Sanhedrin would try criminal cases according to the Pharisaic rules found in the Talmud.

Second, it should be noted that discrepancies exist between what the tractate *Sanhedrin* claims to have existed and what contemporary Jewish writers such as Josephus state. According to Josephus the Sanhedrin met during this period outside the temple (*Wars* 5.4.2 [5.144]; 6.6.3 [6.354]), whereas the Mishna claims that they met in a place inside the temple (*m. Middot* 5:4; *m. Sanhedrin* 11:2). The Talmud, on the other hand, appears to side with Josephus and states that at about A.D. 30 the Sanhedrin went into exile and met outside the temple in the "Trade Halls" *(Hannuth)*, which was located either on the Temple Mount or on the Mount of Olives (*b. Sanhedrin* 41a; *b. Šabbat* 15a; *b. 'Aboda Zara* 8b). Thus the rule in the tractate *Sanhedrin* that a death sentence could be passed only in a special place in the temple where the Sanhedrin met is unclear, since we do not know exactly where it met. In *m. Sanhedrin* 11:4 we furthermore read that a rebellious elder should be put to death during one of the three main feasts (Passover, Pentecost, the Feast of Tabernacles) to fulfill Deuteronomy 17:13: "All the people will hear and be afraid, and will not act presumptuously again."

A third consideration is that even if we were to agree for the sake of argument that all the rules in the tractate *Sanhedrin* were in effect during the time of Jesus (and this is unlikely), who can say that those rules were not or could not have been broken at the trial of Jesus? Early Christians claimed from the beginning that Jesus did not receive a fair trial. Can we accept as proof that Jesus must have received a fair trial before the Sanhedrin the fact that the rules in the tractate *Sanhedrin* demand it? Would anyone claim that in the United States everyone receives a fair trial because that is what the law demands? (Did the laws of Germany protect Jews from sham trials and kangaroo courts during the time of the Nazis?) The information in *b. Sanhedrin* 43a must be understood as counterpropaganda to the Christian claim that Jesus did not receive a fair trial. This attempt to defend Jesus' trial, however, suggests the very opposite. He did not receive a fair trial. Certainly few would argue that for forty days before Jesus' execution an attempt was made to find witnesses on his behalf.

Finally, if the issue ultimately comes down to a conflict between the Gospel accounts of what happened at Jesus' trial and the regulations described in the Talmud, which are we to believe? Certainly any claim that one source is more "objective" than the other is highly debatable. The Gospels, of course, were written from a Christian point of view, but the Talmud was likewise written from an idealized Jewish point of view of what should have taken place. As for dating these sources, if it is argued that the oral sources underlying the Talmud date back to the events, the same claim can be made for the oral sources underlying the Gospel accounts. As for their written dates, the Gospels were written well over a century earlier than the Mishna and more than three or four centuries earlier than the Jerusalem and Babylonian Talmuds. Furthermore, the Gospels were written at a time when eyewitnesses were still alive.

The right to exercise capital punishment in Jesus' day. Some scholars have attacked the historicity of the Gospel accounts of the trial by claiming that the Jews in Jesus' day would have had no need to go to Pilate since they already possessed the right to exercise capital punishment. A number of examples are given to support this claim. One example was the Jewish right to put to death any Gentile who left the court of the Gentiles in the temple and entered into the inner court. A fence separated the court of the Gentiles from the inner court. At the entrances through the fence were warnings that any Gentiles proceeding further would be the cause of their own death. Josephus (*Wars* 6.2.4 [6.126]) explicitly refers to this Jewish right to execute Gentiles in such instances (compare also 5.5.2 [5.194] and *Ant.* 15.11.5 [15.417]; Acts 21:27-36). Yet Josephus's statement actually demonstrates that the Jews did not have the power to practice capital punishment, for he points out that this privilege with respect to the violation of the inner court of the temple was a concession granted by the Romans. The very fact that the Romans permitted the Jewish people in this one instance to exercise capital punishment demonstrates that they did not have that right in other instances.

Another example that is sometimes given to support this claim involves the martyrdom of Stephen. Yet in the account in Acts 7 Stephen's death is not associated with a decision of the Sanhedrin and its right to exercise capital punishment. Stephen was killed through a mob lynching that had nothing to do with any Jewish right of capital punishment.

A third example often given involves the death of James, the brother of Jesus, by Ananus. According to Josephus (*Ant.* 20.9.1 [20.197-203]), Ananus, the high priest, convened the Sanhedrin and with their approval executed James by stoning. Once again, however, this example proves the opposite, namely, the lack of authority of the Jewish leaders to exercise capital punishment. The trial and stoning of James took place during the absence of a Roman governor, for the former governor had died and the new governor had not yet arrived. Upon his arrival the new governor, Albinus, immediately removed Ananus from the high priesthood, because what Ananus had done in putting James to death was illegal.

The right to exercise capital punishment was jealously guarded by Rome. It is even questionable whether a Roman governor during his absence could delegate this authority to one of his assistants. John therefore represents the situation well when he records that the Jewish leaders said, "We are not permitted to put anyone to death" (Jn 18:31). It is interesting in this regard that the Talmudic materials support this claim (*b. Šabbat* 15a; *j. Sanhedrin* 18a, 24b). It seems strange that here, where the Talmudic materials support the Gospel accounts, some critics claim that both are in error.

Conclusion

In discussing the trial of Jesus there is a great need to be sensitive to how these accounts have been understood and used in the past to support anti-Semitism. One of my most distressing experiences as a Christian was viewing the television series *The Holocaust*. In one scene, as women and children are standing naked in line to go to the gas chambers, a Nazi guard states, "We are doing this because you crucified Jesus." Whether Nazi guards actually said this and whether the women and children realized that they were about to be gassed is not at issue. In the past horrible injustices and pogroms have been directed toward Jews on the basis of their being "Christ killers." Christians should be the first to speak out against such evils.

On the other hand, we should not succumb to some politically correct desire to rewrite the Gospel accounts in order to refute this charge. We cannot rewrite what took place in the past. The Gospel accounts clearly portray the Jewish leaders of Jesus' day as being involved in his death. That is also the understanding of the rest of the New Testament (Acts 2:23, 36; 1 Thess 2:14-15), Josephus (*Ant.* 18.3.3 [18.64]), the Mara bar Serapion letter and the Talmud (*b. Sanhedrin* 43a). The high priest and the Sanhedrin were the chief agents in this. The arrest and trial of Jesus were the result of a long-term conspiracy against him (Jn 11:47-57). Not only did they condemn him, but they pressured Pontius Pilate to execute him even though he wanted to release him. No one who accepts the essential reliability of the Gospel accounts can deny that. However, it must always be pointed out that the leaders in doing so circumvented the will of the people.

The strongest hindrance to the Jewish leaders' desire to do away with Jesus was the Jewish people. The very fact that Jesus was betrayed reveals that the leaders could not arrest Jesus openly, because the people would have resisted it. The Gospel accounts clearly indicate that it was not the Jewish people who sought Jesus' death. Rather, it was certain leaders who did so contrary to the desires of the people as a whole. The only time the people appear to side with the leaders is in the cry for the release of Barabbas (Mk 15:13-14), but even here the Gospel writers point out that the chief priests stirred up the crowd to do so. The general portrayal of the Jewish people toward Jesus is positive: "The chief priests and the scribes were looking for a way to arrest Jesus by stealth and kill him; for they said, 'Not during the festival, or there may be a riot among the people' " (Mk 14:1-2). (The self-curse "His blood be·on us and on our children" [Mt 27:25] should be understood for what it is—a foolish and stupid statement by a few Jews who had been stirred up by the chief priests. Although Israel's unbelief had serious consequences [compare Mt 21:41, 43; Acts 13:46; Rom 11:11], this foolish self-curse cannot in any way serve as a justification for anti-Semitism.)

A proper understanding of the trial and death of Jesus does not allow room for anti-Semitism. We must remember that Jesus was a Jew. The disciples, the mother of Jesus and all those who loved Jesus were Jews. The earliest church members were all Jews. This makes the inflammatory statement "The Jews killed Jesus" absurd. Paul in Galatians 3:29 states that anyone who has faith in Jesus has become one of Abraham's children. Thus there is a sense in which every Gentile believer today is a spiritual descendant of Abraham, that is, a "Jewish" believer.

In a deeper sense, however, Christians know that *they* are the cause for Jesus' death. Ultimately it is the believer, for whom Christ died, who is responsible for his death. At the time of the crucifixion, if the Jewish leaders were not present and if no Roman soldiers were on hand, Jesus would still have had to die. The new covenant he brought had to be established by his blood. Thus, if those who enjoy fellowship in this new covenant seek a scapegoat, they need only look in a mirror. Even to blame the political authorities of Jesus' day as primarily responsible for his death ignores the biblical teaching that it was we, who follow Jesus, who brought about his crucifixion. It was our sin that caused his death. The death of Jesus was a divine necessity (Mk 8:31; 9:31; 10:33-34, 45).

There is no room for anti-Semitism in the Christian faith. A more biblical attitude is portrayed by Paul in Romans 9:3: "For I could wish that I myself were accursed and cut off from Christ for the sake of my own people, my kindred according to the flesh."

References

Bammel, Ernst, ed. *The Trial of Jesus*. Naperville, Ill.: A. R. Allenson, 1970.

Blinzler, Josef. *The Trial of Jesus: The Jewish and Roman Proceedings Against Jesus Christ*. Westminster, Md.: Newman, 1959.

Brown, Raymond E. *The Death of the Messiah*, pp. 311-877. New York: Doubleday, 1994.

Bruce, F. F. "The Trial of Jesus in the Fourth Gospel." In *Gospel Perspectives: Studies of History and Tradition in the Four Gospels*, edited by R. T. France, 1:7-20. Sheffield, U.K.: JSOT, 1980.

Catchpole, David R. *The Trial of Jesus: A Study in the Gospels and Jewish Historiography from 1770 to the Present Day.* Leiden: E. J. Brill, 1971.

Corley, Bruce. "Trial of Jesus." In *Dictionary of Jesus and the Gospels*, edited by Joel B. Green, Scot McKnight and I. Howard Marshall, pp. 841-54. Downers Grove, Ill.: InterVarsity Press, 1992.

Green, Joel B. *The Death of Jesus*, pp. 271-92. Tübingen, Germany: J. C. B. Mohr, 1988.

Sanders, E. P. *Jesus and Judaism*, pp. 294-318. Philadelphia: Fortress, 1985.

Sherwin-White, A. N. *Roman Society and Roman Law in the New Testament.* Oxford: Clarendon, 1963.

Winter, Paul. *On the Trial of Jesus.* New York: DeGruyter, 1974.

18
SUFFERED UNDER PONTIUS PILATE, DEAD & BURIED
Despised & Rejected, a Man of Suffering

T HE SCENE OF THE TRIAL BEFORE PILATE WAS THE PRAETORIUM. AL-though this term could be used for the Fortress of Antonia, where the local Roman garrison was housed, it is best to understand it as referring to the Herodian palace. That fits better the reference in Mark 15:16 to the praetorium's possessing a courtyard. Doubtless Pilate would have favored the more lavish accommodations found in the palace over the more spartan lodging available at Antonia.

When the sentence had been pronounced, the execution began. "After flogging Jesus, [Pilate] handed him over to be crucified" (Mt 27:26; Mk 15:15). A flogging *(phragelloō)* was normally part of a crucifixion (Josephus *War* 2.14.9 [2.306]). Luke does not refer to this directly but alludes several times to Pilate's suggestion of giving Jesus a flogging and then releasing him (Lk 23:16, 22). In John another term *(mastizō)* is used to describe the flogging (Jn 19:1), and it is mentioned along with other abuse Jesus received before his crucifixion.

From the praetorium Jesus was led to the place of execution, a small hill that could be seen at a distance. An execution was intentionally a public act, for it was meant to serve as a warning against crime and rebellion. Consequently the site was located near a road so that passersby could witness the execution. The place was called Golgotha in Aramaic, and this translates to Cranium in Greek and Calvary in Latin. In Jesus' day it was located outside the walls of the city (Mk 15:20; Jn 19:20; compare Heb 13:12). Thus they "went out" (Mt 27:32; cf. Mt 21:39) of the city to reach it. Later, when Herod Agrippa enlarged the city with the so-called third wall, this site was within the walls of Jerusalem.

Probably the most likely location today is the Church of the Holy Sepulchre. Traditions from as early as the second century associated this location with Golgotha, and in A.D. 325-335 Constantine chose this site to commemorate the crucifixion. Another site, "Gordon's Calvary," proposed in the nineteenth century has little to commend it.

The route Jesus took to the site of the crucifixion is mostly conjecture. The famous Via Dolorosa assumes that the trial took place at the Fortress of Antonia, which is unlikely. If Jesus was tried at the palace, another route would have been taken. But we must remind ourselves that it is not the *where* of these events that is important but the *what*.

The shape of the cross took varied forms: the traditional cross, or *crux immissa*, in which the vertical beam extended above the horizontal one (like a lower-case *t*), the *crux commissa*, which looked like a capital *T* (the horizontal beam rested on the vertical one), and the *crux decussata*, or crooked cross, which looked like an X. Crucifixion could even take place on a scaffold, where several victims would be crucified side by side. The fact that Jesus carried his cross argues against the last, and several factors favor the use of the traditional cross in Jesus' crucifixion. One is that Matthew 27:37 (compare Lk 23:38) refers to the legal charge's being placed "over his head." The other Gospels also mention this inscription's being affixed to the cross, and it is easier to understand the readability of the inscription if it was placed over Jesus' head (compare Jn 19:19-20).

Leaving the praetorium Jesus was compelled to carry his own cross (compare Plutarch *De sera num. vind.* 554A). Usually this did not involve the entire cross but only the crossbeam, or *patibulum*. The vertical beam, or *staticulum*, was intentionally left in the ground as a constant warning to all. Like a guillotine or hangman's noose in a public square, it was intended to serve as a deterrent from crime. As he carried this crossbeam,

Jesus' strength failed him. The scourging had taken its toll. To assist him the Roman soldiers impressed Simon of Cyrene to carry the crossbeam to Golgotha. (Lk 23:26 words this account in such a way that Simon became the first person who took up the cross and followed Jesus.) Cyrene was the capital city of the province of Cyrenaica in present-day Libya. Mention is made of a synagogue of the Cyrenians in Acts 6:9 (compare also 11:20; 13:1).

Questions have been raised as to the historicity of this reference. (How could Simon have been walking into the city during the Passover, since sabbath rules, which limited the amount one could travel, were in effect?) The historicity of this incident is assured, however, by Mark's reference to Simon as the father of Alexander and Rufus, the father of the readers' friends. It is inconceivable that the readers of Mark would not have inquired from these two men concerning this incident.

Mark also mentions that they "brought" Jesus to Golgotha. This may imply that Jesus needed help after his scourging to walk to Golgotha.

"And They Crucified Him"
It was customary for the victim to carry his cross naked to the place of execution. This added shame and humiliation to his execution. Perhaps it was due to Jewish sensitivity that Jesus was not required to do so, for after his scourging and mocking he was reclothed with his own garments. At the cross these were removed and divided among the soldiers. It was customary for the execution squad to share the clothing of the victim, but, since Jesus' tunic (the chiton, or undergarment) was seamless, the soldiers did not divide it into four parts. (This suggests that four soldiers made up the execution squad.) Instead, they cast lots for it. Normally the Romans crucified their victims naked, but due to Jewish sensitivity they may have allowed Jesus to wear some sort of a loincloth. The fact that Jesus did not bear the cross naked on the way to Golgotha supports this possibility.

Upon their arrival at Golgotha Jesus was offered wine mixed with myrrh (Mk 15:23). Within the Talmud we read,

When one is led out to execution, he is given a goblet of wine containing a grain of frankincense, in order to benumb his senses, for it is written, *Give strong drink unto him that is ready to perish, and wine unto the bitter in soul* [Proverbs 31:6]. And it has also been taught: The noble

women in Jerusalem used to donate and bring it. (*b. Sanhedrin* 43a)
The offer of this drink was a genuine act of compassion. The mixture
of wine and myrrh (both myrrh and frankincense are gum resins from
trees) was intended to bring about a stupefying effect that lessened the
pain of the victim. How it brought this about is uncertain. The dulling
effect of the alcohol in the wine is obvious, but there is no evidence that
myrrh, which is generally associated with embalming and used as a per-
fume, worked as a pain-killing drug. In Jesus' day, however, they apparently thought that it did.

It is unclear if the soldiers themselves offered this drink to Jesus or if
they permitted the women to do so. (Matthew refers to this drink as a
mixture of wine and "gall." In so doing he may have sought to show how
this act fulfilled Ps 69:21, seeing this act as one of mockery rather than
compassion.) Upon tasting the wine, Jesus refused to drink it. He was
committed to drink the "cup" that his Father had given him, and the cup
of wine and myrrh would interfere with that.

The term *crucifixion* can refer to several forms of capital punishment.
There was not always a clear distinction made between the crucifixion
of a victim who was alive and the public display of a corpse of a person
who had been put to death in another manner. *Crucifixion* can also refer
to the impaling of a person on a stake. Such a crucifixion would generally
bring instantaneous death. Such a death, however, did not serve well the
tastes of those who preferred death to be slow and painful. The better-
known form of crucifixion involved hanging a person on a cross of some
kind. This form of crucifixion goes back at least to the seventh century
B.C. and was made popular by Alexander the Great.

As the Roman Empire spread eastward, it soon made use of this form
of punishment. Among the Romans, crucifixion was a form of punishment for the lower classes. (Note how Jesus' self-emptying resulted in
a slavelike death, that is, death on a cross [Phil 2:7-8].) Roman citizens
were spared this form of execution. As a result, tradition tells us that
whereas Peter was martyred by crucifixion, Paul, being a Roman citizen,
was beheaded.

Jews were all too familiar with crucifixion, for even Jewish leaders used
it. In the first century B.C. the high priest Alexander Jannaeus crucified
eight hundred Pharisees who had revolted against him. In 4 B.C. the
Syrian governor crucified two thousand Jews. During the Jewish revolt

in A.D. 66-70 Josephus refers to Titus's crucifying five hundred Jews a day! He states that the number of victims was so great that there were not enough crosses for the victims and no longer room for crosses to be erected. Even allowing for hyperbole, a large number of Jews must have been crucified by the Romans in connection with the destruction of Jerusalem. Crucifixion remained the primary form of capital punishment in the Roman Empire until A.D. 337, when Constantine banned it.

The method of attachment to the cross varied. Tying and nailing the victim were the most common. Since this did not affect any vital, internal organs, death was slow. After being fastened to the crossbeam, the victim was then lifted up with it as the crossbeam was raised by forked poles. The crossbeam was then inserted in a notch in the vertical pole and secured. John 20:25 makes clear that Jesus' hands were nailed to the cross (compare Col 2:14). Luke 24:39 suggests that his feet may have been as well. In actuality the nails were driven not through the palms of the hands but through the wrists, for the hands would not be able to support the weight of the victim. (The Hebrew word for "hand" included the wrist.) The nails were generally driven between the two major bones in the wrists. With the discovery of a crucified man in 1968 whose feet were nailed independently to the sides of the vertical beam, there is no need to question Jesus' hands (wrists) and feet being nailed to the cross.

If the victim was supported only by the nails, he tended to die more quickly than the torturers wanted. As a result, they sometimes placed a footrest, or *suppedaneum,* at the bottom and/or a block of wood, or *sedile,* to support the buttocks. Crucifixion was thus sometimes described as "sitting on the cross." Although this allowed some relief for the body, it was not done as an act of kindness or mercy but as a means of prolonging the agony.

A great deal has been written concerning the "cause" of Jesus' death. Numerous medical doctors have sought to analyze the Gospel accounts, often treating them as if they were carefully written medical reports preserved for a later scientific community. The most commonly described cause of death is asphyxiation, but that cannot be proven. Bodily exhaustion, no doubt, also played a role.

Crucifixion is one of the most abominable forms of torture and execution that the world has ever seen. It is so horrible that only Christians speak positively of it, and that is only because of the redemption Jesus achieved by means of it. Among the Jews it was especially despised due to Deuteronomy 21:23 ("anyone hung on a tree is under God's curse"). This verse was later applied to crucifixion, adding the spiritual horror of the divine curse to the physical horror. Crucifixion involves all that a sadistic and evil torturer could want. The Roman poet Cicero referred to it as "the most cruel and most hideous of tortures" and said that "the very name 'cross' should not only be far from the body of a Roman citizen, but also from his thoughts, his eyes, and his ears" (*Pro Rabirio perduellionis* 5.16). Crucifixion involved lengthy torment.

In some cases the victim would live for days. Flies and insects would eat away at the lacerated back and the wounded hands and feet. One ancient writer referred to the victims of crucifixion as "food for birds of prey and grim pickings for dogs," for birds and animals would begin to feed on them even before they had died. It involved great agony, for the victim found no respite from his pain. There was nakedness and shame and the insults of those who seem always to find a sickening delight in the pain and torment of others. There was the feeling of absolute help-lessness. Slowly, so very slowly, the living corpse awaited the blessing of death. But it would not come until as much pain and suffering were extracted from the victim as possible. Almost any modern form of capital punishment looks amazingly "gracious" when compared to crucifixion.

The time of the crucifixion is described differently in the Gospels. All agree that Jesus was crucified on the eve of the sabbath. However, whereas Mark 15:25 tells us that the crucifixion took place at "nine o'clock in the morning" (literally, the third hour), John 19:14 states that it was "about noon" (about the sixth hour). Matthew and Luke do not give the time, but they must be thinking in terms of Mark's time frame, for they state along with Mark that at noon (the sixth hour) darkness came over the land (Mt 27:45; Mk 15:33; Lk 23:44). Thus although they do not specifically mention the third hour, they seem to assume it.

The best way to resolve this conflict is to remember that time desig-nations in that day lacked the precision of today. Such designations as 10:35 a.m. were impossible. In general one referred to the third, the sixth and the ninth hours (9:00 a.m., noon, 3:00 p.m.). In fact, of the twenty-three specific references to time in the New Testament, all but three of them use these time designations. The exceptions are Matthew 20:9 and John 1:39; 4:52. A person could, of course, be more precise, as these last examples illustrate, but generally people were content to speak in broad terms and refer to the third, sixth and ninth hours. As a result, an event occurring sometime between 9:00 a.m. and noon could quite easily be referred to as occurring at the third hour or the sixth hour. Later demands for more precision should not be imposed on the Gospel writers. Notice the approximate Johannine time designation of "about" noon. John may also have had a theological reason for choosing to use the sixth hour designation over the third hour, for it was at noon that the Passover lambs were slain. Thus according to the Johannine chronology Jesus, the "Lamb of God who takes away the sin of the world" (Jn 1:29, 36), and the Passover lambs were slain at the same time.

We read that Jesus was crucified between two "bandits" (Mt 27:38). This is a better translation than "thieves" or "robbers." The Greek term *lēstēs* is best understood as referring to a revolutionary. It is used of Barabbas (Jn 18:40), who is described as a "rebel" who had committed murder during an insurrection (Mk 15:7). Nothing is said about how they were crucified. The church later saw Jesus' death between two bandits as fulfilling the prophecy that Jesus "was numbered with the transgressors" (Is 53:12). It is unlikely, however, that this Old Testament reference created that tradition, for no reference is made to it in the Gospel accounts. The only allusion to it is found in Luke 22:37. That Jesus was the most important victim that day is evident, for he was placed in the center. It also appears that Jesus' position may have been somewhat higher off the ground. This explains the mocking call for Jesus to "come down from the cross!" (Mk 15:30, 32) and the use of a stick to reach Jesus' mouth (Mk 15:36; compare also Jn 3:14; 8:28; 12:32-34).

It was customary for the charge of the crucified to be displayed during the execution process (Suetonius *Caligula* 32.2 and *Domitian* 10.1; Dio Cassius 54.3.7). Sometimes the victim even wore it around his neck as he bore his cross to the place of execution. In the case of Jesus the title was affixed to the cross and placed over his head. The presence of this inscription, or *titulus*, is witnessed to in all four Gospels. The content of the inscription, which John 19:20 says was written in Hebrew, Latin and Greek, is reported as follows:

This is Jesus, the King of the Jews (Mt 27:37)
The King of the Jews (Mk 15:26)
This is the King of the Jews (Lk 23:38)

Jesus of Nazareth, the King of the Jews (Jn 19:19)
All agree that Jesus was crucified on the charge of being the King of the Jews (of being the Messiah). Pilate informed the public that Jesus was being executed for being Israel's king. This was clearly offensive to the Jewish leaders, who requested Pilate to change the inscription to read that Jesus "claimed" to be king of the Jews. Pilate, however, refused. Whether this was to spite the Jewish leaders for having caused him to do something he had not wanted to do is uncertain. But the irony was not lost on John in reporting this incident: through the inscription the Roman governor became an indirect and unknowing witness to Jesus' messianic claim. Although the Jewish leadership had claimed that their only king was Caesar (Jn 19:15), the Roman governor witnessed to the fact that Jesus was in fact their king. (Compare Jn 11:50 for a similar example, when Caiaphas unknowingly witnessed to the necessity of Jesus' dying for the nation.)

Upon Jesus' crucifixion the mocking began once again. It is apparent that throughout the trial and crucifixion Jesus was the object of ridicule. It occurred at the trial before the Sanhedrin (Mk 14:65), at the hearing before Herod (Lk 23:11), at the trial before Pilate (Mk 15:17) and during the crucifixion (Mk 15:29-32). At the cross the intensity of abuse increased. Soldiers, passersby, the Jewish leaders and even the bandits railed at him. Two main themes dominated the mockery. One was the riddlelike claim that he would rebuild the temple in three days after it was destroyed. The other was the messianic claim that he was the Christ, the King of the Jews. The latter reveals once again that Jesus was crucified for claiming to be the Christ. In light of Jesus' crucifixion by Pilate on political grounds and the inscription "King of the Jews" on the *titulus*, there should exist little doubt that Jesus believed, accepted and taught that he was the Christ. His crucifixion removes all serious doubt.

The Seven Last Words of Jesus
The Gospels present us with seven different sayings uttered from the cross. Luke and John record three each, whereas Mark and Matthew record one in common. Arriving at the exact order in which they occurred is highly problematical. The traditional order is as follows: "Father, forgive them; for they do not know what they are doing"; "Today you will be with me in Paradise"; "Woman, here is your son. . . . Here

is your mother"; "My God, my God, why have you forsaken me?"; "I am thirsty"; "It is finished"; "Father, into your hands I commend my spirit."

"Father, forgive them; for they do not know what they are doing" (Lk 23:34). The manuscript testimony for this saying is mixed. Some of the earliest and best Greek manuscripts lack this verse. As a result, it is uncertain as to whether it was part of Luke's original writing or a later scribal addition. In favor of its being part of Luke is the fact that in Acts 7:60 we have a parallel saying on the lips of Stephen. Since Luke intentionally sought to parallel what occurs in Acts with what occurs in his Gospel, this may indicate that Acts 7:60 is the equivalent in that book to what Luke has recorded Jesus as saying. The "they" to whom Jesus refers includes not only the ignorant bystanders but also the Romans and the Jewish leaders involved in his crucifixion. Although they thought they knew what they were doing, they really did not. (Compare Paul in Acts 26:9, who thought he knew what he was doing in persecuting the church but really did not.)

"Truly I tell you, today you will be with me in Paradise" (Lk 23:43). Although at one time both the bandits crucified alongside Jesus ridiculed him, Luke records that one later had a change of heart. How this came about is not stated. We can only speculate as to whether Jesus' character persuaded him of his innocence or whether it was revealed to him in some supernatural fashion. Luke, however, does not tell us. For him this incident served as another witness to Jesus' innocence. Earlier Herod and Pilate witnessed to it. Here even a bandit acknowledged it. But he acknowledged more: he confessed that Jesus is the King of the Jews, and he requested that Jesus remember him when he entered into his kingly reign.

Jesus' response was the promise that when he entered into the full presence of God (literally, "Paradise"), he would bring the bandit with him. Needless to say, this saying has been an encouragement to many people over the centuries. Salvation is indeed by grace. There is no one so evil, there is no one so hopeless, that they cannot come to Jesus for mercy and find forgiveness and eternal life even in the "eleventh hour."

"Woman, here is your son." . . . "Here is your mother" (Jn 19:26-27). Rather than reading into this saying a deep religious symbolism, it is best to take it at face value. Jesus was concerned for his mother's well-being and sought to provide care for her. He did so by entrusting her into the keeping of the beloved disciple who that day took her into his home.

Whereas earlier Jesus had been responsible for caring for his mother, now in his absence the beloved disciple would care for her.

Where the "brothers and sisters" of Jesus fit into all this is unclear. The idea that Mary remained a perpetual virgin after the birth of Jesus and that his brothers and sisters were simply cousins fits this scene nicely. (The view that the brothers and sisters of Jesus were Joseph's sons and daughters by a previous marriage does not fit as well, and the view that they were Joseph and Mary's children does not seem to fit this action at all.) Nevertheless, the evidence that Jesus' brothers and sisters were true half-siblings, sons and daughters of Joseph and Mary, is convincing. As a result this scene remains a problem. Why did Jesus not entrust his mother to her own children? Could it be that since at this time they did not believe in him (cf. Jn 7:1-5), he did not want to entrust her to "unbelievers"? We simply do not know.

"Eloi, Eloi, lema sabachthani?" . . . *"My God, my God, why have you forsaken me?"* *(Mk 15:34).* This is the only saying from the cross that is found in two Gospels. Both Mark and Matthew state that it took place after "darkness came over the whole land" (Mk 15:33). The Evangelists saw this darkness as deeply symbolic. Darkness is often associated with divine judgment in the Bible (Joel 2:2, 10; 3:15; Amos 8:9; Zeph 1:15; Wisdom 5:6), and the Gospel writers wanted their readers to know that judgment was coming upon the nation. Doubtless their readers saw in the events of A.D. 70 a fulfillment of this. Another fulfillment would be in the kingdom of God being taken from Israel and given to the Gentiles (Mk 12:9; Rom 9:30-33). Along with its association with judgment, darkness is also associated with evil. At Gethsemane Jesus had said, "But this is your hour, and the power of darkness!" (Lk 22:53). The time of the crucifixion was indeed an hour of evil and "darkness."

Numerous suggestions have been made as to what caused this darkness. That it serves a theological purpose is of course true, but this need not mean that the reference to darkness is fictional. One suggestion is that it was due to an eclipse—one way of reading Luke 23:45 is "the sun having been eclipsed"—but this explanation is unlikely for several reasons. For one, the maximum time for a solar eclipse is about eight minutes, and the accounts say that this darkness continued from noon to three in the afternoon. Second, a solar eclipse is not possible during the full moon at Passover time. Other suggestions are sunspots, a volcanic eruption, a sirocco dust storm coming in from the desert, a thunderstorm and so on. We simply do not know what caused the darkness. As for the comment that there was darkness over the whole land/earth, we should interpret this much as we do Luke 2:1 and its reference to Caesar's decree that all the world should be registered. It is descriptive language using hyperbole.

Closely associated with this symbol of judgment is another: the veil of the temple being rent in two from top to bottom. Whether this refers to the outer veil leading into the sanctuary (the Holy Place) or the inner veil leading into the Holy of Holies makes little difference. (In favor of the former is the fact that this veil was visible to the crowds in the temple, whereas the latter was visible only to the priests serving in the sanctuary. In favor of the latter is the reference in Heb 10:19-20.) The use of the passive "was rent" indicates that God was the cause. Whereas the rent veil can serve as a symbol that those who believe in Jesus have direct access to God (compare Heb 10:19-22), it serves here primarily as an omen of judgment. God had forsaken the temple (Mt 23:37-38; 2 Baruch 6:7; *Testament of Levi* 10:3). Soon it would be destroyed. Already through Jesus' death, however, it had been rendered obsolete and was superseded.

"My God, my God, why have you forsaken me?" comes from Psalm 22:1. In his desire to express his agony and sense of feeling forsaken, Jesus quoted a lament psalm. He sensed, like the psalmist before him, that he was all alone. God had left him comfortless. Although he was committed to obeying God's will and suffering death by way of the cross, he could not help but express his agony. There is no need to assume that Jesus had foreknown all that he was now experiencing. It is here more than anywhere else that the cost of his fulfilling the will of the Father becomes clear. It is here more than anywhere else that the Christian community becomes aware of the seriousness and horror of sin.

Turning to his native tongue, Jesus quoted the psalm in Aramaic, in the form that was most familiar to him: "Eloi, Eloi, lema sabachthani?" On hearing this some of the bystanders thought that he was calling for Elijah. In the Greek text such confusion is quite understandable, for the Aramaic "My God" *(eloi)* and the Greek "Elijah" *(Elias)* are reasonably close, but in Aramaic the two terms are not. As a result, it is unclear how or why this misunderstanding occurred. In response someone filled a sponge with the vinegar wine that soldiers usually drank, placed it on a stick and offered it to Jesus. In John this act is described as taking place after the next saying.

"I am thirsty" (Jn 19:28). This cry reveals something of the suffering and helplessness Jesus experienced. The tradition has placed this saying next to the previous one because of the similar response. A sponge filled with wine was offered to Jesus. It is uncertain in Mark if this offer was a form of mockery. Did he expect his readers to interpret this act in light of Psalm 69:21 ("They gave me poison for food, and for my thirst they gave me vinegar to drink")? If so, it would be a hostile act. It is also uncertain in Mark whether the offer of wine was actually carried out. In John the offer was not hostile but friendly, and Jesus accepted it. It is unclear in John whether the soldiers themselves offered Jesus this drink or whether they permitted someone in the crowd to do so. John describes the wine-filled sponge as being on the end of "a branch of hyssop" (Jn 19:29). If this refers to the hyssop associated with the Passover (Ex 12:22; Heb 9:18-20), it is difficult to understand how that kind of hyssop could have borne the weight of a sponge filled with wine. What exactly the term *hyssop* refers to remains unclear.

"It is finished" (Jn 19:30). Jesus knew that his work had been completed. He had been victorious. He had completed the work he had been sent to do. In so doing he fulfilled the will of God and thus the Scriptures. These words are a powerful reminder against any and all who somehow suggest that to the grace shown in the cross something more needs to be added. It is audacious indeed to think that one could somehow add something to Jesus' work. Redemption was accomplished once and for all.

"Father, into your hands I commend my spirit" (Lk 23:46). When Jesus spoke of his death at the Last Supper, he was confident. One day he would share the messianic banquet with his disciples. Here, too, he was confident. Like the psalmist Jesus believed that God would not hide his face but would hear his cry (Ps 22:24) and that he would therefore live (v. 29). Unlike the cry of agony, this prayer of committal is addressed to his "Father."

The Death of Jesus

The specific cause of Jesus' death is not given in the Gospel accounts. Some have suggested that it was from a "broken heart." Others speak of asphyxia. Whatever may have been the physiological cause, the Gospel portrays that even here Jesus was in charge. He gave up his spirit (Mt 27:50; Jn 19:30). The tie between life and the will is mysterious, but those working with dying people often testify how people at a certain point can willingly submit to death. At this point Jesus had accomplished what he had been sent to do. His work was finished; he had successfully run the race that had been set before him (compare Heb 12:1). He now placed himself into the hands of his Father and gave up his spirit.

Jesus' death was accompanied by a number of signs. As already mentioned, the veil of the temple was torn from top to bottom. There was also an earthquake. Rocks were split in two. (Indirect support for these phenomena is sometimes seen in Tacitus *Histories* 5.13, Josephus *War* 6.5.3 [6.288-96], and *j. Yoma* 6:43c, but these references are quite ambiguous.) Tombs were opened, and many of the dead were raised. Those raised entered Jerusalem and were seen by many (Mt 27:52-53). It is unclear how "after his resurrection" (27:53) should be understood. It may indicate that whereas the tombs were opened and the dead were raised to life, those resurrected from the dead did not enter Jerusalem until after the resurrection, or it may indicate that all of this occurred after Jesus' resurrection.

The first signs (veil, earthquake, rocks) were omens of judgment and witnessed to the divine judgment on Israel both then and in the near future (A.D. 70). The resurrection of the dead was a sign witnessing to the arrival of the new age. Probably this resurrection is best understood in terms of the others mentioned in the Gospel accounts. Like Jairus's daughter, the widow of Nain's son and Lazarus, they would again experience physical death. The resurrection from mortality to immortality that Jesus experienced still awaits his return when history comes to an end.

The Synoptic Gospels record at this time a confession by the centurion: "Truly this man was God's Son!" (Mk 15:39; compare Mt 27:54). This confession should be understood in the fullest christological sense. That is the intention of the Evangelists. The lack of the Greek article before "Son" does not mean that we should translate this confession "Truly this man was *a* son of God." In light of the Evangelists' purpose in recording this confession, it must be understood as "Truly this man was *the* Son of God," just as in the titles found in Luke 1:32, 35 and Matthew 27:40, 43, where the article is also missing in the Greek text. The reason given in explanation for this confession is that the centurion saw "what had taken place" (Lk 23:47); that is, he saw "the earthquake and what took place" (Mt 27:54). Having seen (or heard about) these signs and having witnessed the character of Jesus during the crucifixion, the centurion was led to make this confession. Doubtless his understanding of this confession was less rich and full than that of the readers of the Gospels.

In John we read that because the following day was the sabbath the execution had to be brought to completion. It was not permitted among the Jews for bodies to be left exposed in this manner on the sabbath (Deut 21:23). To hasten death one would break the legs of the victims. A name was even given to this procedure—*crurifragium*. This both brought additional shock upon the victim and made breathing more difficult. What a victim would often do during crucifixion when his lung muscles became weary was to press his legs against the footrest or the nails that pierced his feet and thus allow the lung muscles to regain some of their strength. With the legs broken that was no longer possible, and breathing became more difficult. Accordingly, the legs of the two bandits were broken, but it was not necessary to do this to Jesus. He was already dead.

One of the soldiers pierced Jesus' side with a spear, and "blood and water came out" (Jn 19:34). How this should be interpreted is greatly debated. Some have treated this statement as if it were an official autopsy report. Numerous medical studies have been made as to its significance. Yet John's purpose is less physiological than theological. Some have seen this as being aimed at proto-Gnostics, who argued that Jesus did not really die. John's statement plus the following verse are interpreted as refuting such a view by stating that he witnessed Jesus die on the cross. He saw Jesus' lifeblood and water flow from his body. Others have interpreted the blood and water as a reference to Jesus' death as the Passover lamb, with the resulting coming of the Spirit (compare Jn 7:38-39). Still another view is that they refer to baptism (water), which is associated with the coming of the Spirit (compare Jn 3:5), and the Lord's Supper (blood).

The Burial of Jesus
The bodies of criminals were often denied burial. It may very well be that the bodies of the two bandits were simply cast into some pit. This did

not occur with respect to Jesus. His burial is associated with a man named Joseph of Arimathea, a secret believer who was a member of the Sanhedrin (Mt 27:57; Jn 19:38). Luke makes a point of stating that Joseph had not agreed to the plan and action of the Sanhedrin in seeking to kill Jesus (Lk 23:50-51). (This reveals that the "whole council" and the "all" of Mk 14:55, 64; 15:1 are somewhat hyperbolic.) At great personal risk he went to Pilate and sought the body of Jesus. He did this not as a devout Jew who sought to keep the sabbath from being profaned but as a genuine follower of Jesus. Pilate was surprised that Jesus had died so quickly, but after confirming that Jesus was indeed dead he permitted Joseph to have the body.

It is somewhat confusing as to whether Joseph himself removed the body of Jesus from the cross or whether one of the soldiers did. According to John, Nicodemus, who may also have been a secret believer, assisted Joseph in burying Jesus. Placing Jesus' body in a linen cloth, they brought him to a tomb carved out of rock. Luke and John refer to it as a tomb "where no one had ever been laid" (Lk 23:53; compare Jn 19:41). Thus it was a fitting place for the burial of the King of the Jews. (Compare the use of a virgin colt on Palm Sunday [Lk 19:30, 38].) Matthew points out that this was Joseph's own tomb (Mt 27:60) and that he was a rich man (v. 57). Although no explicit mention is made in the Gospels to Isaiah 53:9 ("They made his grave with the wicked and his tomb with the rich"), later interpreters saw this as an example of the fulfillment of Scripture.

In preparing the body, Joseph and Nicodemus would first have washed the body and removed from it the caked dirt and blood. Frequently those preparing a body for burial would cut the fingernails and hair, close the eyes and so on (see *m. Šabbat* 23:5). We are not told all that took place. There is mention of a linen cloth *(sindōn)* used to wrap Jesus, and John refers to "cloths" (19:40, *othonion*). It may be that the Synoptic Gospels concentrate on the major cloth that was used, whereas John points out that there were other pieces, such as a headpiece, as well. Unlike the Egyptians, the Jews did not remove the inner organs and practice embalming. Jesus' body, after being washed, was wrapped with spices (myrrh and aloes). The latter served primarily as deodorants to offset the smell of bodily decomposition. According to John 19:39 the spices used weighed "about a hundred pounds." A Roman pound was about twelve ounces. But even when translated to our system of weights, that appears to be an enormous amount—seventy-five pounds! It is uncertain whether we are to interpret this weight literally or symbolically.

Once they finished their work, the body was laid in Joseph's tomb and sealed with a stone. This tomb was cut out of a rock wall. Such a tomb contained an opening about three feet high. Inside there was frequently room to stand, and as the tomb became used for more and more burials additional rooms were sometimes added. The stone used to seal the opening was probably shaped like a wheel. Lying in a trenchlike track, it would be rolled down the trench to cover the tomb opening, resting securely against a wall. To prepare us for the story of the empty tomb, the first three Gospel writers state that Mary Magdalene and another Mary were present observing the burial procedure.

Matthew states that on the sabbath the Jewish leaders appeared before Pilate. They were concerned over Jesus' saying about rising on the third day from the dead (Mt 27:62-63). Whether this was their understanding of Jesus' riddle concerning the temple being destroyed and rebuilt in three days (Mk 14:58) or whether they had heard about Jesus' passion and resurrection predictions (Mk 8:31; 9:31; 10:33-34) is uncertain. They realized, however, that if the disciples were to steal the body of Jesus and tell the people that Jesus had risen from the dead, "the last deception would be worse than the first" (Mt 27:64). Thus they requested that the tomb be made "secure" against the possibility of theft.

Pilate's reply (Mt 27:65) can be interpreted in two ways: "You have your own guard. You secure the tomb with them," or "I grant your request. I am giving you a guard of Roman soldiers to secure this." Several arguments favor the latter interpretation. (1) The term *soldiers* (*stratiōtais*) used in Matthew 28:12 to describe this guard is almost always used in the New Testament for Roman soldiers (compare Mt 27:27). It is never used with respect to the temple police under the control of the Jewish leaders. (2) In the *Gospel of Peter* 8:31, a second-century work, the guard is understood in this manner. (3) If the guards were Jewish and under the control of the Jewish leaders, why would they be in danger of getting in trouble with the Roman governor for the disappearance of Jesus' body (Mt 28:14)?

Having thus been given a Roman guard, the Jewish authorities sealed the tomb. The latter involved placing a portion of wax at a place where the stone and the wall joined and impressing on the wax the Roman seal. Thus the Jewish leaders and Rome worked side by side to keep the body of Jesus within the tomb. Their power and authority, however, would secure the tomb for only a day, for on Easter all this would be for nothing.

Theories That Jesus Was Not Crucified

In this discussion of the death of Jesus nothing has been said concerning some of the absurd theories that Jesus of Nazareth did not really die on the cross. Most of them are refuted by their own explanations of what supposedly happened.

One such theory argues that it was not Jesus who was crucified but Simon of Cyrene. By mistake upon arrival at Golgotha the soldiers thought that the one bearing the cross, Simon, was Jesus, and they crucified him. Does one really have to refute such a theory by pointing out that confusing a flogged Jesus covered with blood and unable to bear his own cross with a man who was not flogged is impossible? And could the soldiers who started with Jesus somehow forget what he looked like and how he was dressed on the way to the cross? Did the enemies of Jesus railing at him as he hung on the cross forget so quickly what Jesus looked like?

Another explanation, which comes out of a Gnostic setting, is that whereas the body of Jesus was crucified, the real Jesus (his "spirit") was not. Some of these explanations even have the "real" Jesus sitting on the cross during the nailing, laughing in derision at what was taking place. Such a theory is so heavily based on an untenable dualism of body and spirit that it does not require any refutation. It even admits what it seeks by its dualism to deny—that Jesus of Nazareth, the son of Mary, was crucified.

Another theory is that a brother of Jesus was confused with him and crucified in his place. Still another theory, found in the Qur'an, claims that Jesus was not crucified but that a double was substituted: someone was transformed to look like Jesus and was crucified in his place. One theory involves Judas. According to this theory, although Judas agreed to betray Jesus, at the last minute in the Garden of Gethsemane he intentionally kissed another man who was present, and this other man was crucified rather than Jesus.

All these theories require unbelievable error and confusion on the part of those involved in Jesus' death. It is hard to imagine that those who desperately wanted Jesus killed were confused about his appearance and could be so easily mistaken. He was a public figure. He had been teaching openly in the temple. To believe one of these theories we must radically alter the Gospel accounts in a manner that is not credible.

Conclusion
The death of Jesus of Nazareth on the cross is one of the best-known and best-attested events of history. Its denial is not based on evidence but on apologetic motives. The fact remains—Jesus of Nazareth truly suffered under Pontius Pilate, died and was buried!

References

Brown, Raymond E. *The Death of the Messiah*, pp. 880-1524. New York: Doubleday, 1994.

Dodd, C. H. "The Historical Problem of the Death of Jesus." In *More New Testament Studies*, pp. 84-101. Grand Rapids, Mich.: Eerdmans, 1968.

Fitzmyer, Joseph A. "Crucifixion in Ancient Palestine, Qumran Literature and the New Testament." *Catholic Biblical Quarterly* 40 (1978): 493-513.

Green, Joel B. "Death of Jesus." In *Dictionary of Jesus and the Gospels*, edited by Joel B. Green, Scot McKnight and I. Howard Marshall, pp. 146-63. Downers Grove, Ill.: InterVarsity Press, 1992.

_____ . *The Death of Jesus*. Tübingen, Germany: J. C. B. Mohr, 1988.

Hengel, Martin. *Crucifixion in the Ancient World and the Folly of the Message of the Cross*. Philadelphia: Fortress, 1977.

Kiehl, Erich H. *The Passion of Our Lord*. Grand Rapids, Mich.: Baker Book House, 1990.

Lohse, Eduard. *History of the Suffering and Death of Jesus Christ*. Philadelphia: Fortress, 1967.

O'Collins, Gerald G. "Crucifixion." In *Anchor Bible Dictionary*, 1:1207-10. New York: Doubleday, 1992.

Senior, Donald. *The Passion of Jesus in the Gospel of Mark*. Wilmington, Del.: Michael Glazier, 1984.

19
THE RESURRECTION
"Why Do You Look
for the Living Among
the Dead?"

LATE ON FRIDAY AFTERNOON JESUS' BODY WAS BURIED BY JOSEPH OF Arimathea in Joseph's own tomb. Shortly afterward the sabbath (6:00 p.m. Friday to 6:00 p.m. Saturday) began. It was a day of rest, but for the followers of Jesus it was a day of emotional turmoil. The Gospels do not inform us of their experience, for the story of Good Friday and Easter is not about them but about Jesus. Yet almost certainly it was for the disciples a day of sorrow and great confusion. Due to concern over possible theft of Jesus' body by the disciples, the Jewish leaders sought and obtained from Pontius Pilate a Roman guard for the tomb. On the sabbath the tomb was guarded by the seal of Rome and Roman troops. But as Sunday morning began, the single greatest event in human history would take place.

Several time designations associated with the Easter event exist: "after three days" (Mt 27:63; Mk 8:31; 9:31; 10:34), "on the third day" (Mt 16:21; 17:23; 20:19; Lk 9:22; 18:33; 24:7, 46; compare Lk 13:32; 24:21) and "in three days" (Mt 26:61; 27:40; Mk 14:58; 15:29; Jn 2:19-20). (Compare also Mt 27:64.) How do these designations fit a Sunday, or first day of the week, resurrection? What should be observed from the beginning is that for the Gospel writers these diverse designations did not pose a problem. They were understood as alternative ways of saying the same thing. Matthew could use each of these expressions to describe the time of Jesus' resurrection. They fit for him a Friday-afternoon death and Sunday-morning resurrection without difficulty. Keeping in mind the Jewish understanding of time, the sequence of events was thus:

Day One   6:00 p.m. Thursday to 6:00 p.m. Friday, during which the Last Supper, Gethsemane, the trial, the crucifixion and burial took place

Day Two   6:00 p.m. Friday to 6:00 p.m. Saturday, during which the tomb was guarded

Day Three   6:00 p.m. Saturday to 6:00 p.m. Sunday, when the resurrection took place

The only significant temporal difficulty comes from Jesus' saying that "just as Jonah was three days and three nights in the belly of the sea monster, so for three days and three nights the Son of Man will be in the heart of the earth" (Mt 12:40). One cannot fit three literal "days" and "nights" between Friday evening and Sunday morning. It appears, however, that "three days and three nights" is simply another way of saying "on the third day" or "after three days." This can be seen in 1 Samuel 30:12-13, which contains the expression "for three days and three nights." The Greek translation (LXX) is exactly the same as "for three days and three nights" in Matthew 12:40. In verse 13, however, this time designation is described as "three days ago." Thus "on the third day," "after three days," "in three days," "three days ago" and "for three days and three nights" are all expressions the biblical writers used to designate the same period of time.

Difficulties in the Resurrection Accounts
Since several apparent discrepancies are found in the Gospel accounts of the resurrection, numerous harmonizations have been attempted. Some

are more successful than others, but none is totally convincing. Many scholars have despaired of ever arriving at a satisfactory solution. The main difficulties can be summed up as follows: (1) How many women were actually at the tomb? Were there five (Luke), three (Mark), two (Matthew) or one (John)? (2) Who were the messengers encountered at the tomb? Were they men (Mark and Luke) or angels (Matthew and John)? Were there two (Mark and Matthew) or one (Luke and John)? Note, however, that using the term *young man* (as in Mark and Luke) was a conventional way of referring to an angel. Luke makes this identification in 24:4, 23 (compare also 2 Macc 3:26, 33). (3) Were the men/angels located inside the tomb (Mark, Luke, John) or outside (Matthew)? (4) Did Jesus appear to the disciples in Jerusalem (Luke) or in Galilee (Matthew)?

Early on the sabbath some women, led by Mary Magdalene, left Jerusalem for the tomb. The Synoptic Gospels prepare their readers for this by pointing out that Mary Magdalene and another Mary were onlookers during the burial process. Thus the location of the tomb was known to them. In the Easter story, Matthew mentions these two women, whereas Mark refers to the second Mary as the mother of James and Joses (compare Mk 15:40 with 15:47 and 16:1) and adds Salome. The exclusion of Salome's name by Matthew may be due to her playing such a minor role in his Gospel. For John only Mary Magdalene is of importance (Jn 20:1), but Luke adds Joanna and "other women" (Lk 24:10). His mention of all these women fits well the emphasis on the role of women found in his Gospel. Thus the problem of the number of women present at the tomb is not a major one, as long as we do not force John (one), Matthew (two) and Mark (three) to mean that only the women they mention were there.

The purpose of the women's coming was to anoint the body of Jesus. Whether they were unsatisfied with the preparation of the body by Joseph of Arimathea, whether they "just wanted to make sure" that all was done that could have been done or whether it was for some other reason we are not told. The personal reasons for their coming were not important to the Gospel writers. The importance of their coming lay in their being witnesses to the resurrection. Mark mentions that they were concerned over who would roll away the stone for them (Mk 16:3). It appears that they were unaware of the guard that had been placed at the tomb, probably because it was done on the sabbath without great fanfare. Since they came hoping to anoint a dead body, the idea of Jesus' rising from the dead was far from their minds. They were certainly not in a proper frame of mind for having a hallucination about seeing a risen Christ!

Matthew refers to a "great earthquake" (Mt 28:2) taking place at this time and the angel of the Lord rolling back the stone. (This earthquake should not be confused with the earthquake mentioned in Mt 27:51, and to refer to it as an "aftershock" of the former is simply speculation.) Matthew comments that the earthquake brought fear and panic, and the guards fled. When the guards reported what had happened and that the tomb was empty, the Jewish leaders bribed them to say that the disciples had stolen the body while they were asleep. Such a report might have had serious consequences for the soldiers. Sleeping on guard duty could result in execution. Because of this the Jewish leaders agreed to "cover for them" when the governor heard about it.

Coming to the tomb, the women found the stone rolled away. The purpose of the stone's being rolled away was not to allow the risen Christ to leave the tomb (compare Jn 20:19) but to allow the women to enter and see that the tomb was empty. At this point the four Gospel accounts become difficult to harmonize into an understandable unity. That does not mean that they could not be harmonized if additional information were available. At the present time, however, such information is lacking. Something like the following seems to have taken place.

The tomb was discovered empty, and rather than thinking that Jesus had risen from the dead, the women were convinced that someone had come and stolen the body (Jn 20:2, 13-15). An angelic messenger (or messengers) told them that Jesus was not dead but risen. For Mary Magdalene this was confirmed by Jesus himself (Jn 20:16-17). Told to go and inform the disciples, the women left the tomb and proceeded to do so. The report of the women was treated with skepticism by the disciples. They too were not prepared psychologically for the resurrection. The report was considered "an idle tale" (Lk 24:11). Peter and "the other disciple" (Jn 20:3) ran to the tomb to check this out and found it just as the women said. Doubt, however, remained and was not overcome until Jesus himself appeared to them.

The Historicity of the Empty Tomb
Prior to the twentieth century the historicity of the empty tomb has been

accepted by all. This was true both of those who believed in the resurrection of Jesus and of those who denied it. The empty tomb is in reality the earliest historical "fact" associated with the resurrection. It predates even the rise of faith in the disciples. It was accepted by Jewish opponents as early as the first century, for the theory that the disciples stole the body of Jesus (Mt 28:11-15) assumes it. If we take Matthew's account at face value, this explanation of the empty tomb existed already on the first Easter Sunday. In the twentieth century, however, the historicity of the empty tomb has come under severe attack.

A number of arguments have been raised challenging the emptiness of the tomb. Some attack this Gospel tradition as being unreliable and argue that it is very late. Paul, it is said, knew nothing about it. The empty tomb tradition is understood as a legendary addition to the resurrection accounts. It was created by the early church as an apologetic to prove Jesus' resurrection. They reason that since in the minds of most a resurrection must have involved the transformation of Jesus' physical body, it was a logical necessity to say that after the resurrection his tomb was empty. Thus the tradition of the empty tomb was created.

Another objection to the historicity of the empty tomb is that it played no role in the preaching of the early church. This point can be granted with one reservation. The existence of the theory that the disciples stole the body proves that in some contexts the empty tomb was part of the Christian proclamation. Nevertheless, it is true that early Christian preaching of the resurrection emphasized the resurrection appearances rather than the empty tomb (see, for instance, Acts 2:32; 3:15; 5:30; 10:39-41). It was not the accounts of the empty tomb that brought about the rise of faith in the disciples but the appearances of the risen Christ. On the other hand, whereas the emptiness of the tomb did not prove the resurrection of Jesus or give birth to it, the presence of Jesus' body in the tomb would have ruled it out.

Although it has become popular in the twentieth century to deny the reality of the empty tomb, there are powerful arguments against its being an apologetic legend: the multiple attestation of the empty tomb; the proclamation of Jesus' resurrection assumes the empty tomb; women were witnesses of the empty tomb; the fact of the empty tomb was acknowledged by the Jews; the empty tomb was a well-known tomb; Sunday worship is due to the discovery of the empty tomb on the first day of the week; the earliest church tradition of the resurrection alludes to the empty tomb.

The multiple attestation of the empty tomb. The story of the empty tomb is found in all four Gospels and in at least three separate Gospel sources: Mark, M and John. This multiple attestation gives strong support to the tradition. Furthermore, the alleged contradictions found in these accounts lend support to the breadth of the empty tomb tradition within the Christian proclamation. If the accounts in Mark, M and John were identical, then the objection could be raised that they were simply variations of a single witness. The variations found in the accounts, however, argue for the tradition's existing in three different forms of the oral traditions. The testimony of these three witnesses is weighty.

The proclamation of Jesus' resurrection assumes the empty tomb. The early preaching of the resurrection in Jerusalem would have been impossible if Jesus' body still lay in a tomb. Jewish belief in the resurrection necessitated an empty tomb. The proclamation that Jesus rose from the dead did not mean that his soul or spirit continued to live after his death. For Jews, especially those influenced by the Pharisees, resurrection involved the physical body. The presence of the empty grave clothes in the tomb (Jn 20:5-7) presupposes the belief that the body of Jesus had been transformed and that nothing of it remained. The presence of Jesus' body, on the other hand, would have been proof that he had not risen from the dead. The proclamation in Jerusalem that Jesus was alive and risen from the dead meant that his dead body no longer lay in the tomb. It had been transformed from corruption to incorruption. Thus the tomb was empty. It is furthermore inconceivable that those Jews who opposed Jesus and his followers would not have checked for themselves to see if the tomb was really empty. All they would have needed to do to discredit the early Christian proclamation was to produce the body of Jesus.

Women were witnesses of the empty tomb. The fact that the witnesses to the empty tomb were women, whose witness was disallowed among the Jews, makes the fabrication of this account unlikely. If the empty tomb was a late creation by the early church intended to serve as an apologetic witness to the resurrection, why would women have been named as the chief witnesses? The later the creation of the story and the greater the apologetic motive for its creation, the more difficult it is to imagine creating it in terms of almost exclusively female witnesses. Added to this difficulty is the fact that apart from the empty tomb tradition, women play almost no role in the resurrection traditions.

The fact of the empty tomb was acknowledged by the Jews. The fact of the empty tomb was never disputed by Jews in their polemics with Christians. The Jewish explanation for the empty tomb in Matthew 28:11-15 indicates that the emptiness of the tomb was conceded immediately. If it had originated at a late date, there would have been no need to create such a polemic. At such a date one would have raised questions such as "What empty tomb? Where does this new claim that the tomb was empty come from? We have never heard anything about an empty tomb." The fact that the Jewish polemic never contested the existence of the empty tomb indicates that this tradition is very old. Such a concession assumes that from the beginning Christians proclaimed that Jesus' tomb was empty. It probably also indicates that the Jewish leaders had in fact found it empty.

The empty tomb was a well-known tomb. The reference to the tomb of Joseph of Arimathea in the burial accounts, and thus by implication in the account of the empty tomb, is firmly fixed in the tradition (Mt 27:57-60; Mk 15:43-46; Lk 23:50-55; Jn 19:38-42). As a result, the tradition of the empty tomb centers on a specific tomb known to both believers and unbelievers, which would have been investigated. It is furthermore doubtful that such a broad attestation to this specific tomb could have arisen late in the life of the church.

Sunday worship is due to the discovery of the empty tomb on the first day of the week. The early church's celebration of the first day of the week and the transformation of sabbath worship on the seventh day to worship on the first day is best explained by the empty tomb tradition. What was it about the first day of the week that caused a change from Saturday to Sunday as the day of worship in the life of the church? If we look at the traditions concerning the resurrection appearances, they are all built around the "third" day. Yet it is far from clear why the early church would have assumed that the resurrection of Jesus took place on the first day of the week. Given a Friday (to 6:00 p.m.) crucifixion, it is quite possible to conceive of "after three days" as referring to a Monday (6:00 p.m. Sunday to 6:00 p.m. Monday) resurrection. Nothing in the passion predictions or in the resurrection appearances refers specifically to the first day of the week.

The only tradition involving the first day of the week is the tradition of the empty tomb: "When the sabbath was over . . . very early on the first day of the week . . ." (Mk 16:1-2). The one event connected with the resurrection that is clearly associated with the first day of the week is the women's coming to the empty tomb. It therefore appears that the early church celebrated the first day of the week because it was on the first day of the week that the women came and found the tomb empty. The fact that the switch from sabbath to Sunday took place early in the life of the church indicates that the tradition of the empty tomb was known from the beginning.

The earliest church tradition of the resurrection alludes to the empty tomb. One of the earliest traditions concerning the resurrection, found in 1 Corinthians 15:3-8, alludes to the empty tomb. Paul's first letter to the Corinthians was probably written A.D. 54-55. Within it Paul reminds the church of a tradition that he had been taught and that he had shared with them. The exact dating of this tradition is uncertain. It has been suggested, however, that it may have arisen in the late thirties. Although the tradition does not specifically refer to the empty tomb, there is good reason to believe that Paul would have understood it that way.

After stating that "Christ died for our sins in accordance with the scriptures," he adds, "that he was buried, and that he was raised on the third day in accordance with the scriptures" (1 Cor 15:3-4). Some have suggested that the reference to Jesus' being buried simply serves to verify the reality of his having truly died. It is difficult, however, not to interpret the words "died . . . buried . . . was raised" without assuming that the place of burial became empty. For Paul, a Pharisee, a belief in the resurrection of Jesus would have presupposed an empty tomb. (Compare Acts 2:25-31, where David's burial resulted in corruption, whereas Jesus' burial did not. This assumes that Jesus' tomb became empty of that which was liable to corruption [Jesus' bodily remains] when he rose from the dead.)

Nonsupernatural Explanations of the Empty Tomb

The evidence that witnesses to the empty tomb is weighty. Consequently over the years those who denied the resurrection of Jesus have sought to provide some other explanation for the tomb's emptiness on Easter morning. Believing that every effect has some cause, they sought to find some other cause, a rational and nonsupernatural one, to explain the emptiness of the tomb. There are several popular explanations: the women went to the wrong tomb; Joseph of Arimathea took the body; Jesus never died on the cross—he merely "swooned"; the disciples stole the body.

The women went to the wrong tomb. This theory argues that on Easter morning Mary Magdalene and other women went to the wrong tomb. For some reason, whether the darkness of the early morning or emotional turmoil, they made a mistake. They went to a similar-looking tomb, which was empty, and confused this with the tomb of Jesus, which still contained his body.

Several factors argue against such an explanation. For one, there was not a great deal of time between the burial and the arrival of the women at the empty tomb. We are dealing with a period of about thirty-six hours. Could the women really have forgotten in so short a time the burial place of one they loved so? Furthermore, this was no Forest Lawn Cemetery—Jerusalem Branch, where one could mistake tomb 10,358 with look-alike tomb 18,494! This was a private burial tomb. We have no reason for concluding that there were similar tombs in the immediate area that could have been confused with this one. We also know that it was a specific tomb, the tomb of Joseph of Arimathea. This means that the tomb of Jesus was not some amorphous, mass-produced, look-alike tomb. It was a specific tomb, and it is virtually certain that the Jewish leaders would have checked to make sure that the tomb in which Jesus was buried was indeed empty. Finally, if we take seriously Matthew's account of a guard's being placed at the tomb, such a confusion by the women would quickly have been pointed out. It is interesting to note that one of the original proponents of this explanation, even though he still denied the resurrection of Jesus, later rejected this explanation of the empty tomb.

Joseph of Arimathea took the body. According to this theory the owner of the tomb came and took away the body of Jesus. This theory is based on no historical or literary evidence. One can just as well posit that Pontius Pilate stole the body to play a trick on the Jewish leaders in retaliation for what they had pressured him to do. The theory that Joseph of Arimathea took the body of Jesus possesses no more historical evidence to support it than the theory that Pontius Pilate took it. This is the stuff fiction is made of. Furthermore, why would Joseph have wanted to do this? The body of Jesus had received a noble burial. To remove it and place it somewhere else would dishonor it. Arguing, on the other hand, that Joseph wanted to create the myth of Jesus' resurrection assumes that Jesus had predicted his future resurrection, but most critical scholars tend to deny this.

Finally, what are we to do with the Roman guard? If we take this part of the tradition (Mt 28:11-15) at face value, it refutes this theory. If Joseph had taken the body, the guards would have had a perfectly logical story to give to the Jewish leaders. Why explain the empty tomb by saying that while they were sleeping on guard duty the disciples stole the body? They could simply have said, "Joseph, the owner of the tomb, came and took the body." The fact that they did not do so refutes this theory, unless we assume that Matthew 28:11-15 is entirely fictional.

Jesus never died on the cross—he merely "swooned." According to this view, the "swooned" Jesus revived in the coolness of the cave, rolled away the stone and then walked away. This theory proposes that the Roman soldiers mistook Jesus' having fainted on the cross with his having died. Yet the soldiers were so sure of Jesus' death that they did not break his legs as they did in the case of the two bandits. And these guards were well acquainted with death! As soldiers they had a good idea of whether someone was alive or dead. It is unlikely that they would have confused a swooned Jesus with a dead Jesus. And what of the spear wound? Are we to ignore this?

Even if we were to grant, for the sake of argument, that Jesus did not die on the cross, it seems incredible to think that he could have done all that was physically necessary to emerge from the tomb. How did he roll away the wheel-like stone sealing the tomb? How did he roll it back *up* the trench? How did he obtain the leverage needed to do so? Little leverage is obtained in pushing an automobile if instead of pushing it from behind, one pushes it at one of the side doors. Yet if Jesus rolled away the stone, he would have had to roll it uphill by pushing on the side of the stone. We should also note in this regard that the stone is described as "very large" (Mk 16:4).

The most serious objection to such a view came from a scholar who never believed in the resurrection but taught that the Gospel miracles were all "myths." He pointed out that a "swooned" Jesus in need of bandaging and medical treatment could never have given rise to the conviction of the disciples that he had conquered death. At best such a Jesus would have raised feelings of pity, sorrow or protection. He would never have evoked a cry of "Hallelujah, he is risen! Jesus is Lord! He has conquered death!" A swooned Jesus could have elicited feelings of pity from the disciples but could never have given birth to their resurrection faith.

The disciples stole the body. This is the oldest attempt to explain the empty tomb apart from Jesus' resurrection. It likewise faces numerous objections. One is somewhat humorous. If the guards were sleeping, how did they know what took place? Could they really have slept through such a noisy activity as rolling away the stone? A more serious objection is the question of why the disciples would have wanted to steal the body. Why would they want to exchange this noble burial place for something less noble? Are we to believe that they sought to "fulfill" Jesus' prediction that he would rise from the dead?

Most critical scholars have excluded this possibility by denying that Jesus predicted he would rise from the dead. But what conclusively refutes this attempted explanation is that the vast majority of biblical scholars agree that the disciples truly believed Jesus rose from the dead. They could not have believed this if they had themselves removed the body of Jesus from the tomb. It is true that one can find a scholar here or there who may talk about the disciples stealing the body, but such scholars represent the radical fringe of biblical scholarship. Even the author of *The Passover Plot*, who portrayed Jesus' resurrection as a carefully constructed plot, exempted the disciples from that plot. The Gospels make clear that it was not some sudden and unexplainable courage on the part of the disciples to steal Jesus' body that gave birth to the resurrection faith. On the contrary, it was the rise of the resurrection faith that gave birth to the subsequent courage of the disciples.

Other explanations. Several other explanations of the empty tomb can be mentioned in passing. One is that the body of Jesus completely decomposed into a gaseous vapor within thirty-six hours. Thus the tomb of Jesus was empty because his body, bones and all, evaporated by Easter morning. Needless to say that would be miraculous. Bones do not evaporate and disappear in a day and a half. If such a miracle is needed to explain the empty tomb, Christians over the centuries suggest they have a more satisfactory and meaningful one: Jesus rose from the dead!

Another theory is that the tomb was empty because the priestly leaders stole the body in order to prevent the tomb of Jesus from becoming a shrine. The individual who suggested this theory, however, accepted other aspects of the Easter story that refute this. He acknowledged that the high priests sought and were granted a guard for the tomb. Yet why request a guard to protect the tomb from theft and then on the same day perform that very theft? And why not then produce the body of Jesus when the disciples began to proclaim his resurrection? The supreme irony would, of course, be that an action performed to prevent the veneration of Jesus at a tomb shrine ended up leading to much greater veneration of him as the risen Lord.

The witness of the empty tomb remains. The unsatisfactory nature of the theories that attempt to explain the empty tomb is clear. No convincing rationalistic explanation exists. To those who are open to the supernatural occurring in history the gospel explanation remains the most convincing. The women came to an empty tomb on the first day of the week because Jesus Christ had conquered death and the grave. He had risen from the dead. Having said this, it must also be acknowledged that the empty tomb by itself is not sufficient to explain the Easter faith of the disciples. As stated already, the presence of Jesus' body in the tomb would refute such a faith, but its emptiness did not change doubt to faith. Along with the empty tomb, however, are other witnesses to the resurrection of Christ.

The Witness of the Resurrection Appearances
The earliest Christian proclamation was not simply that Jesus died for our sins and that he was raised. It was rather that he died for our sins, was raised and appeared to . . . (compare Acts 2:32; 3:15; 5:32; 10:39-41; 1 Cor 15:3-8). The resurrection of Jesus was never a philosophical abstraction unconnected to history. It was rather a historical event, the results of which were witnessed to by the resurrection appearances of Jesus. The number of the appearances mentioned in the New Testament is quite impressive. They include his appearance to Mary Magdalene (Jn 20:11, 18), the women (Mt 28:1-10), Peter (Lk 24:34; 1 Cor 15:5), the disciples on the way to Emmaus (Lk 24:13-35), the ten disciples (Lk 24:36-40; Jn 20:19-23; 1 Cor 15:5), the eleven disciples (Jn 20:24-29), the eleven

disciples in Galilee (Jn 21:1-23), five hundred disciples (1 Cor 15:6; Mt 28:16-20), James (1 Cor 15:7), and the disciples at the ascension (Lk 24:50-52; Acts 1:3-8). The rise of faith in the disciples that resulted is also an event in history, which biblical scholarship readily acknowledges. But how did this faith come about? What was the "cause" of this "effect"? Again several theories have been suggested.

The most common rationalistic explanation is that the resurrection faith arose due to a series of visions that the followers of Jesus experienced. Some suggest that the disciples were in a highly anticipatory mood of expectation and as a result had subjective visions of the risen Christ. In such situations a rattling window, a glimpse of someone wearing a garment like Jesus used to wear, a voice resembling that of Jesus could all lead to a visionary experience. Others suggest that these visions were produced in the subconscious as the disciples sought to resolve the tensions created by Jesus' death. Is it typical, however, for groups mourning the death of their leader to resolve their tensions by means of visions of the departed having risen from the dead? Attempts to explain the resurrection appearances by such a hypothesis stumble over the state of unbelief present in the disciples.

Such an explanation would seem to require that the women went to the tomb that Easter morning to greet the risen Christ with a rendition of the "Hallelujah Chorus." Why exactly did the women go to the tomb that morning? Was it to greet their Lord in song as the stone rolled away? On the contrary, they went with spices to anoint a dead body! Upon finding the tomb empty, did they jump to the conclusion that Jesus was risen from the dead? No, they thought that someone had taken away his body.

As for Thomas, although his doubt drew a reprimand from Jesus, it illustrates well the disciples' resistance to believing that Jesus had risen from the dead (compare Lk 24:11, 25, 38; Jn 20:24-28). Such resistance is quite understandable. Having been hurt so badly by the death of their Lord, they did not want to open themselves up to the possibility of being hurt again. That would happen if they accepted the report of Jesus' resurrection and it then proved to be false.

Thus we find that the conditions conducive to producing visions were not present among the followers of Jesus. On the contrary their emotional state would have hindered the possibility of any such visions. Two other things should be mentioned in this regard. Visions produced by the subconscious tend to be individualistic in nature. Yet the resurrection appearances occurred among groups of people at the same time. Also, the resurrection appearances contain aspects that are not visionary in nature: Jesus was physically touched (Mt 28:9; Lk 24:39; Jn 20:17, 27); he ate with the disciples (Lk 24:30, 41-43; Jn 21:13, 15 [?]); he had extensive conversations with several people at the same time.

Another explanation of the resurrection appearances, which is somewhat related to the vision hypothesis, is the "telegram" theory: after his death Jesus telegraphed pictures of himself back into the minds of the disciples. Such a view is sometimes encountered in psychic circles, but it suffers from many of the same objections listed against the vision hypothesis. The physical nature of the resurrection appearances clearly opposes such a view. The telegram theory also contains within it a serious moral dilemma, for Jesus is portrayed as deceptively sending back telegraphic visions of himself leading to the false conclusion that he had risen from the dead.

In the early church the greatest witness to the resurrection was the appearances of the risen Christ to his followers. Paul in his list of those who witnessed such an appearance even refers to "more than five hundred brothers and sisters at one time." He then tells the Corinthians that "most of [them] are still alive, though some have died" (1 Cor 15:6). Paul invited his Corinthian readers to check out the eyewitness reports for themselves, for the majority of witnesses to the resurrection were still alive. The number of Jesus' resurrection appearances, the varied circumstances in which they occurred, the number of witnesses involved and above all the character of those who shared this witness brought conviction wherever the gospel message was proclaimed. That message, now found in the New Testament, still brings conviction. Yet along with the witness of the empty tomb and the resurrection appearances is still another witness that can bring assurance and certainty that Jesus rose from the dead.

The Witness of the Living Christ

Throughout the existence of the church countless numbers of people have come to believe in the risen Christ. If asked, some could give a reasoned defense of this hope within them. They could argue both historically and philosophically in defense of their faith. Others with a similar conviction could not. They might simply respond as the hymn writer: "You ask me how I know he lives? He lives within my heart." Such a witness should not be dismissed out of hand. Multitudes of people from every continent and nation, from all races, throughout the centuries have joined together and confessed, "Jesus Christ is risen from the dead." Such a witness is subjective to be sure. But it is a witness that is available to all. The experience of the living Christ is open to all who would seek for themselves to "taste and see" (Ps 34:8).

If, as Christians maintain, Jesus has risen from the dead and sits at the right hand of God, then such a personal and immediate experience of the risen Christ should be available. The overpowering nature of this witness can be seen throughout history as men, women and children have made the supreme witness in martyrdom. They, and we today, know that our Redeemer lives. We have experienced his presence, his power and his love.

The Meaning of the Resurrection

What does the New Testament mean when it says that Jesus rose from the dead? For some this is simply a mythical way of referring to "the rise of faith in the disciples." It is a way of saying that somehow after the death of Jesus, perhaps by way of reflection, his teachings came alive for the disciples. They became convinced of the truth he had taught. Exactly what that truth is usually reflects the particular social and ethical views of the commentator. What the statement "Jesus rose from the dead" means for them is that God helped the disciples to see the value of Jesus' teachings, and as a result they recommitted themselves to his cause. The New Testament does not speak, however, of the resurrection *of the disciples* on Easter but of the resurrection *of Jesus*. Whatever may have happened to the disciples was the result of what happened earlier that day to Jesus.

We should not confuse the resurrection faith with the resurrection itself. They are related as effect and cause. The faith of the disciples is the effect of the resurrection of Jesus. Without the latter the former is a mere illusion. Paul himself states, "If Christ has not been raised, then our proclamation has been in vain and your faith has been in vain. . . . If Christ has not been raised, your faith is futile and you are still in your sins. . . . If for this life only we have hoped in Christ, we are of all people most to be pitied" (1 Cor 15:14, 17, 19).

The Gospel accounts portray the resurrection as something that happened to Jesus, not the disciples. What happened to Jesus (resurrection) affected the disciples (the rise of the resurrection faith), but they are separated in time and nature. What happened to the disciples took place after what happened to Jesus and is different from what happened to Jesus. For the disciples, it involved the rise of faith and its beneficial consequences—justification, forgiveness, reconciliation, peace, eternal life, the promise of a future resurrection. For Jesus, it involved the translation of his body from mortality into immortality. The popular definition in some circles of the resurrection as "the rise of faith in the disciples" confuses an effect with the cause and misunderstands what the biblical writers meant by the term *resurrection*. Only Jesus experienced the resurrection.

When the New Testament proclaims the resurrection of Jesus Christ, it does not mean by this that something happened to the disciples. The latter is, of course, true. Yet even if nothing happened subsequently to the disciples, the resurrection would still be true. The proclamation of the resurrection of Jesus Christ is precisely that—the resurrection *of Jesus Christ*. That resurrection is not the same as the fact of the empty tomb, even if it presupposes it. It is not the *resuscitation* of the body of Jesus to physical life. The resurrections of Jairus's daughter, of Lazarus and of the widow of Nain's son were of this nature. They regained physical life, but subsequently they died. In the case of Jesus, however, his resurrection involved rising to immortality. It was an eschatological event in the fullest sense of that term. All that was susceptible to mortality and evil was transformed into an immortal existence, and in the case of Jesus it involved a return to the glory he possessed before his incarnation and exaltation to the right hand of God.

The Ascension
According to Acts after his death the risen Christ appeared to his followers "by many convincing proofs" for a period of forty days (Acts 1:3). During this period he taught them concerning the kingdom of God. On the other hand, Jesus' ascension in Luke 24:51 appears to have taken place in Jerusalem immediately after the resurrection. But since the same author wrote both accounts, it is clear therefore that in his mind they

do not contradict each other. Not much is written in the Gospels concerning Jesus' activity during this forty-day period, and this lack is "remedied" in various Gnostic works found in the apocryphal Gospels.

Immediately after the resurrection Jesus appeared on several occasions in Jerusalem and its environs. Some of the accounts appear to fit this locale better than others: Mary Magdalene (Jn 20:11-18), the women (Mt 28:1-10), Peter (Lk 24:34; 1 Cor 15:5), the disciples on the way to Emmaus (Lk 24:13-35), the ten disciples (Jn 20:19-24) and the eleven disciples (Lk 24:36-48; Jn 20:26-29; 1 Cor 15:5). Thereupon he appeared as he had promised (compare Mk 14:27; 16:7) to the eleven disciples in Galilee (Jn 21:1-23), to the five hundred disciples (1 Cor 15:6; Mt 28:16-20 [?]) and to James (1 Cor 15:7). Finally, he appeared to the disciples in Jerusalem at the ascension (Lk 24:50-52; Acts 1:3-9).

After the resurrection it is quite probable that the disciples returned to Galilee, for that was their home. They had been in Jerusalem only because Jesus had led them there. Now that the Passover was over it was natural for them to return to their homes in Galilee. For them to return to Jerusalem for the Feast of Weeks (Pentecost), the second of the three major Jewish festivals, is also understandable.

Shortly before the day of Pentecost, Jesus, after commanding his followers to remain in Jerusalem until the promised coming of the Spirit, ascended from their presence into heaven. This marked the end of the resurrection appearances of Jesus. How this fits in with Paul's claim that he had seen the risen Christ is unclear. Paul does, however, mention that his experience was unusual (1 Cor 15:8). With the ascension, the followers of Jesus ceased hoping for or awaiting additional resurrection appearances. Their hope now focused on the parousia. What the church now looked forward to was the day when "this Jesus, who has been taken up from you into heaven, will come in the same way as you saw him go into heaven" (Acts 1:11).

Conclusion

Unlike the death of other great world figures, the death of Jesus did not result in a "Jesus Memorial Society" gathering regularly to remember their departed hero. Events did not permit this. Easter destroyed that possibility. There was no tomb containing the body of Jesus that could serve as a shrine. There was no mausoleum to visit. There was no monument where his followers could go to read odes commemorating "the time he was with us." The tomb was empty. Jesus was not dead. He was alive! He had conquered the great enemy, death. He lived and dwelt with them. And today he continues to dwell in the hearts and lives of his followers through his Spirit. The New Testament and the church ever since shout triumphantly, "Christ is risen from the dead!"

The proclamation of the early church concerning Jesus Christ, however, is not simply "that Christ died for our sins, that he was buried, that he was raised and that he appeared to his disciples." To this confession must be added "and he will come again." The ascension of Jesus furthermore points out that Jesus' return is not capable of being demythologized into some abstract or abstruse sociological movement or event. "This Jesus" who ascended shall return "in the same way." If we accept the meaning that Luke attributes to these words, we can only interpret them to mean that Jesus of Nazareth, who rose from the dead, shall return in visible bodily form just as he ascended.

The "Life of Jesus" is incomplete. It awaits that day when he will return to share the messianic banquet with his followers (Mk 14:25). For those who follow and love him, that is a day prayed and longed for. When the church prays, "Our Father in heaven, hallowed be your name. Your kingdom come. Your will be done, on earth as it is in heaven" (Mt 6:9-10), it prays for his coming. This longing and prayer has even been preserved in the New Testament in the ancient Aramaic prayer *"Marana tha"* (1 Cor 16:22). Until that day the church will continue to "wait for the blessed hope and the manifestation of the glory of our great God and Savior, Jesus Christ" (Tit 2:13), and pray "Come, Lord Jesus!" (Rev 22:20).

References

Bode, Edward Lynn. *The First Easter Morning: The Gospel Accounts of the Women's Visit to the Tomb of Jesus.* Rome: Biblical Institute Press, 1970.

Craig, William Lane. *The Son Rises: The Historical Evidence for the Resurrection of Jesus.* Chicago: Moody Press, 1981.

Davis, Stephen T. *Risen Indeed: Making Sense of the Resurrection.* Grand Rapids, Mich.: Eerdmans, 1993.

Fitzmyer, Joseph A. "The Ascension of Christ and Pentecost." *Theological Studies* 45 (1984): 409-40.

Giles, Kevin N. "Ascension." In *Dictionary of Jesus and the Gospels,* edited by Joel B. Green, Scot McKnight and I. Howard Marshall, pp. 46-50. Downers Grove, Ill.:

InterVarsity Press, 1992.

Ladd, George E. *I Believe in the Resurrection of Jesus.* Grand Rapids, Mich.: Eerdmans, 1975.

Maile, John F. "The Ascension in Luke-Acts." *Tyndale Bulletin* 37 (1986): 29-59.

Osborne, Grant R. "Resurrection." In *Dictionary of Jesus and the Gospels,* edited by Joel B. Green, Scot McKnight and I. Howard Marshall, pp. 673-88. Downers Grove, Ill.: InterVarsity Press, 1992.

Stein, Robert H. "Was the Tomb Really Empty?" *Journal of the Evangelical Theological Society* 20 (1977): 23-29.

Wenham, John. *Easter Enigma: Are the Resurrection Accounts in Conflict?* Grand Rapids, Mich.: Baker Book House, 1992.

Index of Subjects

Index of References